# INTERVIEWER APPROACHES

To the SCPR interviewers who tape recorded their doorstep introductions, thus providing unique insight into the task of gaining cooperation on surveys

# Interviewer Approaches

## Jean Morton-Williams

Dartmouth

Published by
Dartmouth Publishing Company Limited
Gower House
Croft Road
Aldershot
Hants GU11 3HR
England

Dartmouth Publishing Company
Old Post Road
Brookfield
Vermont 05036
USA

**British Library Cataloguing in Publication Data**
Williams, Jean Morton
  Interviewer Approaches
  I. Title
  658.31124

**Library of Congress Cataloging-in-Publication Data**
Morton-Williams, Jean.
    Interviewer approaches / Jean Morton-Williams.
      p.   cm.
    Includes bibliographical references and index.
    ISBN 1-85521-339-7 : $55.95 (U.S. : est.)
    1. Interviewing in sociology.  2. Social surveys.  I. Title.
  HN29.M614   1993
  301'.0723—dc20                                                93-20002
                                                                     CIP

ISBN 1 85521 339 7

Printed in Great Britain at the University Press, Cambridge

# Contents

# Foreword

This book has been needed for a very long time. It is about a critical (perhaps the most critical) aspect of surveys, which for one reason or another has been neglected in the literature. It has also been neglected as a topic for sustained research.

Jean Morton-Williams' work remedies both omissions. It is the product of a lifetime in survey organizations, first at the BBC, then in market research, at Marplan and MIL, and then — for the last twenty years of her career — in social research, at SCPR (Social & Community Planning Research). More important perhaps, Jean's unusual career has straddled at least four separate strands of survey work — qualitative research, quantitative surveys, methodological research, and field management —all of which contribute essentially to this volume. It is no wonder that a book like this has not appeared before if, as seems likely, it needed someone with such a diverse background to write it.

The Survey Methods Centre — now the Joint Centre for Survey Methods at SCPR — to which Jean was attached part-time while also running SCPR's field department, was set up in 1980 (originally in collaboration with City University) as an ESRC Designated Research Centre. Under the direction of Gerald Hoinville in its earlier years, the Centre undertook a programme of statistical experiments and other methodological work designed to achieve a greater understanding of the intricate make-up of social surveys. The Centre's work in that period was very wide-ranging — covering sampling, telephone survey methods, question-wording and question-order effects, interviewer and coder variability, and so on —but none was more important or original than the work under Jean's direction drawn upon in Chapters 5-7.

Up to then, the interchanges involved in negotiating access to a potential survey respondent's home for an interview were shrouded in mystery. There were, if course, 'rules', but the actual process was simply an aspect of an interviewer's craft to which researchers were not granted entry. Yet these exchanges on the doorstep not only determine the all-important response rate to a survey, but also provide the respondents' introduction to the subject matter of the survey, thus creating a mindset which may well affect their answers.

Thanks to that research, solid evidence is at last available about this process, enabling good practice to be distinguished from bad, and allowing interviewer training courses nowadays to take account of what has been learned.

But this book is full of such material, drawn from the author's immense experience, knowledge and appreciation of her field. It combines analysis, insights and evidence, and contains a fund of sound practical detail without ignoring its theoretical underpinning. As a result, survey research courses should never again be able to be so indifferent to the subjects of interviewing and fieldwork management.

When Jean retired in 1988, the Joint Centre for Survey Methods prevailed on her to write further about her work 'now that you at last have the time to do so'! What we had no right to expect, however, was the emergence of such a valuable book which will add substantively and substantially to its field.

# Acknowledgements

The research on doorstep introductions that forms the centrepiece of this book was funded by the general grant for methodological research provided by the Economic and Social Research Council to the SCPR Survey Methods Centre (now the Joint Centre for Survey Methods).

There was much help from my colleagues at SCPR in carrying out the research. Thanks are due in particular to Penny Young who undertook the major part of the analysis of the tape recorded doorstep introductions and carried out the depth interview study with respondents that forms the basis of Chapter 6.

Many thanks also to Roger Thomas, Director of the Joint Centre for Survey Methods, who has been unfailing in his support and constructive comment.

Finally, immense gratitude to the SCPR secretaries who put many drafts through the word processor, in particular to Mary Graham and Lis Box who produced the final camera ready copy.

# 1 Interviewing in survey research

## Survey research comes of age

Survey research is regarded as a relatively young discipline. Although its roots are in nineteenth century Britain and the social concerns of that time arising from accelerating industrialization, it was the Second World War that gave it its real impetus. But it is now more than fifty years since the Second World War started, and those years have seen survey research change from amateur to professional status. In the early days, it was thought that any intelligent person could do a survey: psychologists, sociologists and statisticians were perhaps regarded as being more able than others since they might know about experimental design, sampling, attitude measurement and tests of significance; but in the main researchers found out how to design surveys, write questionnaires, analyze the results and write reports by trial and error. Interviewing also was regarded as a simple process, depending only on a degree of common sense, and interviewers were lucky if they received more than half a day's training; quality control was minimal, being largely confined to identifying cheaters.

As the applications of survey research became more complex and expanded into more areas (marketing, economic, social and environmental planning and evaluation, government policy development, medical research, opinion polling), more and more people found themselves becoming career survey specialists responsible for the training of new recruits to the industry and therefore needing to codify and test their expertise. In the United States in particular, where the notion that questions asked of a carefully selected sample could mirror the views and behaviour of the larger society was greeted with more enthusiasm than in Britain, many academic institutions set up their own survey research centres with full survey facilities; these have been in the vanguard of survey methodological research, in the development of theoretical frameworks covering all aspects of the survey process and in setting up training courses.

In Britain, the failure of the universities to become seriously involved in survey research has been a factor in the slower development of survey professionalism in this country so that higher status still tends to be accorded to the subject specialist than to the survey specialist, who is sometimes regarded simply as a survey facility manager rather than as an expert in survey and questionnaire design, analysis and interpretation. Nonetheless, British organizations have made their contribution to theoretical and technical developments in survey research, notably through the Survey Research Centre (originally at the London School of Economics and then independently under Belson), the Social Survey Division of the Office of Population Censuses and Surveys (OPCS),[1] the Joint Centre for Survey Methods[2] at Social and Community Planning Research, and the Market Research Society's Market Research Development Fund.

Training in survey research is necessarily largely through on the job apprenticeship but this needs to be backed up by accredited formal teaching in theory and techniques. It is perhaps in this area that the survey profession has been most laggardly though there are signs of improvement. In the United States, there are both long and short courses for the social survey researcher ranging from Master's Degree courses to junior and advanced Summer schools. In Britain, where there is less of a division between social and market research with many of the major market research companies undertaking social research projects, there are Market Research Society examinations in survey theory and techniques; some universities, polytechnics and institutes also run short courses, and there is an attempt to get a Master's Degree course in survey methods under way at the London School of Economics.

Survey research can thus be said to have 'come of age': it is no longer true that 'anyone can do a survey'. 'Anyone' can do a bad survey (and still all too frequently does). To do a good survey requires expertise and professionalism at every stage: design, sampling, questionnaire development, interviewing, analysis and reporting, based on an extensive theoretical framework well grounded in practice and methodological research.

The development of survey research has been aided enormously by the revolution in information technology over the last twenty years, a process that is by no means complete. The advent of the personal computer not only makes possible the coordination of processes previously carried out separately and often by hand, but also has the potential to revolutionize the data collection process. Computer applications are widespread in telephone interviewing and laptop computers are already being utilized in personal interviews on continuous and large scale surveys in the United States and in several European countries, including Britain.

An interviewer carrying his or her own computer on an interviewing assignment presents a very different image from the traditional one of the middle aged housewife earning a little pin money. The interviewer has for too long been the Cinderella of the survey industry. Whereas survey researchers demand professional recognition and command high salaries, the survey interviewer is still frequently undertrained, undersupervised, underpaid and undervalued.

The first major programmes of methodological research on interviewers and interviewing were carried out by the National Opinion Research Centre in the US in the late 1940s and early 1950s, and by Belson in Britain in the 1960s. But the pressures on time and costs in carrying out surveys have been such that survey organizations have been slow to do more than pay lip service to the findings.

Nonetheless, standards have gradually improved: considerably more attention is now paid to interviewer training and regular supervision; the Market Research Society has inaugurated an Interviewer Quality Control Scheme which sets out minimum requirements for these and regularly inspects the practices of those organizations that join the scheme. There is a general increase in recognition of interviewers as a vital part of the survey process. However, the status of the survey interviewer remains low and there is a lack of awareness on the part of survey practitioners of the reality of life 'out there' in the field. Too few researchers leave their offices to do some interviewing, or even talk at length to interviewers about what actually happens when trying to persuade someone to take part or when asking the questions. As a result, their expertise is untempered by first hand experience in the frontline. Field management holds the uncomfortable position of trying to bridge the gap by interpreting the researcher's requirements to the interviewers and explaining the interviewers' problems to a not always sympathetic researcher.

This book focuses on one crucial part of the interviewer's task, that of gaining the cooperation of the public on surveys. This aspect has been largely neglected both by methodological research programmes and by those responsible for interviewer training. It is generally acknowledged that good response rates are essential if confidence in the findings is to be justified and bias avoided. It is also recognized that it has become more difficult and more expensive to maintain levels of response over the years. Programmes of methodological research on the interview itself and on computerized data collection are reduced in value if they are not complemented by research on maintaining and improving response rates.

One of the purposes of this book is to convey an understanding of what it is actually like to be an interviewer tackling the demands of approaching someone for an interview 'out there' in the real world (as opposed to the safe haven of a training or briefing session), how they enter into an interaction with an unpredictable other human being and try to marry the demands of this interaction with those of the job. This understanding is based on an analysis of tape recordings made by interviewers of their approaches to members of the public for an interview in their own homes, and the subsequent interaction. This study was carried out by the author at the Joint Centre for Survey Methods and was funded by the Economic and Social Research Council. It constitutes the first methodological attempt to investigate the dynamics of the situation in which the interviewer sets about gaining the cooperation of the public and to identify empirically those aspects of the task that might usefully be tackled through systematic training procedures.

## The place of the interviewer in survey research

Not all survey research depends on interviewers for data collection: self completion questionnaires, usually delivered by post, are widely used for a number of purposes. Postal surveys are relatively cheap compared with interviewer surveys and have the important advantage of avoiding the problems of interviewer effects on survey results. Although they have many useful applications, they also have limitations: there are often problems in ensuring delivery of the questionnaire to the correct sample member and response tends to be skewed towards the more literate sectors of the population. Furthermore, only simple one stage questions can be asked; questions requiring probing to obtain adequate information (such as details of occupation, widely used for determining socio-economic group) or requiring complex filtering depending on the answers given, need the skill of an interviewer.

Survey research that uses interviewers to question samples of people is an immensely flexible tool with a very wide range of applications. It flourishes most in industrialized societies that have the necessary infrastructure of census data and population registers for good sample design, and which also have the wealth to interest those with goods to sell; the rapid expansion of market research since the early 1950s has undoubtedly done much to boost the development of the survey industry. If this book seems to concentrate on methodological work in the social research field, it is a reflection of the fact that it is in this context that most methodological research on interviewing has been carried out. Social and market research practices differ in some respects (primarily sampling approaches and questionnaire length) that affect what is required of interviewers, but basic principles and most aspects of the work are very similar; the research findings can therefore easily be extrapolated from one to the other.

*Survey research worldwide*

During the last twenty years, survey research using interviewers has been increasingly used in developing countries, partly due to multinational programmes set up by the United Nations (such as the World Fertility Survey) and to the growing need for information on the part of international organizations such as the World Bank, as well as on the part of the governments of the countries. The problems of carrying out good survey research in many of these countries are enormous: the contrasts between urban and rural populations, rich and poor, and between different ethnic groups are marked enough in countries such as Britain and the US; but they are minor compared to the differences between various sections of the population in countries such as South Africa, Brazil, Nigeria or India. These differences make it difficult to design samples, write appropriate questionnaires or find and train a suitable fieldforce for carrying out general population surveys.

This book does not attempt to be global in its coverage. Although the issues covered are relevant to survey interviewing wherever it is practised, it is mainly concerned with the problems of gaining cooperation in industrialized societies. Other more qualified writers have written on the special problems and requirements of conducting fieldwork in developing countries (e.g., Warwick and Lininger, 1975).

*The variety of places and people*

The general image of survey interviewing is of an interviewer (usually a middle aged female) knocking on doors to interview a cross section of the general public: this type of in-home interview with a sample of the general population will be the main focus of this book since it is around this paradigm that survey methodology and interviewing techniques have evolved. But although in-home general population samples are the target of a considerable amount of survey research, they certainly no longer constitute the greater part. Much in-home interviewing is concerned with special populations: market research is usually aimed at particular buying groups (housewives, householders, car owners, smokers etc.) and often uses quota rather than random sampling to find respondents; social research surveys are often directed to special needs groups (the elderly, the unemployed, the disabled) or address issues that concern particular sectors of the population such as home owners, council renters, ethnic minorities, school leavers etc.

Not all survey interviewing takes place in the home: some involves sampling and interviewing users of particular facilities, for example, in shopping centres, parks, museums, at the roadside, or on public transport; some market research requires people to go to a local hall to sample products or view commercials.

Many surveys involve interviewing people at their place of work. The wide range of workplace surveys includes studies of trainees and employees on the one hand and of employers, senior managers or people with specific work functions on the other. Special professional groups (e.g., doctors, solicitors or teachers) may also be sampled for particular surveys.

The types of population sampled, the respondent selection procedures and the interview venue can all affect the interviewer's task and the skills required. The topic of the survey may also be important, especially if it touches on areas that people feel reluctant to talk about.

The variety of survey applications is so wide that it is not possible to cover them all. The in-home interview with a random general population sample has been the main vehicle for research into nonresponse and is taken as the normative type of survey for examination in this book. Attention is also given, however, to the different interviewer requirements for quota and random sampling, to the problems in gaining cooperation from certain special populations (such as special needs groups or people at work) or on surveys dealing with sensitive topics.

## Survey interviewers: a declining army?

No one knows how many survey interviewers there are. In the Market Research Society Interviewers' Newsheet, Spring 1989, the statement was made 'that in any one week of the year somewhere in the region of 600,000 interviews are conducted in the UK of which about 70 per cent are face to face'; but interviewing is mostly part-time casual employment with the number of hours worked per week by each interviewer varying enormously; there is therefore no way of estimating the number of interviewers. Some interviewers work only a few hours each week and are happy to have weeks without work; others rely on it as their main source of income and may try to ensure regular work by being on the books of more than one company. Some undertake interviewing only for a short period and turnover of interviewers is generally high. Thus, at any point in time, quite a large proportion of interviewers in the field may have only a few months' experience. However, there are many interviewers who work for a number of years and build up a considerable body of experience; every long established fieldforce is likely to collect a preponderance of experienced interviewers. A survey among interviewers carried out in 1988 by the Field Committee of the Market Research Society[3] with the help of fifteen market research companies, indicated that around three fifths of the members of market research field forces have at least three years interviewing experience, one fifth having ten years or more. Barker (1987) describes two earlier studies in Ohio and New Zealand that show similar results though length of experience tended to be lower in New Zealand, perhaps reflecting the fact that the survey industry has developed more recently there.

The Market Research Society survey also indicated that about half the interviewers worked for only one company but over a quarter worked for four or more. An unpublished survey by SCPR in 1981 among its Panel interviewers (i.e., interviewers who had done at least three surveys for the institute and attended a second phase of training) revealed that 57 per cent had carried out work for other organizations during the previous twelve months, mainly for market research companies but also for other social research organizations.

Traditionally, the 'typical' survey interviewer has been a married woman of mature years whose children are at least into their teens; survey research with its flexible hours and freelance status is seen as providing an ideal way for them to get out of the house, meet people, develop a skill and earn a little money. The surveys quoted above all indicate that this picture is not entirely true: a great many interviewers are under 45: 60 per cent of those surveyed by the British Market Research Society and in New Zealand.

Percentage of interviewers aged over 45:

| | |
|---|---|
| Ohio | 53% |
| New Zealand | 39% |
| SCPR | 54% |
| Market Research Society | 40% |

Around 95 per cent of the members of all the fieldforces studied were women except in the case of SCPR, 15 per cent of whose Panel interviewers were men.

So it appears that a lot of interviewers do not fit the stereotype but come from a variety of other groups to whom flexible hours of work appeal, such as single parents, those in part time or freelance work, those in full time employment who want to earn additional money (especially teachers or those on flexi-time), people who have taken early retirement and people between jobs.

Many surveys take place within specific geographical regions or towns, requiring large local fieldforces to be set up to carry them out; recruitment for these surveys often seems to attract more people from the unemployment register, more men and, in general, a younger population than is the case when recruiting for long term interviewers.

Both the number and the quality of applicants in response to advertisements for survey interviewers depend on several interacting factors such as the extent to which alternative employment, particularly part time, is available, the pay and working conditions and how the work is perceived.

Almost twenty years ago Gorden (1975) wrote, 'There is an unfortunate tendency to consider data gathering as a lower status activity than data analysis or theorising about the data'; this is still generally true and is reflected in low pay and low status for interviewers. As the status of women in the employment market improves with more of them having careers that may be only temporarily interrupted for child rearing, the traditional pool of middle class, educated but occupationally untrained mothers is shrinking; the greater availability of part time work with flexible hours in offices, shops and public services presents alternative opportunities for employment often with conditions that may appear rather more attractive than walking round the streets in all weathers to find respondents, and with no less status than that accorded to interviewing. The work of interviewing is itself becoming less attractive, at least in major cities; on the one hand there is increasing fear of violence to interviewers or wilful damage to their cars; on the other is society's response to high crime rates: entryphones, security gates, gate keepers, and simple refusal to answer the door to strangers, all make access to respondents more difficult.

In Britain there is considered to be an increasingly serious crisis, primarily in London and the South East but also in other major cities, owing to the virtual impossibility of recruiting enough interviewers of sufficient calibre to meet survey needs. Hall & Katryniak (1990) see the face to face interviewer as an 'endangered species' faced with extinction unless the survey industry takes major steps to increase interviewers' pay, status and job satisfaction. Letters and articles in the Market Research Society Newsletter indicate awareness of the problem among senior market research practitioners but the commercial pressure of competitive tendering, in which price and speed are the main criteria on which a research proposal is judged, is seen as perpetuating the situation:

> Sadly, commercial pressure within an increasingly competitive industry such as research can cause agency management to concentrate on those areas to which the client is directly exposed. Accordingly, though illogically, it is fieldwork that is so frequently the poor relation. The amount of time and money spent on fieldwork training and quality enhancement is generally deplorable. Field Managers within an agency tend to be lowest in the pecking order, Field Directors the lowest paid on the Board and interviewers, well we know what they earn!
> (Eamonn Santry, MRS Newsletter, Oct. 1988)

> Bad fieldwork in my experience does not result in any great measure from poorly trained or dishonest interviewers. By far the greatest culprit is the competitive pressure which forces excessive workloads on interviewers... Generally speaking the system rewards the agency which works its interviewers hardest.
> (Jack Potter, MRS Newsletter, November 1988)

Economic recession accentuates competitive pressures but also tends to enlarge the pool of unemployed people willing to be recruited as interviewers, at least for a short time.

It is not only in Britain that there is a shortage of people willing to undertake face to face interviewing: in the United States there have been acute problems in many major cities for some years and the situation is similar in Germany, France and Italy.

There are those who consider that only an internationally accepted increase in the pay and status of interviewers can have any marked effect. Since the current frenetic commercial pressures often result in underprepared and poorly conducted research, there are considerable arguments in favour of fewer more carefully planned and executed surveys in both social and market research. Other practitioners, however, see the role of face to face interviewing to be diminishing; they argue that better paid and more dedicated interviewers can only marginally improve response rates in inner city areas; they see telephone interviewing already becoming in the States as effective a mode of research for large general population surveys and consider it will soon become so in Britain and other countries as well. Face to face interviewing would be reserved for certain sorts of social research, especially that entailing special samples such as the elderly, disabled or unemployed, and for small market research studies such as hall tests, where response problems are much less.

A third possibility, and the least desirable, is that survey organizations should be expected to soldier on under the present conditions with standards of sample coverage and interviewing quality deteriorating. One of the objects of this book is to increase awareness among buyers and overseers of survey research in government, business and the universities, as well as among practitioners, of the conditions necessary to obtain high response rates and to collect good data.

## The interviewer's vital role

Interviewers are the capillaries of the survey process; the point at which the exchange of question and answer takes place. Apart from opinion poll reports in the newspapers, the interview experience constitutes for many members of the public their only source of information about survey research: the interviewer thus has the dual responsibility of asking the questions and recording the answers as intended by the researcher, and also of ensuring that the interview is an enjoyable and worthwhile experience for the respondent so that the public's willingness to cooperate is not eroded. This responsibility is shared by the researchers who can make the interviewer's task easy or, in some circumstances, virtually impossible with an overlong questionnaire, difficult procedures and demanding sampling constraints.

The interviewer's role requires a synthesis of discipline and initiative that is not easy to define or achieve: the strict rules that apply to sampling, respondent selection and the asking of questions require meticulous training and discipline in application; but considerable initiative is also required to persuade a reluctant respondent to take part in the survey, to probe correctly when answers do not conveniently fit the precoded categories given in the questionnaire or to deal with the situations when respondents fail to behave according to the researcher's expectations. The conflicting demands are particularly marked in surveys with preselected addresses: interviewers are under considerable pressure to obtain good response rates yet must always bear in mind that cooperation is voluntary and must be careful not to offend or alarm those they approach.

A major part of this book consists of an analysis and appraisal of the interviewer's tasks in obtaining cooperation, covering both the discipline to follow rules and the requirements for initiative.

**Respondent burden: why do they bother to answer survey questions?**

Researchers sometimes seem to have little awareness of how their questionnaires might appear to members of the public; on occasion they have been known to expect response rates of 80 per cent on a survey entailing a 75 minute interview covering difficult and abstract issues which, though fascinating to the researcher, were largely meaningless to many respondents; or they have expected large numbers of people to keep daily or weekly diaries of activities or to remember in detail what they did, what they bought, how much they spent, etc. When response rates are low, the interviewers or the survey organisers are blamed.

What is truly remarkable is that around 70 per cent or more of a general population sample are willing and able to give around an hour of their time to a stranger on their doorstep, to enter into an interview without knowing in detail what it is going to cover, and to make at least some effort to make sense of the questions and to answer them accurately, even though there is no direct benefit to them for doing so. Research buyers and practitioners should never take this for granted but remember it with gratitude and amazement, doing their best to preserve this state of affairs.

Jack Potter, in his capacity as Chairman of the Professional Standards Committee of the Market Research Society, proposed that the Code of Conduct should include a clause to the effect that: 'Questionnaires must be competently designed and of a length acceptable to the sample of people being interviewed' (MRS Newsletter, September 1991).

In an article in the MRS Newsletter (March 1989) on managing change in market research, Janet Weitz, Managing Director of a market research company, suggests that all graduate trainees should spend their first year as interviewers thus solving in part the problem of finding interviewers to cover London and the South East, contributing enormously to their education as researchers and thirdly, 'Bringing interviewing in-from-the-cold and firmly placing it where it belongs as a fundamental part of good research'. Such a bold suggestion has much to recommend it. In the last analysis, survey research depends on the willingness of people to be interviewed, on their being able to understand the questions and being prepared to give full and thoughtful answers.


**The interview takes place in a social context**

The survey interview has been defined as 'a conversation with a purpose' (Bingham and Moore, 1934; Moser and Kalton, 1971; Powney and Watts, 1987); but it is a 'conversation' that obeys few of the rules of ordinary conversational interaction since the interviewer assumes the role of questioner and the respondent is placed in the role of answerer. Most people in industrialized countries are familiar enough with the concept of a survey to understand in broad terms that they will be required to answer questions. This is not always the case, however: an interviewer who had been working in an area of London with a large Asian population remarked, 'The trouble is, if you ask an Asian how many children they have, the polite answer is "Three; how many do you have?"' In other words, the Asian respondent expected the interview to follow the usual rules of mutual disclosure used in polite conversation. The survey interview is thus a rather specialized form of social interaction with its own rules, but these have to be compatible with the broader framework of the social conventions of the population being studied. The survey interview thus takes place within a broad social context. The unique interactive event of the individual interview must operate within the framework of the socially accepted norms:

> It is important to establish the larger context of the interview situation lest we myopically focus on the techniques of the interaction and forget that the relationship between interviewer and respondent is determined to a great extent by how their roles fit into the larger society, and that this relationship either inhibits or facilitates the flow of certain types of information.
> (Gorden, 1975)

Survey practitioners working within their own culture in a Western industrialized society tend to take the social context for granted since the accepted ways in which surveys are conducted have developed within it and been influenced by it. Those undertaking survey research in developing countries tend to be more sensitive to these issues; Warwick and Lininger (1975) sometimes found that prospective respondents had no concept or understanding of research and that the whole notion of engaging in a question and answer process was very foreign; whether or not the headman was interviewed first could vitally affect cooperation and accuracy of information given, as could sex and/or race of interviewer. There might also be fear that the information could be used to harm individuals or the community.

Such concerns are not entirely irrelevant in industrialized societies with a longer tradition of survey research, as the interviewer's remark on Asian respondents quoted above indicates. Ethnic matching of interviewers and respondents has long been recognized as important in surveys to do with racial issues but the possibility of different concepts about and attitudes towards the survey process is often ignored and simply left to the interviewer to cope with.

Although ethnic cultural differences are the most obvious, there are also likely to be differences in reaction to being approached for an interview between social class, age, religious and regional groups, some being more likely than others to regard it as an intrusion or to fear the effects of giving information.

The overall image of survey research has suffered from the increase in 'sugging' ('Selling Under the Guise' of doing a survey). The Market Research Society Interviewer Card Scheme, which attempts to ensure that all accredited market research interviewers carry a card with their photograph, is an attempt to make it possible for members of the public quickly to establish that the person approaching them is a bona fide interviewer. Leaflets to leave with respondents after they have been interviewed thanking them for the interview and telling them a bit about the ways survey information is used also help to educate and reassure the public. Social research organizations such as SCPR and Social Survey Division of OPCS issue their own interviewer cards and leaflets which set out the rights of respondents to refuse to be interviewed. A letter describing the purpose of the specific survey and what organization it is being carried out for is also sent in advance or handed over by the interviewer. Similar practices are followed in other countries. These measures all play a part in informing prospective respondents about survey research and reassuring them that the information will not be misused.

In surveys where the population to be sampled is a circumscribed one, such as residents of a housing estate or in an institution, or employees of a single firm, it is particularly important to consider the social context within which the survey will take place: to discover what the hierarchies and power structures are, what are likely to be the attitudes towards the survey sponsor, how much respondents are likely to talk to each other about the questions, and so on. For example, a survey in a manufacturing company's factory was threatened with a possibly biasing loss from the sample of many of the Roman Catholics selected for interview because the questionnaire contained a question on the use of contraception that one respondent felt was not justified by the subject matter. He expressed his indignation to his fellow Catholics, many of whom decided they would not agree to be interviewed. The crisis was averted by the removal of the offending question which was of peripheral value. This is an example of the dangers that can attend the inclusion of sensitive questions that are not central to the theme of the survey and illustrates the need for the interview as a whole to make coherent sense in terms of the frame of reference of respondents.

When an interviewer approaches a private household to seek an interview, the social rules governing the approach to a stranger within their own home must be obeyed, and also those that apply to making requests of a stranger. These rules include notions of privacy and territory. A stranger on the doorstep must state their business from outside the door; it is not permissible to cross the threshold until invited to do so. The survey interviewer is more rigorously constrained by these rules than is the door-to-door salesman since information obtained by pressurizing tactics is likely to be of limited value and such practices blur the distinction between selling and interviewing, rebounding to the detriment of survey research.

Within the framework of society's rules, the interviewer employs a number of strategies and tactics to persuade the selected person to take part. These have to be adapted responsively as the interaction between the interviewer and the contacted person develops. The experienced interviewer will acquire a considerable repertoire of persuasive approaches which may vary in their effectiveness and in their acceptability in terms of what is considered to be appropriate to the interviewer's role.

The interviewers' own image of their role and of survey research is an important element in their morale and in their success in obtaining co-operation. It is necessary for survey organizations to convey to their interviewers a sense of the value of the research in which they are participating, the fundamental importance of their role as data collectors and the professional level of expertise that they are expected to practise. It is only by emphasizing this perspective that interviewers are enabled to withstand the alternative undermining perspectives of themselves as intrusive snoopers, or as askers of silly questions, portrayed on occasions by the media or by antagonistic respondents.

## Ethical considerations in survey interviewing

An implicit system of values is part of the social context within which survey research takes place, governing not only the social norms of what is permissible behaviour but also what is ethically acceptable. It is apparent from what has been said about the interviewer's role that there is an inherent conflict between the job task of maximizing respondent cooperation and ethical considerations governing the lengths to which an interviewer may go in persuading people to give an interview; sometimes survey agencies unwittingly put interviewers under quite unfair pressures to improve response rates in their anxiety to reach a target that may not be realistic in view of the questionnaire type and length, the subject of the survey, the sort of respondent being approached or the amount of money paid to interviewers for the work. Although there are a number of legitimate steps that can be taken to optimize response, the level of response that a particular survey will achieve is not only the result of the resources devoted to the fieldwork but of the characteristics of the survey. It is thus in one sense a finding of the survey, to which pointers should be obtained from a preliminary feasibility study. Some surveys, through no fault of the interviewer, are so unacceptable to members of the population approached that it is doubtful whether they are of sufficient value to be worth undertaking, at least without drastic revisions in form that may entail restricting the objectives of the study.

The responsibility for pressurizing interviewers rests in the first place with field management, but they too are under pressure to 'do a good job' according to implicit standards set by researchers and funders of research. It is unethical of research practitioners and buyers to abrogate their responsibility in this matter; interviewers cannot reasonably be asked to do the impossible and then blamed for not achieving it. Research has shown that this type of pressure can lead to cheating as a way of resolving the dilemma (Crespi, 1945).

More recently, ethical issues in social research in general have been reviewed: the International Statistical Institute Ethics Committee has drawn up an international Code of Practice for statisticians. The Social Research Association worked in parallel with them and adapted the statisticians' code to produce ethical guidelines for those engaged in all kinds of social research; these are described as 'an outline of what the Association recommends as good professional practice' rather than a strict code of conduct. The Market Research Society, which first published its Code of Conduct in 1954, issued a revised and updated version in 1989. These all give extensive coverage to the rights of those from whom or about whom data are collected and also consider the obligations of researchers to society at large, to funders and employers and, in the case of the Social Research Association's Guidelines, to colleagues. However, none of them gives any specific attention to the obligations of researchers to interviewers or considers what desirable professional behaviour towards them should be. Interviewers are the public face of the research team yet are rarely thought of as colleagues; they are usually the most inexperienced and least informed part of the research team yet their role is vital, not only in collecting accurate data but in enhancing the reputation of survey research among the public and in dealing with problems and pressures that arise in the field. Interviewers represent the researcher and the sponsor in the field and respondents may frequently fail to distinguish between these three functions. Researchers and sponsors need to be more aware that the instructions they give to interviewers can often be in conflict with the rights of the respondents as perceived by the interviewer. Future versions of Codes of Conduct should give more consideration to the interviewer's perspective and to the researcher's obligations to interviewers.[4]

Consideration for the rights of the interviewer is closely tied up with awareness of the rights of the respondent. The appropriate sense of researcher responsibility is admirably expressed by Warwick and Lininger:

> We also emphasize that survey research must respect the freedom, dignity and privacy of the groups under study. We thus reject the notion that the researcher has a right, in the name of science or some other higher end, to deceive respondents, misrepresent the nature of the study, or prowl unchecked into the private lives of individuals.
>
> (Warwick & Lininger, 1975)

Gorden (1975) defines ethics as 'the application of social values to concrete behaviour', and points out that, in the 'world of deeds and action', ideals can very easily be thrown into conflict. What seems self evidently right from one perspective can seem grossly unethical from another. As Gorden indicates (op. cit.), in survey research there are perspectives from the point of view of the sponsor, society at large, researchers, interviewers and respondents.

An undertaking that has been given to respondents more or less from the beginning of survey research is that the information they give will be treated as confidential and used only for purposes of the research; there will be no comeback, for example, in the form of sales pressures or the reduction of benefits.  This is why survey researchers so bitterly resent 'sugging'; it makes it appear that researchers are breaking a tenet of their code on which the trust of the public is based.

Survey organizations, especially those involved in social research, now usually give explicit expression to respondents' rights, either in explanatory letters or, more usually, in leaflets given to respondents. These leaflets frequently also give a brief exposition of the purposes of survey research, how samples of participants are selected, what happens to the data, and may include a short description of the survey organization.  (See Annex to this chapter for a copy of part of SCPR's leaflet for respondents.)

In addition to undertakings of confidentiality and use of the information only for research purposes, informational leaflets given to respondents usually also cover:

- their agreement to participate
- the interview itself
- the use of the data

## Agreement to participate

It is generally agreed that it should be made clear to prospective respondents that participation is not compulsory (though the interviewer will put forward legitimate persuasive reasons as to why they should take part).  It is also generally felt that respondents have a right to know in advance what the survey is about, who the sponsor is, and how the data will be used. But sometimes to disclose such information might bias responses; for example, market research companies are rarely able to say which manufacturer has commissioned the survey; to do so might lead to answers over favourable towards their client's brand due to the common tendency to try to give answers that please, or simply to increased awareness of the particular brand. Often, interviewers themselves do not know who the sponsor is.  Similarly, in studies of reactions to traffic or aircraft noise, it is common to try to establish whether noise is uppermost in people's minds as an important local issue and whether a particular type of noise is seen as more or less annoying than other noises, before respondents are made aware of the specific research interests.  In these cases, it is considered that it should be explained to respondents why a full description of the purpose of the survey cannot be given; where possible, the full explanation should be given at the end of the interview. In particular, it is considered unethical knowingly to mislead the respondent as to the purpose of the survey.

*The interview itself*

Respondents should know that they can change their minds about participating in the survey at any time and can ask to have their questionnaire torn up. They should also be aware that they can decline to answer any particular question that they find unacceptable. However, they do not have the right to see the questionnaire itself which is the property of the research agency. This is occasionally a point of contention between respondent and interviewer and an example of a clash of view points: respondents are inclined to think that, since they have agreed to answer the questions, they have a right to see the questionnaire and what has been written down; the researcher, on the other hand, feels that the questionnaire itself with its detailed instructions to interviewers is a confidential document and should not be seen by others until the survey is complete. Interviewers are usually instructed to tear up the questionnaire and cancel the interview if a respondent is very insistent on seeing it.

It is recognized that respondents may have second thoughts after the interviewer has left and may want further information or even to have their questionnaire destroyed. It is therefore considered that the explanatory letter or the descriptive leaflet should contain a name and telephone number that respondents can contact. This is especially important in research among special groups such as the elderly whose helpers or relatives may have misgivings about the legitimacy of the survey, or on surveys covering detailed personal information, especially if it is of a sensitive nature.

*The use of the data*

Through a description of the purpose of the survey or subsequent amplification, the participants should be given some general idea of the use to which the data will be put. The problems here are often more acute for social research projects than for market research, the broad objectives of which are usually fairly unambiguously to do with increasing market share or with product or advertising development. It is rather facilely assumed by many that it is self evident that social research is for the good of 'society', but some people may strongly disagree with the policies of the particular government in power and feel that research sponsored by them is likely to be misused. Others may feel that certain sorts of information might be used for the advantage of the larger society but that their own interests would not be served. Surveys about road or airport development, the disposal of nuclear waste or ways in which the unemployed make use of the 'black economy' might come into this category. It is not sufficient to assure respondents that the information they give will not be used in any personal way to their disadvantage; they must also be able to judge whether the survey findings in general are likely to lead to action that may have a negative effect on them.

What has been set out above are the main ethical issues that affect interviewers and respondents and the currently accepted guidelines to interviewers when a conflict of values arises. But there are no absolute standards and it is impossible to draw up a complete set of rules. What is important is that research sponsors, practitioners and interviewers should be aware that there is an ethical viewpoint to all aspects of survey work and that they should know what standards have been established. It is the responsibility of the professional organizations who have drawn up the Codes of Conduct to ensure not only that their members are familiar with the details of the code, but that funders of research know what ethical conventions have been adopted by the profession so that the perceived need for information is not allowed to outweigh other ethical considerations.

## Exposition

Chapter 2 starts with an appraisal of response rate trends and types of nonresponse and seeks to identify what sort of people tend to be missed from coverage by surveys. This is followed in Chapter 3 by an analysis of the complex set of tasks required of an interviewer in approaching members of the public and setting up an interview and, (in Chapter 4) by an overview of the range of different methods currently available to field management to optimize response.

Chapter 5 presents an analysis of the doorstep interactions between interviewers and members of the public approached for an interview based on tape recordings made by interviewers. The different types of situation with which interviewers have to deal are categorized and the ways in which people express reluctance to participate are identified and evaluated in terms of the effectiveness with which interviewers respond to them. The effects of an experiment in scripting the introduction to be used by interviewers are described. Interviewer performance is evaluated and an attempt made to define the characteristics of a good survey introduction.

In Chapter 6, the request for an interview is examined from the viewpoint of members of the public; why they agree to participate is investigated through analysis of depth interviews with respondents and evaluated in the light of theoretical research from social psychology.

In Chapter 7, a 'Social Skills' approach is used in an analysis of the strategies and tactics that can be adopted by interviewers when approaching members of the public for interview. Social Skills theory rests on the premise that adeptness at handling social interactions is a learned skill, albeit mainly informally learned in the process of growing up; through suitable analysis of the components of the skill, training procedures can be developed that will enhance the individual's ability to achieve the goals of an interaction (for example, to persuade someone to give an interview). In Chapter 7, the social skills required by an interviewer to achieve low rates of refusal are identified through analysis of detailed discussions with field supervisors and interviewers.

Chapter 8 discusses the problems of recruiting interviewers of sufficient calibre and the requirements for training to ensure optimum response rates. A training scheme using social skills training techniques is presented in Appendix II.

Telephone interviewing continues to grow as a method of data collection. Many of the principles that apply to face to face interviewing are also relevant when the interview is conducted by phone but require some adaptation. The particular requirements to obtain good response on telephone surveys are examined in Chapter 9.

This book concentrates on surveys of the general population interviewed at home. In the final chapter there is a review of the special problems and different tactics and skills necessary to obtain interviews on a range of other types of survey. Included are other types of sampled populations (employers, professional people, the elderly or handicapped, and ethnic minorities etc.), other types of survey situation (workplace, street, places of leisure etc.) and other types of survey such as those requiring repeat interviewing and surveys on sensitive topics.

### Notes

1    Formerly the Government Social Survey.
2    Formerly the SCPR Methods Centre (see Foreword).
3    The results of this survey are unpublished but were made available to the author.
4    The Market Research Society is currently considering extending its Code of Conduct to include the rights of interviewers. These revisions are expected to be incorporated into the Code in 1993.

## Annex

## Respondents' rights

The following is incorporated into a leaflet that SCPR interviewers leave with every respondent:

*The entitlements of those taking part*

Your participation is entirely voluntary. Once you have agreed to take part you may still change your mind during the interview and withdraw information you have already given. Also, if you prefer not to answer any questions, you may simply decline to do so.

You are entitled to know the general purpose of the study and the identity of the funder. Normally we prefer to give these details before the interview but occasionally, for technical reasons, we may ask you to wait for them until the end of the interview. You may be assured, however, that we will never deliberately mislead you or hold back information that we think would make you uneasy about having taken part.

Your privacy will be protected. The information you give will be used for research purposes only and will never be linked with your name or address for any other purpose.

You will be given a letter or leaflet about the survey and a telephone number in case you require further information.

# 2 Nonresponse

Asking the questions from the questionnaire is only part of the interviewer's work - and some would say it is the easier part. For inexperienced interviewers in particular, knocking on the door, establishing whom to interview and persuading them to participate constitute the most daunting aspects of the job. It is estimated that, when random sampling is used, only a third to a half of the time that the interviewer spends in the field is devoted to interviewing (Sudman, 1965; van Staveren, 1990), the remainder is taken up with the process of setting up the interview. Yet these functions frequently have comparatively little time and attention devoted to them in training.

The interviewer's task in obtaining the interview varies considerably according to the method of sampling used, the main distinction being between quota and random sampling. When quota sampling is employed there is no onus on the interviewer to call again at an address to contact someone who is out or who is too busy to be interviewed right then, nor to try to persuade the reluctant respondent; records of failure to obtain an interview with a potential respondent are rarely kept. In contrast, when a random sample is taken, the interviewer is enjoined to make considerable effort to interview every eligible person and to keep detailed records of success or failure. It is therefore random sample surveys that have provided the main basis for research to evaluate interviewer performance in obtaining the interview and to examine the factors that operate for and against good response rates.

The object in this book is to examine the task of obtaining the cooperation of members of the public in surveys from every angle: in this chapter, an overview of patterns of nonresponse provides a context in which to review the wide variety of tasks required of interviewers in both quota and random sample surveys in setting up the interview, the difficulties interviewers face and the field management tools that can assist them.  As a preliminary step, it is useful to describe briefly the standard practices used for selecting random samples of the adult population in the United Kingdom.  The particular method presented is for a sample that entails interviewing one adult per household.  It is recognized that, in many surveys using random samples of the population, the unit of study is the household or the requirement is to interview every adult household member.   However, the procedure outlined below exemplifies the basic principles of general population sampling and is the one used in the research on doorstep approaches described in Chapter 5.

### Multi-stage random sampling

A survey sample is carefully designed so as to provide interviews with a cross section of the target population in sufficient numbers for the results to be reliable; the sample size is usually determined by the complexity of analysis required since any subgroups that are important to the objectives of the study must be large enough for separate analysis.  In survey research comparisons between subgroups in the sample are often more important than estimates relating to the population as a whole.

A random sample consists of names and/or addresses selected systematically from a list that hopefully comprises the entire population that is being studied.  To obtain a sample representative of all adults in Britain, it is necessary to select addresses since there is no accessible comprehensive list of individuals; for example the electoral register consists only of those eligible to be electors and who have taken the trouble to register.  Both the electoral register and the Post Office's Postcode Address File (Small Users),[1] however, can be used as sampling frames for addresses, the latter being regarded as the more complete and up to date.  To arrive at a sample of individuals for interview, the interviewer selects one adult from those resident at the address, using an impartial random procedure.

Except in very localized surveys, a sample drawn by selecting addresses randomly across the whole survey population would be geographically very scattered, making interviewer travelling costs unacceptably high.  Samples are therefore drawn in stages so as to produce representative, but geographically clustered, samples.

At the first stage a number of area units (primary sampling units) is selected by a random method; these units might be wards or polling districts for an electoral register sample or postcode sectors for a Postcode Address File sample. Information available from the National Census or other sources about the location, the degree of urbanization, the administrative and the socio-economic characteristics of these first stage units is generally used to stratify the selection - that is, to ensure that different types of areas (e.g., inner cities, rural areas etc.) are selected in the same proportion as they occur in the country as a whole. It is also important to know the number of addresses within each area, so as to control the probability with which addresses and individuals are eventually selected.

When the first stage areas have been selected, a small number of addresses (typically about thirty) is selected within each. A convenient way of doing this is to divide the total number of addresses in the area by the number ($n$) to be selected in the area to give a sampling interval ($i$); take a random starting number between 1 and $n$ and then select the $n^{th}$ unit, the $(n+i)^{th}$ unit, the $(n+2i)^{th}$ unit and so on until the required number of selections has been made.

This procedure ensures that the addresses selected comprise an unbiased and representative sample (within margins of sampling variability) of the adult population living within the first stage sampling units selected, and thus of the adult population of the whole country.[2]

## What do we mean by 'nonresponse'?

Not all the addresses selected will yield an interview. In order to appraise the success of a survey in covering its target sample, a set of conventions has been generally adopted. The first distinction is between those eligible for inclusion in the survey and those ineligible. None of the lists from which addresses can be selected is perfect: they may contain addresses that are empty or have been demolished and the Small Users Postcode Address File includes small nonresidential business premises as well as private residential addresses. For various reasons, it is usual to omit from general population surveys those who live in institutions such as hotels or old people's homes. The presence of ineligible addresses of these kinds on the sampling list is an inconvenience; they reflect the shortcomings of the sampling frame and are not relevant to the issue of response on the survey. They are therefore designated as 'deadwood' rather than 'nonresponse'; they are subtracted from the total issued sample before the response rate is calculated. Levels of nonresponse are thus based on the total eligible sample, not the total issued sample. Experience with a particular sampling frame establishes overall what level of 'deadwood' to allow for when selecting the sample: a sample drawn from the electoral registers will usually yield only 1-2 per cent 'deadwood' while about 12 per cent of a Postcode Address File (Small Users) sample will fall into this category, mainly because of the inclusion of small business premises. The total number of selected addresses has to be increased to allow for this loss from the issued sample.

In order to achieve an interviewed sample of a specific size, allowance also has to be made for nonresponse, that is, failure to achieve an interview at in-scope addresses. There are two main categories of nonresponse, 'refusals' and 'noncontacts', each of which covers some subsidiary groups:

Refusals include:

- complete refusal by someone at the address to give any information, so that the eligibility of residents for interview cannot be established nor a respondent selected;

- refusal by the selected person;

- refusal by someone else on behalf of the selected person (usually on behalf on an elderly, sick or handicapped person that a carer considers would be distressed by the interview);

- broken appointments: if the selected person makes an appointment to be interviewed at a later point and then proves impossible to contact despite several calls, this is usually regarded as a hidden refusal rather than a noncontact.

Noncontacts include:

- failure to make contact with anyone at the address after a minimum of four calls;

- failure to contact the selected individual after a minimum of four calls;

- the selected individual is away (e.g., on holiday, working or in hospital) for the remainder of the fieldwork period.

Other reasons for nonresponse include being ill at home or being unable to give the interview through disability, senility or lack of adequate of English (though sometimes proxy interviews may be permissible).

An example of a response rate analysis is given as an Annex to this chapter.

## Trends and variations in nonresponse

It is generally considered that in urbanized western societies it is becoming more and more difficult to obtain good response rates. This contention is difficult to prove or disprove because surveys vary in many ways that can affect their acceptability to members of the public.

Steeh (1981) studied trends in response for two major repeated surveys in the US from 1951 to 1979 and concluded that refusal rates had increased substantially since the 1950s; in a more recent study in which an attempt was made to adjust for variations in such factors as topic salience, type of sponsorship and number of permitted contacts to obtain the interview, Goyder (1987) indicated a distinct increase in nonresponse during the 1970s.

In Britain, studies of response trends have concentrated mainly on continuous and repeated surveys in which sponsorship, interview length and questionnaire content remain similar over time (Lievesley, 1986; Market Research Society, 1976 and 1981). Three surveys examined in these studies started at the beginning of the 1970s or earlier; of these, the commercially sponsored National Readership Survey shows an upward trend in refusals (but not noncontacts) in the early 1970s and again in the early 1980s. The other two surveys were both government sponsored: the Family Expenditure Survey and the General Household Survey; over two decades they show fairly constant noncontact rates but more erratic refusal rates; however, there is no overall upward trend. Surveys of more recent origin, such as the government sponsored Labour Force Survey launched in 1973 and SCPR's British Social Attitudes Survey which started in 1983 and is funded by a consortium of charitable trusts and government agencies, show very similar patterns.

The conclusion thus seems to be that while there is a tendency for refusal rates to rise, it is not irreversible: but all the survey agencies involved in these studies report the need for constant vigilance and effort to maintain response levels; whenever response has started to drop, new field management measures are likely to have been introduced or more resources put into such tactics as reissuing refusals to another interviewer.

There is a fear that if response starts to decline on continuous or repeated surveys, there will be reduced confidence in the comparability of data from different waves; there is thus considerable pressure on field managements to maintain response levels. Walsh (1976) has shown how organizational measures over a period of time can bring about a marked improvement in response rates; it is the experience of most field organizations engaged in repeat or continuous random sample surveys that this is so but also that the improvements can only be maintained by constant attention and frequent new approaches. It thus seems that good response is in part dependent on interviewer morale rather than being a simple function of field procedures and survey characteristics.

*Response varies by region*

Steeh (1981) showed that in the US both refusals and noncontacts tended to be higher in large cities than in smaller cities and rural areas; in Britain, response in Greater London is consistently lower than in other parts of the country (Lievesley, 1986); in a study of constituency characteristics, Hoinville (1980) showed that response was related to population density and was lowest in metropolitan inner city areas in general, though not as low as in Greater London. The type of areas that showed the second lowest average response rates were those identified by ACORN[3] cluster analysis as suburban commuter areas which are mainly high social status areas and also areas where people tend to return late from work.

*Reasons for trends and variations*

Many reasons have been put forward to explain the increasing difficulty in obtaining good response rates:   Goyder (1987) found correlations between response trends and a general increase in concern with privacy issues; Colombo (1983) also speculates that extensive public debate about the intrusiveness of questions on the 1971 Census in Great Britain may have contributed to reduced response to government surveys.

Increased crime rates and public response in terms of entry phones, reluctance to answer the door at night, gatekeepers etc. have been cited as underlying the problems in inner city areas:   House and Wolf (1978) found that the crime rate of an area was the best predictor of refusal rate. Weeks et al. (1980) showed that there had been a substantial decrease in the proportion of adults at home during the week and that this trend was most marked in inner city areas.

Public attitudes towards surveys are also thought to have changed due to the increased amount of survey work carried out, leading in some areas to over exposure and consequent irritation.  The growth in 'Selling Under the Guise' of survey research ('sugging') has also made the public more suspicious of the survey interviewer.

There are clearly many factors that affect people's willingness to be interviewed.   That trends of increasing nonresponse can be halted indicates that the process of obtaining the interview is dynamic and fluid and that the perceptions and attitudes of the people approached play a vital role.  These factors are examined in greater depth in Chapters 4 and 5.   There are, however, features of the survey itself and of the interviewers that affect response.

*Survey topic and interview length affect response*

The term 'Salience' is used to indicate whether a survey topic is perceived as being of interest and relevance to those approached for an interview; it includes notions of whether the survey is likely to benefit the respondent, society in general or a particular subsection of it and the extent to which respondents feel they have something to say on the subject.

It has long been apparent that there is little difficulty in obtaining well above average response rates for surveys on topics with high salience, even when the questionnaire is an hour or more in length.  High salience surveys are usually confined to subsections of the population (such as mothers of young children on topics to do with health and nutrition, disabled people on aids or benefits, or residents of a particular area about development plans), but studies such as the National Crime Survey, where a general population sample is asked about crimes perpetrated against them or their property, also have high salience.  Surveys of opinions of general issues, for example, the British Social Attitudes Survey which covers a wide range of topics, elicit less cooperation because people feel insufficiently informed about the issues and cannot see that participation will benefit them, or people like them, in any particular way.

When the topic's salience is low, then questionnaire length is likely to have more effect.  in an experiment on a telephone survey that used a shortened version of the British Social Attitudes questionnaires, a forty minute interview received 11 per cent more nonresponse than a twenty minute interview on the same subject (Sykes and Collins, 1987).  Goyder (1987) has shown through multivariate analysis that topic salience is the more important variable but that interview length has an independent effect when topic salience is held constant.

Salience is not the only characteristic of the survey subject matter to affect response: some surveys may be highly salient but obtain low response because people are reluctant to discuss the topic with a stranger (such as personal financial matters, family planning or sexual behaviour); Belson (1975) describes in detail the development work undertaken to obtain a satisfactory level of response in a survey among teenage boys on their involvement in criminal acts.

*Experienced interviewers tend to get higher response*

A dip in response to the General Household Survey in 1981 was attributed by OPCS to a recent recruitment drive for interviewers that had resulted in a higher proportion of inexperienced interviewers in the fieldforce (Colombo, 1983).  Durbin and Stuart (1951) found that overall nonresponse was 14 per cent higher for inexperienced (and largely untrained) interviewers than it was for fully trained and experienced Government Social Survey interviewers; the increase in nonresponse was mainly due to a larger proportion of refusals.  In an analysis of 61 surveys carried out by SCPR, interviewers who had worked for the institute for more than five years were found to obtain higher response rates than less experienced interviewers (Lievesley, 1986).  Couper & Groves (1991) found a positive correlation between the length of time interviewers had worked for the US Bureau of the Census and overall response rate and that the effect was most noticeable over the first few years and then tended to tail off.

It is probable, of course, that the effects of experience are confounded with a certain amount of (self) selection; new interviewers who find it particularly difficult to obtain cooperation may drop out of interviewing or be weeded out by their managers.  This implies that those who take up interviewing vary in the level of appropriate social skills that they bring to the job.  There seems to have been no research to develop ways of appraising these skills as part of the selection process, though they are undoubtedly intuitively assessed by the recruiting officers.

In order to improve interviewer performance in obtaining cooperation, it is necessary to identify the basic social skills that provide a good foundation for becoming a successful interviewer and also to establish the nature of the more specific skills that are learned through experience so that they can be taught in basic training rather than left to develop through trial and error.

## Does nonresponse matter?

If we could be sure that nonrespondents did not differ from those interviewed, there would be less need to worry about response levels since the survey results would not be affected. Any differences, however, might indicate that certain sections of the population are under represented; this could seriously affect the accuracy of the survey, particularly if it is concerned with minority groups in the population.

The higher the level of nonresponse, the more there is a likelihood that differences between respondents and nonrespondents could bias the survey results. It is therefore important to collect information about nonrespondents. There are several ways of doing this:

*a) Comparison with population data.* The most common is to compare the characteristics of the interviewed sample with those of the general population using, for example, census data, government statistics or some large government survey with a very high level of response.

*b) Comparison with an external source.* Occasionally, information might be available from another source about both respondents and nonrespondents; this is sometimes the case where samples are drawn from special lists such as the register of the unemployed or lists of council tenants; in 1971 and 1981, OPCS were able to extract census data relating to individuals sampled in the General Household, Family Expenditure and Labour Force Surveys.

*c) Data collected by interviewers.* Sometimes it is possible for interviewers to collect some information about nonrespondents when they call at the address, though usually only for a couple of variables and rarely for all nonrespondents.

All three of these methods have the limitation that comparisons can usually be made on only a number of very general characteristics.

*d) Analysis by number of calls at address.* A fourth method is based on the assumption that those who require the most effort in terms of number of calls to obtain the interview are similar to those not interviewed; hence comparison of the characteristics of those interviewed after one, two, three, four or more calls is taken as a pointer to types of possible bias in the sample. This method has the advantage that it is not restricted to a few general population variables but can be applied to those of importance in the specific survey being undertaken; it is only valid for identifying the characteristics of noncontacts since refusal is as likely to occur at first calls as at later calls.

## Who are the nonrespondents?

Because of the number of different ways of assessing whether non-response bias is likely to exist, and also because much of the research has concerned survey specific variables, it is difficult to establish whether there is a consistent tendency for certain sections of the population to be under represented. The pattern that emerges indicates that response tends to be lower among those in smaller households, especially one person households; associated with this is lower response among the older age groups, young adults (20-24) and those without dependent children. Response is lower also among those in lower socio-economic groups, the less well educated, those in lower income groups and the self employed. (Lievesley, 1986; Rauta, 1985; Redpath, 1986; Goyder, 1987; DeMaio, 1980.)

What is apparent from the literature is that certain types of people tend to be consistently under represented on most surveys but that others may be under represented on specific surveys. The picture is confusing because this general overview does not distinguish between those who refuse and other types of nonrespondent, especially noncontacts.

## Refusers and noncontacts are different

As Lievesley (1986) points out, if there are differences between refusers and noncontacts, the biases resulting from these two sources may offset each other. The evidence suggests that this is to some extent the case: in a methodological survey carried out at SCPR, an attempt was made to recall on refusers and noncontacts to collect some basic demographic data about them. Successful contact was made in 78 per cent of the cases. Compared with respondents, noncontacts were more likely to be male and in the younger age groups; they were considerably more likely to be single, to be working and to live in rented accommodation and flats. Refusers in general were more similar to respondents but were a little more likely to be female, to be in the older age groups, to be married, to own their accommodation outright and to live in semi-detached houses. Benson et al. (1951) also showed offsetting bias when they found that refusers tended to be of lower economic status and to be less well educated whereas noncontacts were more likely to have college degrees and higher incomes (variables that could not be covered in the SCPR survey).

In the SCPR survey, both refusers and noncontacts had smaller average household size than respondents, showing that in this respect the amount of bias is compounded by the two types of nonresponse.

There is clearly some correlation between the various characteristics described for each type of nonresponder: single people are more likely than married people to be young and to live in rented accommodation; men are more likely than women to be working. If all the characteristics associated with not being contacted by the interviewer are considered together, we have a picture of a young single working male living in rented accommodation; the lifestyle stereotypically associated with this group is such as to make it difficult for an interviewer to make contact.

The difficulties of collecting sufficiently detailed information about nonrespondents and the dangers of imputing differences from comparisons between those interviewed after only one or two calls and those who were only contacted or persuaded after several calls mean that the profiles of refusers and noncontacts are rather sketchy and may be lacking in important dimensions. Although it is some comfort that there is evidence that distortions to the sample caused by noncontacts and refusals offset each other, there may be other variables on which only one of the types of nonrespondent differs from respondents. Furthermore, one category of nonresponse may be higher than the other; for example, on SCPR ad hoc surveys, noncontacts usually exceed refusals; on repeat government surveys such as the General Household Survey or Family Expenditure Survey, on which enormous resources are expended to achieve a high response rate, noncontacts are very low and are far exceeded by refusals. Despite the rather confusing evidence, it is clear that some sections of the population tend to be under represented in surveys and that any survey with a low response rate may well contain biases specific to that survey. Response levels must therefore continue to be a matter for concern.

In addition to devoting effort and resources to obtain a high response rate, all possible ways of evaluating the representativeness of the sample should be used. The number of calls made to get the interview should be recorded by interviewers and included in the computerized data set so that key variables in the survey can be analyzed by number of calls in order to look for possible pointers to bias due to noncontact in the sample. Interviewers can also usually find out at least the sex, household size, type of dwelling and possibly approximate age of most nonrespondents so that the deficiencies in the achieved sample in those respects can be assessed.

It is common practice to compare the achieved sample with the population as a whole in demographic terms; information is usually available for general population samples from the Census (which may be out of date towards the end of the decade) or from large government sponsored surveys with high response rates, such as the General Household Survey. Comparisons are usually made on such variables as age, sex, socio-economic group, household size, and region. It also makes good sense to include in the questionnaire questions relevant to the subject of the survey that are specifically designed to replicate information already available about the population being sampled; for example, surveys on health might include some questions used in the General Household Survey in order to make comparison possible.

All these measures provide information for appraising the representativeness of the achieved sample: to what extent can the information be usefully used to correct the sample by weighting? Opinions vary among sampling statisticians as to the wisdom of such a course but some (e.g., Moser and Kalton, 1971) recommend that it should be done provided that:

1. the population information is reliable;

2. the variable or variables on the basis of which the sample is to be weighted is known to be related to important information being collected by the survey.

There are dangers in weighting the sample to correct for apparent bias in that it may exacerbate hidden unrepresentativeness on other variables. There is no sure way of avoiding bias except by achieving a good response rate. Although the representativeness of the sample should be appraised, the information can best be used to estimate the extent to which it falls short and to indicate the direction and degree of possible bias, rather than as a panacea through weighting.

## Quota sampling

Some survey practitioners argue that a well constructed quota sample can be as good as, or better than, a random sample with a poor response rate since the quota controls ensure that the achieved sample represents the target population in terms of selected variables such as age, sex, socio-economic grade and economic activity status (working/not working etc.). Most face to face market research surveys use quota sampling but, on major surveys, the first stage, that of selecting interviewing areas, is usually carried out according to strict random sampling principles; the interviewing areas may be wards but are often smaller units such as census enumeration districts; the interviewer selects people for interview within the defined area to fit preset quota requirements in terms of such variables as age, sex, economic activity status and social grade.

Quota controls can be interlocking or independent; a common form of interlocking control is to set separate age and economic activity status quotas for men and women, so that age and economic activity status are independent of each other but are interlocking with sex. Age is usually

divided into three categories, ranging from 16-35 to over 55 years. There
are six categories within the socio-economic grading system generally used
in British market research:

A       Senior management and professional
B       Middle management and professional
C1      'White collar' workers, junior management, clerical
C2      Skilled manual workers
D       Semi skilled manual workers
E       Unskilled manual workers, those living on state benefits or
        pensions.

The top two (A and B) and the bottom two (D and E) are usually
combined to give four categories. For women, whether they are working
or not is usually an important quota control. Clearly, the larger the
number of categories and the more quota controls interlock, the harder
the task for the interviewer. (For more detailed information on varieties
and complexities of quota sampling, see Rothman & Mitchell, 1989;
Worcester & Downham, 1986.)

*Appraisal of quota sampling*

The claim that quota sampling can be as good as, or better than, random
sampling relies on two assumptions: that the behaviour and attitudes to
be measured are related primarily to the variables used as quota controls;
secondly, that they are not associated independently of these controls with
factors underlying nonresponse nor with the characteristics of those likely
to require more than one call to obtain an interview. People who are out
a great deal, who are very busy and unwilling to be interviewed
immediately or live in small households, are likely to be under
represented; those at home during the day such as those without paid
jobs, shift workers or people who work at home, and those whose work
takes them into the street such as maintenance workers, may be over
represented, unless the variable is one of the quota controls or the time
at which interviewers work is strictly controlled (Moser & Stuart, 1953;
Sudman, 1966).

There is some evidence that the proportion of those contacted on a
quota sample who refuse to be interviewed can be quite massive. For
example, in a quota sample survey on hours of work for women and men
for the Equal Opportunities Commission, interviewers were asked to
record how many refusals they met with: the report cites that 'there were
1,749 estimated refusals for the 1,412 successful interviews obtained
(Marsh, 1991). This provides enormous scope for certain sorts of people
to be under represented and more research is required to make closely
controlled comparisons between the samples obtained by the two
methods.

Quota sampling can have other short comings. Each interviewer's quota specification is usually the same, at least within broad regions and often for the country as a whole; but areas are likely to vary considerably in age and especially social grade composition. This can be another source of bias, especially in analysis of subgroups.

Bias can also arise from the opportunity that the interviewer has to exercise some choice in which dwellings or which people to approach: the flat with the large dog, the house with filthy windows and decaying furniture in the garden or blaring forth loud music and the dwelling with an entryphone can be avoided. There is also a great temptation to interviewers to slide a 50 year old into the 55+ group or a C1 into a B social grade when there is difficulty in filling the last gaps in the quota. The establishment of socio-economic grade by two or three questions on the doorstep has been found to be very unreliable (Marsh, 1986; Rothman, 1989).

## Comparisons of quota and random sampling

There has been relatively little research to evaluate empirically the differences between quota and random sampling and much of what there is is quite old (Moser & Stuart, 1953; Sudman, 1966). There is one recent study by Marsh & Scarbrough (1990) in which a comparison was made of samples obtained by quota and random methods on a survey about response to unemployment carried out in an East London borough and a town in East Anglia. Half the interviews in each locality were sampled by each method. According to the best estimates available, the unemployment rate was 13 per cent in both localities. Screening methods were adopted to increase the number of unemployed persons in both samples to 40 per cent of the total. For the quota sample, the quota controls were age and sex, the latter interlocked with economic activity status. Interviewers were instructed to record all refusals.

The refusal rate was, as expected, much higher for the quota sample: 45 per cent, compared with 29 per cent for the random sample.

The primary sampling units for both samples were polling districts; these each included a number of smaller census enumeration districts. As a measure of the extent of clustering of the samples, the enumeration district of each address was ascertained. It was found that the quota sample was one and a half times more clustered than the random sample; in other words, the interviewers using quota sampling methods confined themselves to relatively small sections of their allotted areas. Furthermore, analysis of the neighbourhoods in which respondents lived, using the ACORN classification, showed that the quota sample was less heterogeneous than the random sample, indicating possible selectivity of types of neighbourhood to interview in on the part of the quota interviewers. Additional evidence of selectivity was provided by the fact that in the London borough 20 per cent of the interviews were conducted in the wrong ward. The unemployment rate (an index of the 'roughness' of an area) in the quota sample neighbourhoods was lower than in those for the random sample and the amount of variation in employment levels was less.  As the authors say:

> This suggests that the quota interviewers interpreted the latitude about whom to interview as latitude about where to interview, perhaps even targeting different areas to secure interviews with employed and unemployed people.
> (Marsh & Scarbrough, 1990)

The two samples were compared to try to establish what types of bias each might produce.  The types of bias looked for were those that had been found in the rather sparse and dated earlier studies.  The findings were not always in keeping with those of earlier research, which were themselves not always consistent.  This suggests that the effects of quota sampling may vary according to the differing constraints imposed by the quota controls, not only because of the way in which interviewers select neighbourhoods in which to search for people to fill their quotas, but also as a result of 'snowballing', the practice of asking respondents to advise where other eligible people might be found.

In this study, there was some indication that the quota sample was biased towards the more easily accessible people; the women were biased towards those in households with children; in general, there was a bias towards people in public sector employment (rather than private) and against the extremes of the income range.  On the other hand, men were under represented in the random sample but not in the quota sample because gender was a quota control.  It must be borne in mind that the response to the random sample was only 62 per cent and was therefore unlikely to be free of nonresponse bias.

*Random location sampling*

An alternative method being increasingly adopted by some leading market research companies is 'random location sampling' (van Staveren, 1990). Based on methods developed in the United States (Sudman, 1966; Stephenson, 1978), this system combines aspects of both random and quota sampling.

A large number of very small interviewing areas (usually census enumeration districts) is selected, the selection of points being stratified by region and geodemographic variables available through ACORN or other classificatory data bases.  The use of very small sampling points means that variation between points is maximized while variation within points is minimized.  The reduced variation within points, it is argued, removes the need for complicated quota controls, especially socio-economic grade which is notoriously unreliable.  The first quota control is gender; among women, further controls are working status and the presence of children; among men, usually the only control is time of interview, the number of interviews that can be taken before 4.00pm being restricted. The theory is that likelihood of being at home is the only major variable not controlled through the selection of points.

It has been calculated (van Staveren, 1990) that the number of half hour interviews achievable per day by this sampling method is seven to eight, compared with only about five on a random sample and nine on an ordinary quota sample, and that design effects are only a little larger than those for random samples and considerably less than for ordinary quota samples. These advantages are based on interviewer assignments being very small (usually one day's work), which rely on the questionnaire and survey procedures being familiar enough, or simple enough, for preparatory time on the part of the interviewer to be minimal.

*In conclusion*

For many purposes quota sampling can give perfectly adequate results, especially for target populations such as housewives where nonresponse might be minimal. For general population samples, random location sampling can provide a considerably improved sample for a relatively small extra cost, provided that the questionnaire is relatively short (around 30 minutes or less) and simple, not requiring interviewer briefings. But for longer and more complex surveys, the verdict has to be that probability sampling is preferable, despite its greater cost, since nonresponse will be less and there is no opportunity for the interviewer to exercise choice over where or whom to interview. What is more, the necessary keeping of detailed records of calls and of nonresponse means that sampling errors can be estimated and the extent and direction of possible bias assessed.

**Reusable samples?**

Some research studies call for a second interview or several more interviews, to be conducted with the same respondents. It is known that, although there is some loss at the second and subsequent interviews, response is usually high among those who have already been interviewed. An important question to be considered is whether, and to what extent, a sample selected for one survey could be used on another survey provided, of course, that respondents agree to further contact. Many survey agencies conduct very large scale national population surveys from time to time or conduct on-going data collection surveys such as omnibus surveys into which a number of clients can buy. The British Market Research Bureau is one such agency that has experimented with using sub samples drawn from a large database of general population surveys for telephone interviews (Hahlo, 1992).

Hahlo argues that around half of the population say they have been interviewed on a survey before and that the existence of the uncontaminated respondent is a myth. In a comparison with a freshly drawn sample, he showed that there were no significant differences between the answers of the two samples to factual or behavioural questions; on awareness questions, the reinterviewed sample tended to mention more brands which could be attributed to respondents trying harder; Hahlo suggests that the reused sample gave a more accurate assessment of awareness.

The results of questions on attitudes to market research were not significantly different although there was a consistent trend for the reused sample to be more positive in their attitudes.

The literature on longitudinal surveys and panel use is clearly relevant to the debate as to whether and in what circumstances members of a sample used for one survey might be selected to participate in another. The cost savings and lack of differences in results indicated by Hahlo's study suggest that the question of reusing surveys should not be dismissed but should be investigated through further research studies to determine what type of surveys might use this approach, what time gap should be left between visits, and how many times a respondent can be interviewed before boredom sets in and patience wears out.

The indications are that selecting a sample from a database pool of previously interviewed respondents about whom a body of information exists can be at least as good as a fresh quota sample. The method has also been used on occasion on random samples as a means of finding a sample of people with particular characteristics or experience as an alternative to expensive screening surveys. To what extent this procedure could be taken further remains to be explored.

### Notes

1   Samples from the Postcode Address File can be purchased from the Post Office or a number of commercial agencies.
2   Those requiring more information on random sampling methods are referred to Kish (1965), Butcher (1988) and Lynn & Lievesley (1991).
3   ACORN ('A Classification of Residential Neighbourhoods') was the first geodemographic system in which cluster analysis techniques were applied to small area statistics from the Census; all enumeration districts and postcode sectors were then classified into descriptive categories based on the results (Webber, 1979).

## Annex

## A typical analysis of response

### (From the First British National Crime Survey)

| I  Addresses | No | % |
|---|---|---|
| Issued (Electoral Register Sample) | 14280 | 100 |
| Found to be out of scope | | |
|    - vacant/derelict | 442 | 3.1 |
|    - business/industrial premise only | 23 | 0.2 |
|    - demolished | 22 | 0.2 |
|    - institution | 18 | 0.1 |
|    - other reasons | 7 | 0.05 |
| Assumed to be out of scope | | |
|    - not traced | 91 | 0.6 |
| Total out of scope | 603 | 4.2 |
| Total in scope | 13677 | 95.8 |

| II  Selected Persons | | |
|---|---|---|
| Total assumed to be in scope | 13677 | 100 |
| Interviewed | 10898 | 79.7 |
| Not interviewed | 2779 | 20.3 |

| *Reasons for nonresponse* | | |
|---|---|---|
| **Refusal (total)** | **1744** | **12.8** |
|    - selected person refused | 1032 | 7.5 |
|    - refusal on behalf of selected person by someone else in household | 314 | 2.3 |
|    - complete refusal of information | 295 | 2.2 |
|    - broke appointment and could not be recontacted | 103 | 0.8 |
| **Noncontact (total)** | **785** | **5.7** |
|    - no contact with anyone at address | 382 | 2.8 |
|    - selected person not contacted | 251 | 1.8 |
|    - selected person away/in hospital | 152 | 1.1 |
| **Other reasons for no interview (total)** | **250** | **1.8** |
|    - selected person senile/incapacitated | 122 | 0.9 |
|    - selected person ill (at home) | 75 | 0.5 |
|    - interview not completed | 23 | 0.2 |
|    - selected persons could not speak adequate English | 22 | 0.2 |
|    - other reasons | 8 | 0.1 |

# 3 The interviewer's tasks in obtaining interviews

Preparation for fieldwork and setting up the interviews require organizing ability, a thorough grounding in the procedures and skill in presentation and persuading. Good and bad interviewer approaches are vividly illustrated by McFarlane-Smith (1972) in the introduction to her book 'Interviewing in Market and Social Research'. A vignette of the good interviewer presents her as positive and polite in approach but maintaining a professional distance; she gives a brief well constructed factual introduction that enables the respondent to perceive the goal of the interview; she checks the respondent's eligibility for the interview before starting; she answers questions about the length of the interview and the use of the information truthfully and reassuringly; she has all her materials well organized in businesslike folders. The bad interviewer, on the other hand, carries her materials in a shopping bag; she is over effusive and apologetic in her introduction and interacts in a social and gossipy way, expressing her own opinions about the subject matter; she makes herself at home by hanging up her coat and using the toilet; she fails to give her or her company's names or to establish the eligibility of the respondent until after the interview has started.

McFarlane-Smith sets out the accepted wisdom of the day which has changed little in basic principles since 1972. It is based on a mixture of experience, common sense and idealism concerning the image of the interviewer that the survey industry would like to project: an image of a cool, charming, well trained, impartial professional. In what follows, the requirements of this initial part of interviewing work are set out, together with the ways of tackling them that have evolved through experience and through striving to improve response, reduce bias and save money.

## Initial preparation

Each interviewer asked to work on a particular survey will receive instruction on the conduct of that survey. On social research surveys in Britain, this will usually take the form of a one day 'briefing' conference and written instructions. On market research studies it is more likely to consist of written instructions only, with amplification from regional field staff if required. In the United States, the size of the country tends to make personal briefings prohibitively expensive; instead, postal training schedules are developed. For major and ongoing surveys, these may be quite elaborate, involving dummy interviews both with the supervisor by telephone and with members of the public. All major survey organizations provide their interviewers with a manual which constitutes a permanent reference book for use when interviewing; while some cover little more than the basic definitions of social grading and household status categories and the specific administrative procedures of the organization, others include instruction on the basic principles of all aspects of the interviewer's work (e.g., McCrossan, 1991; SCPR, 1984a).

Interviewers are also issued with an identity card which bears their photograph. Most social research organizations issue their own cards but the British Market Research Society has gone some way in establishing a single market research interviewer's card under its aegis; all companies subscribing to the scheme undertake to observe certain standards in the conduct of fieldwork. The interviewer's identity card is regarded as a very important aid in helping interviewers to establish the legitimacy of the survey and thus in obtaining cooperation. Interviewers are enjoined to carry their manual and their identity card whenever they are working and to show their card to each person that they approach for an interview.

Before visiting the interviewing area, the interviewers need to do a certain amount of preliminary preparation:

1.  they should go over the questionnaire and instructions carefully and make sure all is understood;

2.  they need to prepare and learn a brief introduction to the survey and to think of answers to likely questions about the survey until they have absorbed all the necessary background information;

3.  they must check that all the materials required have been supplied, (they should have already checked that their interviewer's identity card is up to date);

4.  it is helpful to organize the materials into pocket folders or plastic pockets for ease of access in the field;

5.    on a random sample, the interviewer should examine the issued addresses for legibility and completeness or, for a quota sample, make sure the quota requirements are understood;

6.    if the interviewer does not have a map of the area, then one of the first tasks on the first visit to the area would be to buy one. The random sample interviewer then needs to locate the addresses geographically and make notes about the proximity of streets to each other so that a sensible route can be planned each time the area is visited. The quota sample interviewer must identify the location and the boundaries of the interviewing area.

The materials supplied to the interviewers will include general ones that are common to most surveys and others that are specific to the particular survey. General materials will include administrative forms such as pay claims, records of returned work and envelopes for returning questionnaires to the office. There may also be a general leaflet about survey research and its use and this may include information about the organization undertaking the survey work.

Materials specific to the survey are likely to include:

1.    *The questionnaires,* which might consist of different versions for different subsets of the sample or self completion supplements;

2.    *Show cards or other visual aids* for use during the interview. Cards should usually be of a good size (A5 is commonly used) and have large lettering that can be read by most respondents without their reading glasses; they should be laminated so that they stay clean and should be kept together by the use of rings;

3.    *Written project instructions* which should cover how the sample is to be selected, how the survey is to be introduced and how any particularly tricky questions are to be dealt with. They would also include any definitions of categories specific to that survey that might be required in establishing whom to interview or in administering particular sections of the questionnaire. Project instructions are usually written by the researcher but should always be vetted by field management who should be more in tune with how to communicate to interviewers. Attention should be given to the use of clear unambiguous language and good lay out;

On a general population random sample survey there would also be:

4.    *The addresses* at which interviews are to be sought. These may come in the form of lists, photocopies of pages of the electoral

register or, more commonly these days, computer generated labels that are attached to individual address record forms. These forms also contain the requirements for recording details of calls at the address and the final outcome (e.g., Interviewed, Refused, No contact, Ineligible and so on). On random samples, a record of what happened at each issued address is extremely important for evaluating the success of the survey. It is helpful to obtain as much information as possible about all calls at the address (day, time and outcome) so that the problems of gaining cooperation can be appraised, especially if an address is reissued to another interviewer. The design of the address record form should therefore be given careful consideration and should include full instructions on how to complete it. Usually, each field work organization develops its own standard layout which can be modified to meet the needs of individual surveys. An example is given in Appendix I;

5. *An explanatory letter* for leaving with the respondent; this normally briefly describes the purpose of the survey, introduces the sponsor and the survey organization, gives some indication of how the address was selected and how the information will be used, and gives assurances that confidentiality will be preserved. The letter usually gives an address and phone number through which members of the public can obtain more information about the survey and is signed by someone with authority and prestige. It is usually on the sponsor's headed paper. The explanatory letter is another means of establishing the interviewer's and the survey's credibility; it can be used to help obtain cooperation and to allay suspicion at the first contact, or left with the respondent after the interview to ensure that they have a record of what the survey was about, who it was for and where the interviewer came from;

6. *Respondent selection forms* might also be required if the interviewer has to administer a random selection procedure to select one person for interview from those resident at the address. The respondent selection form might be combined with the address record form (an example is given in Appendix I);

On a quota sample survey:

7. *Instructions as to the quota requirements* and quota record keeping forms.

A judicious use of different coloured paper helps the interviewer to identify quickly which item of survey material is which.

## The first visit to the interviewing area

If possible, interviewers make their first visit to the area in daylight. On most surveys, the first thing they have to do is to visit the local police station to inform them about the survey; this helps to establish the bona fides of the interviewer and to pre-empt problems caused by people suspicious of the interviewer's activities phoning the police. Police stations vary in the attention they give to an interviewer's visit and it is not unknown for the police to deny having heard of a survey despite it; SCPR has found it best to provide interviewers with a standard letter to the police on which the interviewer fills in the name of the police station, their own name, identity card number and car registration number, the name of the sponsoring organization, the project identification number and the fieldwork dates. A copy of the explanatory letter provided for respondents is attached to the standard letter. Interviewers are also instructed to make a note of the name of the officer to whom they speak and of the time and date of their call.

While it is still daylight, most interviewers want to establish that they have correctly identified their interviewing area and that they can find the streets in which their addresses are situated; this is particularly the case in rural areas where roads are less clearly marked and where houses are sometimes known by names rather than numbers.

If the area is in an inner city, the interviewer will also establish whether any parts of it are particularly unsavoury and best visited only in daylight. The police are often helpful in warning interviewers about potentially dangerous areas, though in some interviewers' opinions they are often over cautious.

The interviewer on the spot is the best person to judge whether or not it is likely to be dangerous to attempt to interview in the area or, as is more likely, in some parts of the area. The field managers and researchers have to be prepared either to pay for someone to accompany the interviewer or to accept that certain addresses cannot be covered adequately. The accompanying escort is sometimes required to guard the interviewer's car rather than the interviewer; thankfully, damage to or theft from interviewers' cars is more common than damage to their persons; but neither is, so far, a frequent occurrence in Great Britain.

Women interviewers' husbands are often reluctant for their wives to interview in areas with a bad reputation and their feelings have to be respected. It is thus common practice when male interviewers are available to give them the assignments in the rougher areas. However, men too can be in danger and may need to work in pairs in some areas, at least after dark. At least one British fieldwork organization has issued its interviewers with personal alarms. This is a reasonably inexpensive way of safeguarding interviewers and of increasing their confidence.

## Finding addresses

Experienced interviewers become very adept at tracking down hard-to-find addresses.  A problem may arise for a number of reasons: the sampling frame may be out of date or the address may have been wrongly or inadequately recorded on it; or the address may have been wrongly or only partially copied when the sample was drawn; sometimes the available maps are too small or are inaccurate or out of date due to demolition or new building, and sometimes the British way of naming streets or numbering houses or flats is confusing.

The first recourse in searching for a hard-to-find address is to ask local shop keepers or roundsmen.  If that fails, the local post office or police station may be able to help.  The local post office should be able to provide access to the Postcode Directory for the area and this can be used to locate addresses if the postcode is given.  The local council office should be able to help in establishing whether an address has been demolished and also in locating blocks in council estates.

Before the interviewer spends a great deal of time searching for an address, the office should be asked to check that it has been accurately copied from the original sampling frame.  Apart from miscopying, there are pitfalls into which the inexperienced sampling clerk may easily fall; for example, in the electoral register, village or area names may be put once as a subhead; electors' names, house numbers and street names are then listed below without the village or area name.  The clerk may assume that all the streets are in the town or a larger area that gives the constituency its name, or fail to notice that there has been a change from one village or area to another.  Similarly, addresses in blocks of flats on large council estates may cover several pages in the register and the name of the road on which the estate is situated may appear only once at the beginning.  The interviewer may thus be given flat numbers and block names but no street name.

Searching for addresses can be time consuming, frustrating and costly.  It is therefore important that the sampling frame should be as up to date and accurate as possible and that care should be taken to copy the complete address accurately, with an awareness that doing so may not be as straightforward a task as it appears to be.

## Establishing eligibility of the address

Having found the address, the interviewer's next task is to establish whether it is occupied or not and whether it is residential, or business premises or an institution that would normally not be eligible for inclusion in the survey.  Whether the premises are vacant cannot always be determined by observation alone and the interviewer may make enquiries among neighbours, being very discreet as to the purpose of the visit.  No attempt should be made to describe the survey as a garbled message about it may be passed on; on no account should an interviewer try to obtain any personal information from neighbours as this could result in justifiable charges of snooping.

To be ineligible for inclusion, business premises or institutions must have no residential unit at the same address, which usually has to be established by enquiry at the address; small institutions such as hostels or small old people's homes have to be distinguished from communal dwellings of other sorts by asking a few questions about number of residents and how the running of the place is organised so that a definition which the interviewer will have learned, can be applied.

## Making contact at the address

Interviewers are usually instructed to make at least four calls at an address to try to obtain an interview, each call being on a different day of the week and at a different time: it is stipulated that at least two of the calls should be during the evening or at the weekend. Often, interviewers make many more calls in between those demanded by the rules. Again, a discreet and generally worded enquiry as to when is likely to be a good time to find someone home might be made of a neighbour if a couple of calls have proved fruitless.

Experienced interviewers often remark that they have noticed a decline in people's willingness to answer their doors after dark, or else there is a widespread habit of leaving on lights and television while out. Other barriers may make contact difficult such as wardens of sheltered housing or the increasingly numerous entryphones. Even experienced interviewers often find dealing with entryphones difficult because the sound quality is usually very poor and traffic noise makes conversation difficult. In these conditions, it is virtually impossible to convey the desired information, to establish authority for the survey or to make an impression of being a trustworthy and friendly person, all of which play a part in gaining cooperation. The canny interviewer will usually try to persuade the person on the other end of the entryphone either to come to the main door or to admit them by saying that they have a letter about the survey to give them.

### The etiquette of making contact

When the interviewer makes contact at the address, there is an accepted way of proceeding that is based partly on conventions of social politeness, partly on the logic of the task to be accomplished and partly on experience as to what seems to encourage participation in the survey. The order may vary slightly but broadly the steps are as follows:

1.    the interviewer greets the person who answers the door, introduces themselves and the organization for which they are

working, e.g., 'Good afternoon; I'm Nigel Brown, an interviewer working for ..... Here is my identity card;'

2.    they then check that they are at the correct address and if so;

3.    briefly introduce the survey stating who it is for and its general purpose or content, e.g., 'We are doing a survey for the Department of the Environment on what it is like living in this area;'

At this point the person at the door may ask a question or indicate suspicion or reluctance to take part. The interviewer must react adroitly to this with appropriate information and/or reassurances. Providing the conversation is allowed to continue, the interviewer proceeds to establish who should be interviewed; on a general population random sample survey,[1] the interviewer would:

4.    explain that it is necessary to select one person at random from those resident at the address, a procedure that, with the person's help, will take only a minute or two;

5.    carry out the respondent selection procedure.

If the person contacted turns out to be the person selected for interview, the interviewer will then explain about the survey a little more fully and ask for an interview. If another is the selected person, the interviewer will ask to speak to that person, if necessary calling back up to three more times if the person is out. If contact was made at the address only on the fourth call, the interviewer might have to make up to three further calls (seven in all) to try to obtain the interview. When the selected person is contacted, the interviewer has to show their identity card and introduce the survey from the beginning as misleading information may have been given by the person first contacted.

When a person has been selected for interview, only that person may be interviewed; substitution is not allowed. The reason for this is often difficult to explain to the diffident or reluctant selected person who may suggest that someone else in the household or a next door neighbour would be a better informed and more interested respondent. The interviewer not only has to have a grasp of the basic principles of sampling, but be able to explain them convincingly and simply to someone who may have no concept of what a 'sample' is.

Occasionally, one family member will try to protect another by assuring the interviewer that the selected person will definitely not want to take part, that their English is too poor or that they are too senile or handicapped to do so. This may be true but interviewers should, where it is possible without giving offence, ask to see the person to establish the situation for themselves. In some surveys, proxy interviews with another adult household member may be permitted, at least for sections of the questionnaire dealing with factual information. Sometimes another member of the household is able to act as interpreter between the interviewer and the selected person. The researcher must make it clear whether or not proxy interviews or the use of interpreters are allowed.

At any point during the contacting, explanatory and respondent selection procedures, the interviewers may have to deal with requests for information or expressions of distrust or reluctance. They have to be familiar with information that can be used to amplify the description of the survey, its funding, its purpose and how the information will be used, and also to be skilled in putting this over, in using the explanatory letter and general leaflet to establish the legitimacy of the survey, and in conveying by their manner, expression and way of talking, the professional and trustworthy nature of their own role. The dynamics of this process, the ways in which reluctance are expressed, how members of the public feel about being asked for an interview and the social skills required by the interviewers are the focus of intensive investigation and analysis in Chapters 5, 6 and 7. The purpose here is to indicate broadly the range of knowledge and skills that are required of the survey interviewer in obtaining the interview on random sample surveys. The requirements are somewhat less stringent when quota sampling is used as the reluctant or hard to contact person can be replaced with someone more willing, but the basic principles are the same.

## The respondent selection procedure

In both random and quota sampling, the interviewer has to establish the eligibility of people for interview, a procedure that depends for its accuracy on the correct definition of certain categories. The interviewer has to be thoroughly familiar with these definitions as they often have to be used on the doorstep in circumstances where reference to written instructions is impossible.

The definitions that might have to be applied in establishing eligibility for interview may include any of the following:

*Residence at the address:* in a sample of addresses, only those normally resident at the address are eligible for interview; whether someone is resident is unambiguous in most cases but special rules apply to those working or studying away from home or in hospital or prison (McCrossan, 1991; SCPR, 1984a).

*A household:* the sampling instructions may require the interviewer to identify how many households live at the address and to select one by a random procedure or to select a person from each household there. To count as one household, a group of residents must either share at least one meal a day or share the living accommodation (i.e., a living room or sitting room). This latter alternative qualification was added by OPCS at the time of the 1981 Census to reflect changing social patterns in which family meals are less common.

*Household status:* sometimes the survey is confined to people who fulfil particular roles in the household; on many market research surveys only 'housewives' are interviewed, defined as the (female) person responsible for the cooking and catering; on others the 'Chief Income Earner'[2] of the household may be the target, defined as the person with the largest income, whether from employment, pensions, state benefits, investments or other sources. A third definition of household status that is sometimes used is that of the Householder; this is simply an adult member of the household who is legally responsible for the accommodation (SCPR, 1984a). There can be more than one Householder in a household, in which case some additional criterion for selection of a respondent has to be adopted; this may simply be to select the male out of a male/female pair or the elder out of a same sex pair; or a random procedure may be used.

There may be other specific definitions of categories of respondent to be learned for a particular survey and there are almost certain to be other standard definitions that have to be applied during the interview itself (such as marital and economic activity status). The interviewer must have a detailed knowledge of the definitional rules, including those governing marginal cases, and also be prepared to learn new rules when social changes dictate revision of the standard definitions.

When a random sample of addresses is used as the basis for selecting individuals for interview, (e.g., from the electoral registers or the Postcode Address File), it is the interviewer's responsibility to select that individual by a strictly impartial procedure. Methods are usually based on that designed by Kish (1949). At addresses where there is only one household in residence (the majority of cases) this involves:

1.  identifying all those in the household who are eligible for interview (e.g., those aged 16 and over); if there is only one, then that person is asked for an interview;

2.  listing those eligible in order, usually alphabetical order of first names;

3.  referring to a two-way grid in which the column is identified by the number of eligible people in the household and the row by a random digit, usually the last digit of the address serial number. (See table 3.1.) If the sample is produced by computer (or at least entered on computer prior to the production of the interviewers' address record forms) then it is possible to generate a series of random selection digits, equivalent to one row of a

selection grid, separately for each sampled address (see Appendix I). Whichever method is used, it is important that the method is unambiguous and can be reproduced and checked by a supervisor recalling at the address.

**Table 3.1**

**Example of respondent selection grid**

Address serial number: 1 3 5 7    selection digit    | **7** |

Eligible people listed at the address = 3 :    Anne      **1**  selected person
                                               Frank     2
                                               Thomas    3

| Selection digit | No. of eligible people | | | | | | | |
|---|---|---|---|---|---|---|---|---|
| | **2** | **3** | **4** | **5** | **6** | **7** | **8** | **9** |
| 0 | 1 | 2 | 3 | 2 | 1 | 5 | 4 | 7 |
| 1 | 2 | 3 | 1 | 4 | 3 | 6 | 5 | 9 |
| 2 | 1 | 2 | 2 | 5 | 4 | 3 | 1 | 4 |
| 3 | 2 | 1 | 4 | 3 | 5 | 7 | 6 | 8 |
| 4 | 1 | 3 | 2 | 1 | 6 | 2 | 1 | 6 |
| 5 | 2 | 1 | 3 | 5 | 1 | 7 | 4 | 2 |
| 6 | 1 | 2 | 4 | 3 | 2 | 5 | 3 | 1 |
| 7 | 2 | 1 | 3 | 2 | 4 | 1 | 7 | 5 |
| 8 | 1 | 3 | 2 | 1 | 3 | 4 | 2 | 6 |
| 9 | 2 | 2 | 1 | 4 | 5 | 6 | 8 | 3 |

In a multi-household address, an adaptation of this procedure is often used as a preliminary to selecting one household in which to carry out the interview.

In Postcode Address File samples, no names of residents are available; a random selection has therefore to be made at every household with more than one resident. When addresses are selected from the electoral register, it is possible to use a modification which reduces the number of households at which the selection has to be made to about 25 per cent of the sample: the sampling clerk not only copies down the address but the names of all electors listed as living there. A star is put against the name of the elector on whom the counting procedure alighted when the address was selected. The interviewer checks whether all those listed are still living there and that there is no one else there not listed who is eligible for the survey; if all the registered electors are still living there and there is no one else eligible, then the starred elector is taken as the selected person. If there has been any change, the interviewer must list all eligible residents and carry out the selection procedure.[3]

Once a person has been selected, only that person can be interviewed; no substitution is allowed, even if that person is away or sick for the whole of the fieldwork period.

New interviewers sometimes find this selection procedure difficult to grasp and daunting to administer on the doorstep so early in their interaction when they have not had time to develop any rapport with the person they are talking to. Discussions with new and experienced interviewers have suggested a number of ways of making the procedure more efficient and easier to put over:

> The interviewer should explain to the contacted person: 'It may not be you I need to ask for an interview; I have to select one person from those living here by a special procedure.'

> The steps that the interviewer has to go through and the questions that have to be asked to arrive at the selection of the correct person should be set out in questionnaire style so that the necessary questions are asked correctly, terms are defined where required and all the steps are followed systematically. The use of such a questionnaire requires training and considerable practice but, once grasped, can be administered in a few minutes.

> The interviewer can tell the contacted person, 'To find out whom I should ask for an interview, I have to complete this very short questionnaire' and ask for their help in the process. It is then possible to ask to step into the light to complete the questionnaire if that is necessary.

> If the selection grid has to be used, the interviewer should explain: 'I have to use this table so as to pick one person completely at random.'

An example of a combined address record form and respondent selection questionnaire for a sample drawn from the Postcode Address File is given in Appendix I.

The interviewer's tasks in making contact at the address, selecting a respondent correctly and gaining cooperation have been described in some detail in order to demonstrate the wide ranging skills and knowledge that are compressed into what may only take three to five minutes. But these few minutes are crucial to the success of the survey and are often over dependent on personal flair and experience.

Research to appraise the effectiveness of different strategies and approaches, analysis of the skills involved, and the development of more efficient training methods all help to reduce this dependence.

**Other types of contacting work**

Interviewers are often called upon to undertake other sorts of sampling and contacting operations. In the United States, lists of addresses are not as available as in Britain; random sampling therefore often involves an intermediate role for interviewers: when the interviewing areas have been selected, interviewers visit them and list all the individual housing units in the selected streets. The listing may be returned to the office for a random selection of units to be made for inclusion in the sample or the interviewers themselves may perform the selection, following carefully set out instructions. The process of listing requires meticulous accuracy and careful recording of addresses.

Sometimes the survey is targeted at a minority of the population for whom no special list is available from which a sample can be drawn. A very large sample of addresses may be drawn and interviewers asked to carry out a short screening interview at each address to establish whether or not a member of the target group lives there. Sometimes, any adult member of the household can give this information. To reduce the amount of work involved, addresses may be selected in small clusters, e.g., five adjacent addresses; such an approach was used in a national study of the extent to which people had suffered a misfortune in the previous year (Wood, 1979). If the incidence of the minority group is not known, the total screening operation may have to be done in two parts, the first part being designed to establish the incidence and to determine the size of the screening sample required. It is much easier to keep control of the screening operation if it is done separately from the interviewing. High response is necessary at the screening phase as any addresses not covered remain in an ambiguous situation: it is not known whether there is anyone eligible there or not. Nonetheless, the requirements of the interviewer at the screening phase are rather different from those at the interviewing stage. It is usually fairly easy to train new interviewers to undertake the screening whereas the interview itself may require highly skilled and experienced interviewers; different fieldforces may therefore be appropriate for the two tasks.

Some surveys may not require interviewers to knock on doors but may take place in the street or a number of other places. The interviewer may have to master a method of randomly selecting passengers at railway stations or at airports, visitors at exhibition sites or tourist attractions, or motorists at the roadside. Such samples, known as 'flow samples', are designed according to strict probability sampling principles and records of nonresponse are kept so that the efficiency of the operation can be evaluated. Perhaps the most famous British survey that uses flow sampling is the International Passenger Survey conducted on a continuous basis by OPCS at sea and airports.

In America, a great deal of face to face market research is now carried out in shopping malls which frequently also provide venues at which new products or advertisements can be tested; quota sampling methods are used but clearly the population from which the sample is selected is confined to those who shop in malls and may well be biased towards those who shop there frequently and/or spend long periods of time there. The British equivalent is street interviewing and recruitment for hall tests in shopping centres which are likely to suffer from the same sampling limitations. In mall or shopping centre interviewing using quota samples, the interviewer usually has a broad quota to fill in terms of age, sex and social grade, but more important may be usage of a particular product category, such as cigarette smokers, or being in a particular situation, such as having children. The interviewer spots someone who appears to them to fit their quota, approaches them and tries to establish their eligibility in as few questions as possible.

## Notes

1   On other sorts of survey, the interviewers may have a named person to ask to speak to or may have the task of identifying a household unit and then selecting an appropriate household member as a respondent; on yet others, every adult member of the household may be asked to give information.
2   'Chief Income Earner' has recently (July 1992) replaced the outmoded 'Head of Household' definition to identify the person who determines a household's socio-economic grade on the National Readership Survey, a survey based on a random sample that is used as a basis for setting quota targets on many market research surveys.
3   The addresses where the random selection procedure has been used should be weighted at the analysis stage, the weight being the number of eligible people at the address divided by the number of electors at the address.

# 4 Field management options

It has already been indicated that falling response rates can often be raised by special organizational measures and additional effort and resources. The gain always has to be weighed against the cost of these measures.

Some of the fieldwork management options available are primarily designed to reduce the number of noncontacts; among these are increasing the number of calls at an address, lengthening the fieldwork period and controlling the times at which calls are made. Other measures mainly affect the refusal rates, such as incentive payments or sending a letter in advance. Reissuing unproductive addresses to another, more experienced, interviewer is mainly aimed at converting refusals but can also reduce noncontacts.

It has been seen that the kinds of people who refuse to participate in surveys are different from those not contacted. It is perhaps therefore not surprising to find that in a study covering records of 61 ad hoc SCPR surveys, there was found to be no correlation between interviewers' refusal rates and their noncontact rates: an interviewer who is good at persuading people to participate may or may not be good at making contact with the selected person (Lievesley, 1986). To appraise interviewers' response rates and to take the appropriate corrective action requires the two main components of nonresponse to be looked at separately.

Sometimes it is apparent in advance that it is going to be difficult to get a good response rate on a particular survey, for example, an hour long interview on a general population sample covering a topic of low salience. Other surveys may be unusual in design, in respondent burden or in demands on the interviewer and it may be impossible to predict public response to being asked for an interview. Yet others may be of a type that have always obtained good response in the past and there may be some confidence that there will be no problem this time either. When it is known that getting cooperation is likely to be difficult, a range of techniques to optimize response can be built in advance into the organization of the survey.

The repertoire of techniques for improving response that is available to field management is limited by the principles and ethics of professional survey research; some of those used by time-share sales firms would not be acceptable. The main measures have been evaluated at least to some extent by research.

## Number of calls and calling patterns

When random sampling is used, the minimum number of calls that an interviewer must make at an address before classifying it as a 'noncontact' has to be stipulated; each of the calls has to be on a different day of the week and at a different time of the day. Within this overall pattern, interviewers may make additional calls when in the area and near the address, but they are not allowed to make more than the stipulated number of calls without authorization if it involves a further journey to the area, otherwise costs would tend to be excessive.

On the National Readership Survey, a minimum of three calls at an address was stipulated until 1977; in that year, the minimum number of calls was increased to four in an effort to combat falling response rates; the effect was to decrease overall nonresponse from 26.9 per cent to 23.9 per cent with a notable reduction in the categories, 'known to be away temporarily' and 'out at 3 (or 4) or more calls' (Market Research Society, 1981). An experiment in the United States in which the minimum number of calls was reduced from four to three resulted in a big increase in the number of noncontacts (Steeh, 1981). It is now common survey practice to stipulate that there should be a minimum of four calls at an address, each call on a different day and at a different time.

It is often assumed that, given adequate resources and persistence, the number of noncontacts could be reduced to almost zero. There may be some truth in this but experience indicates that the ways in which interviewers organize their interviewing time is as important as the amount of time and money available. OPCS interviewers on the General Household Survey work under the 'four calls' rule outlined above; nonetheless, within this framework they may make as many as ten calls at an address with little additional expense; this is achieved by organizing their addresses geographically and coordinating their recalls at addresses where they have not yet made contact with the other calls they have planned in that area (e.g., at addresses not yet approached or where appointments have been made). This policy has resulted in a noncontact rate of less than 3 per cent, compared with the average of around 10 per cent on the National Readership Survey and most SCPR ad hoc surveys (Lievesley, 1986).

The hard to contact respondents inevitably cost more to interview than those found at home on the first or second call; but the cost of additional calls can be minimized as long as the number of journeys that the interviewer makes to the assignment area does not escalate. In order to keep costs down, OPCS decided that the number of visits interviewers on the General Household Survey made to their area would have to be limited; it was feared that response rates would suffer, but this was not the case; costs were somewhat reduced. This can only have been achieved by interviewers using their time in their areas more efficiently or by extending the average time spent in the area.

An analysis was carried out on three SCPR general population random sample surveys on which the minimum number of calls stipulated was four but interviewers could make more provided they did not make additional journeys unless the fourth call resulted in an appointment. As table 4.1 shows, the number of additional interviews achieved drops off rapidly after four calls; nonetheless, response was significantly increased by making extra calls at fairly low marginal costs (Lievesley, 1986).

**Table 4.1**

**Distribution of interviews by number of calls
needed to achieve them**

| Call no. | Interviews achieved | |
|---|---|---|
| | % | Cumulative % |
| 1 | 30 | 30 |
| 2 | 32 | 62 |
| 3 | 19 | 81 |
| 4 | 10 | 91 |
| 5 | 5 | 96 |
| 6 | 3 | 99 |
| 7 or more | 1 | 100 |
| | 100 | |

(Base: 8029 interviews achieved in 3 surveys.)

In this study, the average number of calls per issued address was 2.5 and the maximum at any one address was twelve.

The evidence suggests that interviewers should be instructed to make up to four calls at an address, if necessary, to obtain a result, each call being at a different time and on a different day, but that they should also be trained in assignment management and make further calls when near the address, even if they have already called on that day or at the same time on a previous day. However, the number of calls is not the only factor: in an experimental survey in which area effects were controlled,

Lievesley (op. cit.) found that there was significant variation between interviewers in their noncontact rates and also an interviewer/area interaction; a 'poor' interviewer in a 'poor' area was five times as likely to get a noncontact as a 'good' interviewer in a 'good' area. As Lievesley says:

> An obvious explanation is that some interviewers were more diligent and persistent. The evidence did not support this since interviewers who had lower noncontact rates were not calling more frequently. An examination of their characteristics showed that interviewers with low noncontact rates were more likely to be employed in other full time jobs in addition to interviewing. This indicates that perhaps it is not maximum availability which is important but WHEN the interviewers work.

The implication is that interviewers with full time jobs are restricted to undertaking their interviewing at times when people are more likely to be at home. This is supported by Durbin and Stewart (1951) who found that LSE student interviewers (who mainly worked in the evenings and at weekends) obtained 51 per cent of their interviews at the first call, compared with Government Social Survey (now OPCS) interviewers who obtained 35 per cent of their interviews at the first call. They also found that 36 per cent of the first calls by LSE student interviewers resulted in an interview compared with 26 per cent of those of the Social Survey interviewers.[1] Lievesley found that only a fifth of first calls by SCPR interviewers resulted in an immediate interview whereas around 30 per cent of subsequent calls did so. Although 23 per cent of first calls resulted in an arranged appointment for the interview, 36 per cent were noncontacts. This puts in question the policy of allowing interviewers complete freedom as to when they make their first calls. The desire of interviewers to scout their area in daylight is understandable and may be advisable in areas that contain very scattered or difficult to find addresses or parts that may be dangerous to visit after dark; but it seems likely that the efficiency of first calls in achieving contact at the address could be much improved if they were made in daylight hours at weekends or in the late afternoon. This is borne out by the finding that interviewers who are reluctant to work at weekends have higher noncontact rates than those willing to do so (Lievesley, op. cit.).

An analysis by Lievesley of times of calls and their outcomes on three general population random sample surveys showed that in an uncontrolled situation, around three fifths of first calls were made on a weekday before 4.30pm; a fifth were made on a weekday evening and a similar proportion at the weekend.

It is not possible to lay down any hard and fast rules about the best times for interviewers to call since at least around a quarter of calls at any time are likely to result in no contact; but Lievesley's analysis shows that, in general, for Britain as a whole (ignoring possible area differences), the best times to make contact are:

- weekday evenings, after 4.30pm but especially after 6.30pm
- Saturday evenings, after 4.30pm
- Sunday mornings, before 2.00pm
- Sunday evenings, especially after 6.30pm.

At these times, between a quarter and a third of calls on average resulted in no contact, compared with around two fifths or more at other times. Weeks et al. (1980) found a similar pattern in the United States with regard to weekdays but weekend findings differed: Saturday was the best day overall for making contact but 10.00am to 4.00pm was better than the evening. Sunday showed a similar pattern to weekdays with evening being the best time to make contact.

A good time to make contact at an address may not necessarily be the best time to carry out the interview: at certain times people may be more likely to say it is inconvenient at that time or even to refuse altogether. Lievesley found that contacts resulted in interviews in around only two fifths of the cases. Times that were particularly bad for a contact to result in an immediate interview were:

- 12.00 to 2.00pm on every day of the week except Sundays
- 4.30 to 6.30pm on Saturdays
- 6.30pm or later on Sundays.

The best times for obtaining interviews at time of contact seemed to be:

- after 4.30pm on Mondays
- after 6.30pm on Tuesdays
- before noon on Saturdays and Sundays
- after 6.30pm on Saturdays.

Some of these 'contact/interview' situations would have been the outcome of appointments made at previous 'contact/no interview' visits. The apparent cooperativeness of contacts on Monday and Tuesday evenings may well be due to the fact that weekends are a good time to make contact but not always a good time to interview, presumably because of family commitments, so the contact results in an appointment rather than an interview.

In a study in Wales, on which the interview could be taken with any resident aged 16 or over, it was found that time of day was more significant than day of the week in determining whether or not a call at an address resulted in an interview; calls made after 5.00 pm were the most successful and those made in the morning were least successful (Swires-Hennessy & Drake, 1992).

The only rules about the organization of calls at addresses usually laid down for interviewers are that:

-       a minimum of four calls must be made to try to obtain the
        interview; each call on a different day of the week and at a
        different time of the day;
-       at least two of the calls should be during the evening or at a
        weekend.

Availability to work both during the evening and at weekends would seem
to be a prerequisite for an interviewer to obtain a low noncontact rate
and to minimize the number of calls necessary to make contact.
Research is needed to investigate the effects of imposing more stringent
limitations than are set at present on interviewers' calling times, including
time of first call.

## Reissuing noncontacts and refusals to another interviewer

If the overall response rate on a survey is below that which is deemed to
be satisfactory, or if an individual interviewer's response rate is
particularly poor, it is common practice to pass the noncontacts and
refusals to another interviewer to make an additional attempt to obtain
the interview. Going back to people known to have refused to cooperate
requires a considerable degree of self confidence and tact; usually the
task is given to experienced interviewers of known persuasive ability who
have received special instruction on how to make an approach under
these circumstances.

It has been found by SCPR that reissuing noncontacts and refusals can
raise overall response by as much as 4-5 per cent, though more commonly
by 2-3 per cent. In an analysis of over forty surveys carried out by SCPR
during the 1970s, around half the reissued noncontacts were located and
interviewed and about 40 per cent of the refusals were converted (Market
Research Society, 1981). From follow up interviews with refusers
(Lievesley, 1986), it was found that many had refused because the time
was inconvenient and they had not appreciated that the interviewer could
call again. There is thus little evidence of a hard and fast refuser
category but more an indication that the selected person's reaction is
influenced by circumstances and mood at the time of the interviewer's
call.

Usually addresses for reissue are selected on the basis of a number of
factors that include the extent to which there is a cluster of sufficient size
to make the alternative interviewer's visit an economical proposition, the
availability of a suitable interviewer within reasonable travel distance and
an appraisal of the likelihood of conversion, based on the first
interviewer's comments about the refusal. In an experiment (Lievesley,
op. cit.), the interviewers were asked to rate each refusal in terms of its
likelihood of being converted. A random half of all refusals were then
reissued to a second interviewer who did not know what the first
interviewer's rating had been. Interviews were achieved with 34 per cent

of the reissued sample and there was a marked correlation between the initial interviewer's assessment of convertibility and the final outcome. If the assessments had been used as a basis for selecting half the refusals for reissue, the conversion rate would have been 43 per cent. It was estimated that applying the usual criteria about scatter of addresses and availability of interviewer would have reduced the conversion rate only slightly, to about 38-39 per cent, but would have been more economical. It thus appears that initial interviewers' assessments of convertibility can add to the efficiency of reissuing but whether the increase obtained by using only this criterion would justify the cost of covering the very scattered addresses that are likely to result is debatable. OPCS found on the General Household Survey that when addresses for reissue were selected purely on the basis of economy without regard to likelihood of conversion, 30 per cent were converted and the cost per achieved interview was 166 per cent of the set cost per interview (Williams, 1988).

In order for interviewers' assessments of convertibility to be useful, it was found necessary to give them special instruction which included explaining the extent to which refusals were usually converted by another interviewer.

On the British Social Attitudes Survey carried out annually by SCPR, selected noncontacts and refusals are nearly always reissued. In order to optimize the effectiveness of the operation, letters have several times been sent to the reissued addresses in advance of the second interviewer's call. Noncontacts and refusers receive a different, appropriately worded, letter and, because in most cases the respondent selection procedure has been completed, the envelope can be personally addressed. The letter apologises for what may be perceived as over persistence and explains why response is so important while making it clear that cooperation is voluntary. It is signed by someone in a position of prestige or authority.

Although no formal appraisal of this practice has been undertaken, interviewers report that it makes their task easier in that they are expected by the selected person and their visit is backed by the authority of the survey organization or sponsor. It also reduces costs as some recipients of the letter phone the office, either to make an appointment or to refuse to participate. This practice of sending letters to reissued addresses is used routinely on repeated social surveys in the United States.

The question has to be asked, is it necessary to reissue addresses to another interviewer rather than simply ask the original interviewer to make further calls on noncontacts and to try to convert refusals? An experienced interviewer will often on their own initiative make an attempt to convert refusals and will usually have very few noncontacts because of the skilful way calls are handled. Westerhoven (1978) got interviewers to make unlimited recalls on addresses, including calling again on refusers and achieved a final response of 95 per cent; the final achieved sample included 12 per cent who were contacted after more than four calls and 25 per cent who had initially refused but later agreed to be interviewed.

If no other interviewer is available to travel to the area or if the numbers to be reissued in the area are small, then asking the initial interviewer to make further attempts may bear fruit, especially if the interviewer is of proven calibre. However, it is generally agreed that better results are obtained if addresses are reissued to another experienced interviewer; the respondent may be more impressed with the importance attached to their participation by the appearance of another interviewer; a new approach may be more successful than the original one, and the second interviewer may be less restricted in the times at which they can call than the initial interviewer, thus being able to catch up with the more elusive noncontacts.

### Letters to respondents: in advance or at the time of the interview?

In social research using random samples, it is general practice to provide a letter for sample members; the ground usually covered by such a letter has been described in Chapter 3. Most commonly, this letter is part of the interviewers' armoury when they call at an address. It is used to establish the legitimacy of the survey and to reassure respondents about the use of the data and the trustworthiness of the interviewer. It can be produced at any time deemed useful during the introduction of the survey and the persuasion process. If not used then, it must be left at the end of the interview.

When a sample is drawn from a confidential source, such as the unemployment register, doctors' lists or employers' records, then it is necessary for a letter to be sent in advance to the sampled people to ask permission to pass on their name and address to the survey organization. This letter covers much the same ground as the explanatory letter carried by interviewers but also asks them to write or phone if they do not wish their name to be passed. A time limit of a couple of weeks is given.

Some ethical purists have argued that putting the onus on sample members to 'opt out' is intrusive in that many who do not wish to be interviewed will not get around to responding within the time limit. However, it is found that if those prepared to be interviewed are asked to 'opt in' the response is so low as to be impractical. An 'opt out' procedure is therefore usually adopted but a sentence is added to the effect that even if they do not reply to the letter, they are still at liberty to refuse to be interviewed when the interviewer calls.

Surveys requiring an advance letter of necessity are usually among special populations and on subjects of high salience on which response is not a problem. Falling response rates on general population surveys that do not necessitate an advance letter have led survey practitioners to experiment with them. When samples are drawn from special lists, they usually consist of named individuals and the advance letter can be addressed personally to the selected individual; but general population samples usually consist of addresses at which the interviewer has to select a person for interview. Advance letters can therefore only be addressed to 'The Householder' or to 'The Residents'.

In the main, experiments in sending a letter to sample members in advance have not indicated that it has any significant effect on response. However, a test conducted by OPCS in 1986 on the General Household Survey produced an improvement in response from those receiving the letter that was highly significant (Clarke et al., 1987). There was also some small reduction in the average number of visits needed to obtain an interview, though this saving in field costs has to be offset against the administrative costs of clerical time and postage in sending out the letters.

OPCS decided on the basis of these results to send advance letters to all sampled addresses on the General Household Survey and a year later the improvement in response rates had been maintained.

In the United States, the Survey Research Centre (SRC) at Michigan University and a number of other leading American social research institutes have routinely sent advanced letters to sample members for some years. SRC experience has indicated that the letters are most effective when they are brief and general rather than detailed and when the gap between the arrival of the letter and the arrival of the interviewer is short.

They argue that long introductory letters are unlikely to be read and that in a long letter it is more difficult to choose a level of language appropriate to all members of the sample; thirdly, a long letter reduces curiosity and gives too many possible handles on which to hang reasons for refusal (Warwick and Lininger, 1975). Letters are normally despatched by the interviewers rather than by the office, so that they can be sure to call shortly after its arrival.

Interviewers used to be dubious about the value of advance letters, feeling that they were better able to put over the survey in person, adapting their approach as they appraised the reactions of the person to whom they were talking. In a survey among the elderly carried out by SCPR in 1972 an advance letter was sent; there were several occasions when a written refusal arrived in the office but, when this was passed on to the interviewer, it turned out that a visit had already been made to the elderly person and an interview obtained!

More recently, however, many interviewers have come to feel that an advance letter helps them, especially in inner city areas where entryphones abound and people are often reluctant to open their doors to strangers.

In the OPCS experiment, 92 per cent of interviewers were 'strongly in favour' or 'in favour' of the use of an advance letter, 74 per cent feeling that it helped them gain cooperation; only 7 per cent thought it was a hindrance. They reported that 84 per cent of respondents remembered receiving the letter.

Interviewers commented that the letter helped in the following ways:

1)    it allayed suspicion so that they had to spend less time establishing their credentials;

2)    it was a more professional way of seeking an interview which in turn made the interviewers feel they were doing a more professional job;

3)    it was helpful with specific types of respondent, the elderly being most frequently mentioned.

The main disadvantage was that refusals were more adamant (Clarke et al., op.cit.).

Advance letters are now being sent out on other OPCS repeat surveys with apparently beneficial effects on response.

The content and style of explanatory letters can very usefully be investigated during the piloting work on the questionnaire, especially for major ongoing surveys or where a very high response rate is essential; for example, in the National Household Seroprevalence Survey carried out by the Research Triangle Institute in the United States (Moore et al., 1989), high response was important because the aim was to identify HIV-positive respondents, a characteristic that might be associated with nonresponse. As part of the pilot work, they carried out intensive interviews to understand how and why people of varying risk statuses decide whether to participate in the study; one feature investigated was the introductory letter (which was to be mailed by interviewers in advance of their call). They found that the members of the low risk group liked a general letter that did not mention AIDS but that a sample of high risk respondents (gays and drug users) preferred a more specific letter with more detailed explanation and emphasis on confidentiality.

**Telephone appointments**

Research has shown that making first contact by telephone instead of by a personal call at the address can reduce the average number of calls necessary to achieve a result (Sudman, 1967; Scott and Jackson, 1960) with only a minor increase in nonresponse; but common sense suggests that when the first approach is made by telephone it should be preceded by a letter of explanation to lend authority to the survey. Bergsten et al. (1984) report on an experiment on a survey among elderly people eligible for Medicare in which half were sent an advance letter which was followed by a telephone call while the other half were sent the advance letter only; response to the advance letter and telephone call was 1 per cent lower than it was for those who received only an advance letter, but there was a 20 per cent saving in data collection costs.

In Britain, making appointments by telephone has not been seriously considered except for special samples because of the lack of telephone penetration. This situation is now changing and the enormous increase in telephone surveys may mean that people are becoming more accepting of such an approach. In general, it is felt that it is easier to refuse a faceless voice on the telephone than someone standing on the doorstep; but further research is needed to test appointment making by telephone which could lead to considerable cost savings. However, the cost savings in the field have to be offset against the difficulty and expense of obtaining telephone numbers for addresses where the names of residents are not known as in Postcode Address File samples.

It is possible that advance letters and telephone appointment making could be helpful in increasing response among people in particular circumstances, for example, those with entryphones or gatekeepers, or the very affluent.

## Monetary incentives

Payment to respondents for participating in a survey obviously adds considerably to costs. Results from experiments have been inconsistent (Ferber and Sudman, 1974) or have shown only minor increases in response (Dohrenwend, 1970). In a mail survey, it was found that a cash incentive yielded a higher response rate but inferior data when tested against external sources (Hansen, 1980). The implication is that introducing a financial transaction may be at variance with the motivations and self perceptions that normally lead people to participate in surveys, cutting across a friendly response to the interviewer, feelings of altruism or an acceptance of the survey as intrinsically valuable and important. Some field managers report that their interviewers do not like offering a financial incentive to take part, particularly as the sum offered is usually derisory to most people approached; but being able to offer, at the end of the interview, the option of a voucher to buy goods at a chain store or payment to a charity of their choice has been found to improve interviewer morale as they felt they had something to offer in return for the time the respondent had given.

There is evidence, however, that when the survey requires a lot of hard work on the part of the respondents, a financial incentive is appropriate and effective: Ferber and Sudman (1974) report that offering compensation obtained higher response when sample members were asked to keep written records of expenditure. Payment is sometimes made when respondents are asked to keep a diary (e.g., of journeys undertaken, of leisure time behaviour or television viewing) and OPCS always offer payment to those taking part in the Family Expenditure Survey (FES); an increase in the monetary incentive on the FES in 1981 was accompanied by an improvement in response rate.

There are considerable administrative costs in making financial payments to respondents as it is clearly not acceptable to ask interviewers to carry large sums of cash around with them when they go interviewing. The money has to be sent from headquarters as quickly as possible after the questionnaires have been received and in a form that can be cashed by the respondent who may not have a bank account.

## Reducing respondent burden

When the task required of respondents is time consuming and demanding, an alternative to offering payment is to discover through piloting and discussions with interviewers which aspects of the survey are particularly daunting and off-putting and to try to ameliorate them.

In an SCPR survey about how people budget their time, a short interview followed by keeping a seven day diary of all activities was compared with one longer interview in which respondents were asked in detail about the previous day. Response to the seven day diary was only 40 per cent; it was considerably higher (60 per cent) to the one day recall interview though still not good.

Butcher (1986) reports an investigation on the National Travel Survey (NTS), sponsored by the Department of Transport. The NTS had been carried out four times since its inception in 1965, involving on each occasion an initial interview, a seven day diary kept about each member of the household's travel, and a final interview at which the diaries were checked, additional information about each journey was collected and the journey information coded onto documents ready for punching. Response rates on the third and fourth surveys in the series were considerably lower than for the first two and OPCS were asked to investigate how to raise response.

After some modification to procedures, a pilot was carried out but, surprisingly, the proportion of households fully cooperating was as poor as it had been on the previous survey (58 per cent). The main problem appeared to be the length of the pickup call which sometimes lasted as long as three hours and was very tedious. A number of steps were taken that reduced the average pickup call to 30 minutes: the diary was redesigned to collect more information about journeys so that the interviewer had to collect less information, short walks were recorded only for the final day of the diary period instead of for every day and the interviewer performed the coding operation at home instead of at the respondents' house. On the second pilot a response higher than that in the first two rounds of the Survey was obtained. A continuous National Travel Survey has now been instituted, following the methodology developed in the second pilot; response is regularly around 78 per cent.

## Interviewer motivation

Research by Cole (1956) suggests that the interviewers' interest in the survey and their conviction that it is of value can affect response rate; Butcher (op.cit.) puts forward the view that the interviewer's response to reduced burden is as important as that of respondents: the interviewer is more likely to put over the survey convincingly and with enthusiasm if what is asked of respondents is regarded as reasonable and enjoyable. Not only respondent burden but also the use of monetary incentives and sending an advance letter seem sometimes to have an effect by operating through the boost they give to interviewer morale; interviewers feel more justified in asking respondents to undertake diary keeping if they can offer some small payment for the time taken; an advance letter can lend them authority if the survey is a demanding one.

The effects of interviewer morale are difficult to quantify but field managers are convinced that it plays an important part in achieving a good response. One of the purposes of personal briefings should be to give the interviewers a thorough grounding in the background, objectives and use of the survey so that they understand its importance and can identify with its aims. They should also by the end of the briefing understand the reason for any procedures or rules that make their own task arduous. Butcher (op.cit.) describes how an easing of certain rules governing the conduct of a survey seemed to lift interviewers' morale even though the rules hardly ever needed to be put into operation: the interviewers simply felt that their task was more manageable.

Lack of adequate pay for interviewers to cover the time and complexity of the survey can affect the amount of effort they are willing to put into getting a good response rate. Bonus payments for interviews achieved above a certain target sometimes have an effect in raising response though it tends to be ephemeral. It is very difficult to devise a bonus system that is perceived as being fair since areas vary considerably in ways that cannot be known in advance. It is also important to strike a balance: high response at the expense of data quality is likely to be the outcome if obtaining the interview is seen to outweigh all other considerations. In setting payment rates and budgeting for fieldwork, the amount of record keeping demanded of the interviewer should be borne in mind as well as the length and complexity of the interview and the difficulties of obtaining cooperation.

Frequent contact between the interviewers in the field and a field management representative, usually in the form of a local area organiser, supervisor or field assistant, is an important element in maintaining morale. Interviewing is a lonely job and advice, sympathy and reassurance can do much to maintain enthusiasm. It is important that those fulfilling the liaison function with interviewers in the field should be provided with regular up to date information about each interviewer's progress on each survey so that they can spot the interviewer who is getting a lot of refusals or noncontacts, or who is simply falling behind schedule.    Through weekly contact with interviewers, they become sensitive to drops in morale and quickly find out the causes.  Steps can then be taken to support the interviewer or to modify procedures.

### Length of fieldwork period

When quota sampling methods are used, interviewers' assignments are usually small and the time allowed to complete them may be a week or less.  For random samples, longer fieldwork periods are necessary to allow for the required number of call backs, especially to catch people who are sick or away on holiday, or to enable appointments to be made with busy people who are only contacted after three or four calls.  Usually at least a month is required and maybe longer during the holiday season. Surveys with long questionnaires (over 30 minutes) require longer fieldwork periods to allow appointments to be made.

Interviewers are usually exhorted to try to make contact at every address in their assignment within the first week but for various reasons this is not always possible; many interviewers are restricted in the number of hours they are able to devote to their work (often only 15-20 hours a week); they must always be ready to take the interview at the visit at which they first make contact if the selected person is willing.  Contact therefore cannot be attempted late in the evening or close to an appointment for an interview already set up. The first few days' work may well result in a fairly full schedule of appointments that make it impossible to attempt further contacts at sensible times of the day for some days.  If people at an address are out a lot, the interviewer may not be able to establish who the selected person is until towards the end of the fieldwork period and may then find that that person has just gone away for two weeks.  For reissuing to be sufficiently productive to be worth undertaking, at least a further couple of weeks needs to be allowed to carry out this work.

### Piloting

The pilot for a survey is usually regarded only as part of the development work for the questionnaire; and it is all too often a small scale and rather cursory test fitted in to an overtight and already rigidly planned time schedule and budget.  Often the pilot sample is not drawn in the same way as it will be for the main study so does not provide a proper test of the extent to which people will cooperate.

As has already been indicated, pilots can be used to test out and investigate the way in which the interviewer introduces the survey, the explanatory letter, and reactions to an advance letter or a telephone approach.  Any major survey, and especially one likely to be difficult to get people to participate in, or where high response is essential, should be preceded by both small scale development studies and a larger feasibility survey; the sample should be drawn in the same way as that for the main study and be of sufficient size to provide a proper assessment of any problems in gaining cooperation. Interviewers can be usefully instructed to record information about those who refuse to take part and also to ask for reasons for the refusal. Both those who participate and those who refuse should be asked for their reactions to the subject of the survey as presented in the interviewer's introduction and the explanatory letter. The pilot interviewers' opinions should also be sought about the introduction and procedures, the acceptability of the task asked of respondents, and any other features of the survey affecting cooperation. There should preferably be a debriefing session rather than simply telephone conversations with the interviewers: the differences in opinions between interviewers as to the ease or difficulty in putting over the survey can lead usefully into a discussion of their different approaches and provide a deeper understanding on the part of the researcher of reactions to the survey and how to optimize response. It can also give clues as to features of the survey that might affect interviewer morale and how to ensure that they maintain a positive attitude towards the survey. The contribution that adequate piloting and discussions with interviewers can make to the success of a survey is often undervalued.

It has usually been assumed that all prospective respondents should be approached in more or less the same way, with the same introduction and explanatory letter; some American survey organizations have realized that interviewers intuitively adapt their introduction to fit the perceived requirements of the person approached and have sought to apply this principle to tackle the problem of low response in inner city areas. Through pilot work, the approach is adapted to be persuasive to those living in particular circumstances in particular areas. While no research has been published, the results in terms of improved inner city response rates are reported to be encouraging.

### Monitoring progress

Piloting and feasibility studies can go some way towards indicating problems in response rate and enabling measures to be taken to optimize response, but problems may still arise, perhaps in certain areas of the country or with particular interviewers. An essential tool of modern field management is the ability to monitor progress on a regular basis; this requires interviewers to send in their questionnaires and records of refusals or other nonresponse after each day or two in the field and for the outcome to be quickly processed so that every week during fieldwork, response can be appraised overall, within regions and by interviewer.

The diagnosis of the problems, and decisions how to respond to them can be greatly enhanced by the types of records that interviewers are asked to make of their calls at the address. Firstly, the date and time of each call and its outcome can help plan future calls, whether by the same interviewer or another. Secondly, if the interviewer is asked to rate each refusal on the likelihood of it being converted to an interview, this can result in more cost effective reissuing of addresses. Thirdly, any information about the address or its occupants that might be related to response should be recorded; for example, that there is an entryphone or caretaker, that the selected person is on holiday or works shifts, and so on.

Problems can be dealt with at two levels: in the first place, management decisions can be taken in conjunction with the researcher as to whether any general steps need to be taken to improve response (such as reissuing to other interviewers or sending letters); secondly individual interviewers' problems can be investigated.

The problems highlighted at the individual interviewer level might be lack of progress so that the fieldwork time schedule is threatened, poor response or a high number of noncontacts. These problems are best tackled by the front line regional field management team; regional supervisors or field assistants therefore need to be sent progress figures for the interviewers in their area on a weekly basis; they should speak to all those who are behind schedule or who have any significant number of refusals or noncontacts. This weekly contact with interviewers enables any fall in morale to be diagnosed and dealt with and work to be reallocated to another interviewer if it seems that the time schedule will not be met; advice can also be given as to how to improve response or to track down noncontacts. Interviewers are usually instructed to hold on to the response record forms for those they fail to contact after four calls at the address and to keep trying every time they pass near the address. A decision can then be taken towards the end of the fieldwork period as to whether to undertake a general reissuing of all (or most) refusals and noncontacts, whether to reissue in certain areas, to confine reissuing to the assignments of a few unsuccessful interviewers, to ask interviewers to make further journeys to their area to try to find those not contacted, or to accept the response rate without further attempts to raise it.

## Note

1    OPCS requirements with regard to interviewers' working hours and their training in assignment management have changed considerably since 1951.

# 5 The first contact

The first encounter between the interviewer and residents at a sampled address is a dynamic process: those contacted bring to it attitudes and preconceptions concerning strangers at the door in general and survey interviewers in particular which will be confirmed or modified by the ensuing interaction and focused into an acceptance or refusal of the interview. The first few minutes on the doorstep can thus be crucial to the success of the survey, yet there is a dearth of research on how to introduce a survey or how to persuade people to take part. Previous literature has contributed to the development of an accepted wisdom based on commonsense and the informal reports of interviewers; the most useful expositions have interpreted the accepted wisdom within the framework of an analysis based on psychological theories of motivation (e.g., Kahn and Cannell, 1957; Gorden, 1975; Warwick and Lininger, 1975). Turner and Martin (1981) offer a useful comparison of the instructions given to interviewers for making contact and obtaining cooperation as set out in the interviewers' manuals of three major American social survey organizations: the University of Michigan Survey Research Center, National Opinion Research Center and the Bureau of the Census; they reveal a general consensus of approach but considerable variation in emphasis.

In this chapter the results are presented of a study carried out at SCPR by the Survey Methods Centre[1] to find out what actually happens on the doorstep when an interviewer approaches an address and initiates the process of trying to obtain the interview (Morton-Williams and Young, 1986 and 1987).

**Tape recorded doorstep introductions**

In this study, interviewers were asked to carry miniature cassette recorders and to record the entire process from their initial introduction to the final acceptance or refusal of the interview by the person selected as respondent. A simple tape recording was considered to be the most useful and practical approach despite its obvious limitations: one of the limitations of tape recordings is that they can capture only verbal interactions; it is quite likely that body language such as smiling, gaze, dress and physical appearance, plays an important part on both sides of the interaction. Secondly, the presence of a tape recorder might affect the way in which the interviewers performed, either by leading them to be on their best behaviour or by making them nervous. Thirdly, recordings might be of too poor a quality for transcription because of traffic noise or distance from the contacted person.

There was also the question of the ethics of tape recording people without their knowledge or prior consent and of the acceptability of such behaviour to those contacted. It was decided that, since no personal information was requested at this stage beyond the names of those resident at the address, it would not be an infringement of ethical standards to tape record the interaction provided that an explanation was given at the end of the introductory process and permission was sought at that point to keep the tape recording. If there was any objection, the tape recording was to be immediately erased.

To establish whether such a study was feasible and likely to be valuable, a small scale trial was carried out using field training officers. This showed that it was possible to obtain audible tape recordings with mini-cassette recorders held on the interviewers' arms and that members of the public very rarely had any objection to being recorded. It also showed that extremely rich and valuable information could be obtained even though only verbal behaviour could be studied. The possibility that interviewers might be on their best behaviour did not detract from its value since it was apparent that much could be learnt about the difficulties that interviewers encounter on the doorstep and the ways in which their skills prove unequal to the task despite their best efforts.

*The objectives*

The study had three objectives which were essentially exploratory and descriptive:

> Firstly, to identify the different types of doorstep situation within which the interviewer has to try to put over the survey, select the appropriate respondent and obtain cooperation;

> Secondly, to examine interviewers' initial approaches at the address and their later strategies in attempting to gain cooperation;

Thirdly, to find out how respondents express reluctance to take part, the points in the procedure at which it occurs, and how interviewers deal with it.

### The survey vehicle

The survey on which the study of doorstep introductions was undertaken used a shortened version of the questionnaire designed for the Survey of British Social Attitudes carried out annually by SCPR. It provided a good test of interviewers' skills in obtaining cooperation since it was on broad general subjects, could offer no direct benefits to respondents and did not have a well known sponsor; it was the type of survey on which it is known to be difficult to obtain high response rates. The interview took about 25 minutes and was therefore shorter than on most social surveys. It was introduced as being a survey to investigate people's attitudes to a range of social issues affecting Britain today.[2]

### The interviewers' task on the doorstep

The interviewers' task in introducing the survey and establishing whom to interview was the standard one used on most general population samples. A random sample of addresses was drawn from the electoral registers for the survey areas. One adult aged 18 or over had to be selected by the interviewer using a respondent selection sheet that involved the modified Kish method described in Chapter 2. Sixteen of the total of thirty interviewers on the survey were each asked to record ten of their doorstep interactions and 141 viable tape recordings were obtained.

The interviewers asked to record some of their introductions were instructed to carry out two or three interviews before starting to record in order to get used to introducing the survey; they were then asked to tape record the next ten of their introductions whatever the outcome, so that there would be no selection in order to show themselves in a good light on the one hand or to demonstrate how awkward the public could be on the other. They were to ask at the end of the introductory procedure for permission to keep the tape recording, explaining that its purpose was purely in order to see how interviewers introduced the survey on the doorstep and reassuring them that it would be used only for this research purpose.

All the interviewers participating in the study were women and, although they represented a range of experience, none of them was new to interviewing.

### Experiment in scripting the survey introduction

One way to improve the efficiency of the interviewers' performance on the doorstep might be to give them a more comprehensive script than is usually provided and to ask them to try to keep to it. An experiment in using a scripted introduction was incorporated into the survey. Fourteen interviewers working on the survey were asked to keep to the script provided as far as was possible; five of these were among those asked to tape record some of their doorstep introductions.

### Advance letter experiment

Letters were sent in advance to half the addresses in the sample to describe the survey and to say that an interviewer would be calling within the next two to three weeks. Alternate addresses were selected to receive the letter and these were marked on the interviewers' sample issue sheets so that they knew whether or not a letter had been sent to each address. Of the 141 addresses where a tape recording was successfully made of the interviewer's approach, 73 had been sent an advance letter. We were thus able to make some appraisal of its effect on the interviewers' approach and the response to it.

### Interviewers' and public's reactions to the tape recording

Since the initial doorstep interaction presents a situation in which the interviewer has to deal with the unknown, it is not surprising that using a tape recorder at this point was not very popular. A few of the interviewers on the study who were asked to record some of their doorstep introductions refused to do so. The majority of the interviewers who agreed to take part in the experiment said that they were initially apprehensive about tape recording their introductions and some said that they remained worried about it throughout. About half said that they thought tape recording might have had some effect on the way they introduced the survey because it made them feel that they ought to be word perfect and remember to include all the information; but only two said they would not be prepared to take part in a similar study in the future.

The interviewers reported that most of the people involved were surprised at being told they had been tape recorded but were happy with the explanation. In only 4 per cent of attempted tape recorded introductions did the person object and ask for it to be erased. In 2 per cent of the cases the interviewer either forgot to ask or the person who refused closed the door too quickly for the request to be made. It would take an iron nerve to knock on the door again in such a circumstance!

### Analysis

The recorded interchanges between interviewer and contact were transcribed but in carrying out the analysis both transcripts and recordings were used as many nonverbal nuances could be picked up from the tapes. The analysis used both quantitative and qualitative methods and covered:

1.  the type of doorstep situation with which the interviewers had to cope (ranging from a terse refusal by the first contact to having to make several visits to contact the selected person);

2.  the information given by the interviewers:

    -   in their brief opening remarks to their first contact,
    -   after the contact's first response up to the end of the respondent selection procedure,
    -   after the respondent selection procedure (divided into speech directed to a contact who turned out not to be the selected respondent, to a contact who was also the selected respondent and to the selected respondent who had not been the original contact);

3.  how the person being spoken to responded at each of these points and what sort of reluctance was expressed;

4.  how the interviewers coped with expressions of reluctance.

**The model of the doorstep situation**

The first step in the analysis of what happens on the doorstep was to map out what the interviewers have to go through simply to arrive at the point where they speak to the selected person to try to persuade them to do the interview. Figure 5.1 below presents a model of the interaction paths which the interviewers had to follow to try to obtain cooperation. The boxes at the ends of the paths (in capital letters) indicate the persuasion point; sometimes interviewers did not manage to speak to the selected respondent, in which case the box at the end of the paths indicates the final outcome (e.g., 'Proxy refusal', 'Out - no contact').

The diagram shows that in a small number of cases (7 per cent), the interviewer was not permitted even to ask the necessary few questions to establish who should be interviewed. These constituted a quarter of the refusers on the survey, a result that is remarkably consistent with DeMaio's (1980) findings that 25 per cent of refusals on a Bureau of the Census survey occurred before or during the initial introduction.

In the majority of initial encounters at addresses the interviewers successfully established whom to interview and in just over half, the person first contacted turned out to be the selected respondent; in a further 12 per cent of contact situations the selected respondent was in, though not all were spoken to. At a quarter of the addresses, the selected person was out, requiring one or more further visits in order to speak to the selected respondent. Thus overall, once contact was made

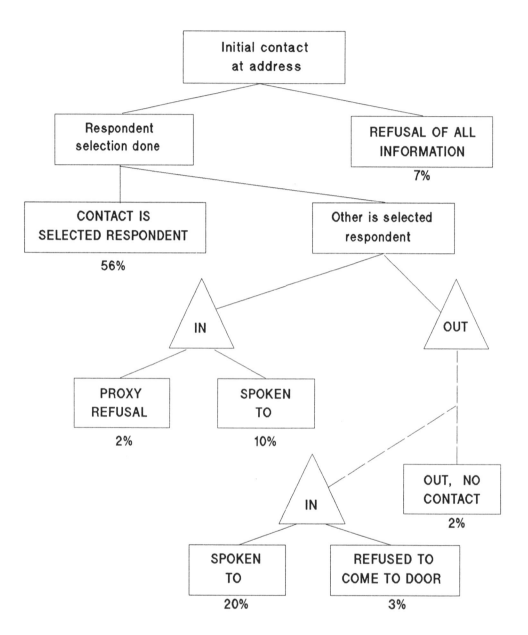

Key: Boxes with captions in capital letters indicate the selection point or,
if selected person was not seen, the outcome.
Broken lines indicate that there may be more than one return visit involved.

Figure 5.1    Model of doorstep situation up to persuasion point
( Base 136 classifiable doorstep situations.)

at the address, interviewers were able to carry out the respondent selection procedure and, sooner or later, to speak directly to the selected person at over four fifths of the addresses: in 7 per cent of the cases no selection procedure could be done and in a further 7 per cent the interviewer was not able to speak to the selected person.

It was apparent that the longer the chain of events between the initial contact and the persuasion point, the less likely it was that an interview would be obtained: over four fifths of those cases where the first contact turned out to be the selected respondent resulted in an interview compared with less than two thirds where the selected respondent was out. There are several possible reasons for this; in the first place, those who are in when the interviewer calls are likely to be biased towards the less active and busy members of society; men and young people, who are more likely to be active outside the home, have been shown to be harder to contact. It is also probable that where there is more than one household member at home, the younger and possibly the more sociable and helpful ones are likely to answer the door; in other words, answering doors and answering surveys are correlated activities. On the other hand, it is also clear that the longer and more complex situation that arises when the contacted person is not the selected respondent taxes the interviewers' social skills to a greater extent than does the simple one to one situation, especially when the interviewer has to deal through a third party and to call back at the address.

## Corroboration from a larger study

Since the numbers in the study of doorstep introductions were small, some corroboration and amplification of these findings were sought by an analysis of interviewers' records of calls at each address on the 1985 British Social Attitudes Survey which comprised 2500 sampled addresses. The results were similar: at 53 per cent of the addresses where the respondent selection process was completed, the contacted person who provided the selection information was the eligible respondent (compared with 56 per cent in the study of doorstep introductions). When the contacted person was the selected respondent, the response rate was 84 per cent; it fell to 72 per cent when another household member was the selected respondent.

As table 5.1 shows, the difference in response was not due to increased personal face to face refusal on the part of those who were not the initial contact, but to proxy refusals and to people being unavailable for interview. Proxy refusals include cases where the selected person gets another household member to tell the interviewer that they do not wish to be interviewed. Unavailability for interview comprises those who are not contacted (which may include some hidden refusers who avoid the interview), those who are away or in hospital and those incapable of giving an interview because of ill health, disability or poor english. These are all groups unable or unlikely to answer the door to the interviewer.

**Table 5.1**

**Outcome by whether selected respondent or other was
first contact at address**

| | | Total first contact at address was: | |
|---|---|---|---|
| | | Selected Respondent | Not Selected Respondent |
| Base: all addresses at which respondent selection done | 2111 | 1121 | 990 |
| | % | % | % |
| Interviewed | 79 | 84 | 72 |
| Unproductive: | | | |
| Personally refused | 12 | 12 | 12 |
| Indirect or proxy refusal | 3 | 1 | 4 |
| Broke appointment | 1 | 2 | 1 |
| Not contacted | 1 | - | 3 |
| Away/in hospital | 1 | - | 2 |
| Unable to give interview (ill at home/senile/no English) | 2 | 1 | 4 |

(Source: analysis of records kept by interviewers of the 1985 British Social Attitudes Survey. Percentages do not always add to 100 per cent due to rounding.)

The analysis of this larger survey also extends our knowledge of the interviewer's task in obtaining the interview by providing a picture of the number of calls they had to make at an address to get as far as establishing whom to interview, and of the extent to which they had to make additional calls to obtain the interview. It covered all calls made at the address, including calls additional to those meeting the criteria of 'different day/different time'; it might thus include cases where two calls were made on the same day.

The correct respondent was identified at the first call at the address in just over half the cases where the selection procedure was carried out but a fifth of addresses required three or more calls before the interviewer was able to establish whom to interview (table 5.2).

**Table 5.2**

**Number of calls at address before establishing
whom to interview**

| | | |
|---|---|---|
| Base: All addresses where selection procedure done | | 2111 |
| | | % |
| Respondent selection completed at: | - 1st call | 57 |
| | - 2nd call | 22 |
| | - 3rd call | 11 |
| | - 4th call | 6 |
| | - 5th call | 4 |

It is apparent that in a fairly large minority of cases a considerable amount of perseverance is required on the part of the interviewer to make personal contact with a selected sample member so that agreement to do the survey can be sought.   Even when the correct person for interview had been identified, the interviewer had to call again to conduct the interview at about half the addresses, sometimes more than once (table 5.3).

The British Social Attitudes Survey interview lasted about one hour so a fairly high incidence of appointment making would be expected.   It would be interesting to see whether more restriction of the timing of interviewer calls to evenings and weekends would reduce the number of calls necessary to obtain the interview.

### Table 5.3

**Number of calls at address to obtain interview after completion of respondent selection procedure**

| | | |
|---|---|---:|
| Base: all addresses at which interview obtained | | 1661 |
| | | % |
| Interview obtained: | - at same call as selection procedure | 48 |
| | - one call after selection procedure | 31 |
| | - two calls after selection procedure | 11 |
| | - three calls after selection procedure | 5 |
| | - four or more calls after | 5 |

## Putting the message over

When interviewers contact someone at a sampled address, the rules of politeness demand that they say who they are and state their business.

In the study of tape recorded introductions, the interviewers were asked to put over the following items of information in their initial opening speech to the person contacted:

1. to check that they were at the correct address;
2. to give their own name;
3. to say that they were working for Social and Community Planning Research;
4. to show their identity card;
5. to mention that SCPR was an independent research institute;
6. to give a brief description of the survey along the lines: 'We are approaching a cross section of the public to find out how people feel about a whole range of social issues';
7. to say that the address had been selected from the electoral register.

This would lead into the respondent selection procedure.

If the person selected for interview was not the initial contact at the address, the interviewer was expected to repeat all items, apart from checking the address, when the selected respondent was contacted.

There were a few additional items of information which could be given as part of the initial introduction or used later after establishing whom to interview:

8.  that the survey was funded by the Economic and Social Research Council;
9.  that the results would be helpful to government departments;
10. that their answers would be treated in confidence;
11. that the interview would take about 25 minutes.

The interviewers varied quite a lot in their initial approaches, some saying very little indeed by way of introduction and moving into the respondent selection procedure as quickly as possible; others gave more extensive introductions. Most of them developed an approach and said much the same thing to each of their contacts but a few tended to vary their initial introduction from address to address. Even the most consistent interviewers on occasion had their initial introduction interrupted by the contact and as a result might not convey all the items of information that they usually included. It is thus not surprising that table 5.4 shows that even the most basic information was not delivered in the initial introduction at every address. The first column in table 5.4 tabulates information given in the interviewers' first statement before any significant response from the contact; the second column shows what additional information was given after the contact had responded with a question, comment or expression of reluctance, but before the respondent selection procedure was completed. Responses such as 'yes' or 'mm-mmm' were not counted as significant.

*Checking the address.* Interviewers are always instructed to check that they are at the correct address at the beginning of their initial introduction. Despite the tape recording, it was done in this survey at only just over half the addresses; at a further 10 per cent the name was checked instead, using the information from the electoral register given on the sample issue sheet. At two fifths of the addresses there was no initial check though the respondent selection procedure provided an implicit check on names at a later point in the procedure. Ten of the sixteen interviewers usually (but not invariably) checked the address while three were more likely to check the name; three rarely checked either until the respondent selection procedure.

Since they were to some extent on their best behaviour in this study, these practices presumably reflect what the interviewers consider to be an appropriate approach; in discussions, some have expressed the view that checking the address does not provide the ideal opening gambit for putting over the survey, particularly when streets are named and houses numbered very clearly.

*Introducing themselves by name.* At almost every address, the interviewers gave their own name; there was one, however, who simply introduced herself as 'an interviewer' in most of her tape recorded contacts.

**Table 5.4**

**Information put over by interviewer in initial introduction**
**(i.e. before completing respondent selection sheet)**

|  | Initial [a] 'speech' % | Additional [b] information % | Total [c] mention % |
|---|---|---|---|
| Base: 136 recorded initial introductions |  |  |  |
| Checks address | 53 }63 | 3 | 56 |
| Checks name instead of address | 10 | - | 10 |
| Gives own name | 92 | 1 | 93 |
| Mentions identity card | 35 | 3 | 38 |
| SCPR, a survey research organization | 96 | 2 | 98 |
| Independent/nonprofit institute | 35 | 2 | 37 |
| Describes survey topic | 70 }78 | 14 | x |
| 'Doing a (social) survey' | 8 | - | 8 |
| Taking random sample/cross-section (electoral reg. not mentioned) | 11 } 53 | 8 | x |
| Addresses selected at random from electoral register | 42 | 1 | x |
| Gives explanatory letter | 5 | 11 | 16 |
| Sponsored by ESRC | 4 | 4 | 8 |
| Length | - | 6 | 6 |

a   Initial introduction up to beginning of respondent selection procedure or to significant response from the contact if sooner.
b   Additional information given to contact after some significant response before completion of respondent selection procedure.
c   The total of the previous two columns; items marked x are not addable as interviewers sometimes repeated themselves.

*Use of identity card.* The identity card was mentioned at only 38 per cent of the addresses but it is probable that it was actually shown in many more cases since all SCPR interviewers are aware that it is compulsory to do so.

*Social and Community Planning Research.* At most addresses mention was made of SCPR (mainly using the full name rather than initials), a social research organization, but only around a third of contacts were told that it was an *independent* organization or institute.

*Describing the survey.* The majority of contacts (70 per cent) were given a brief description of the survey in terms of its subject matter in the initial introduction but some were told only that 'I am doing a survey'; some were either not told this information until later or inferred it from other information given. In most cases the omission was due to the contact interrupting the interviewer's initial speech.

*Explaining why the address was selected.* At many addresses there was no mention in the initial introduction of a random sample of names being selected from the electoral register; this was sometimes due to interruption from the contact but also reflected individual interviewers' styles, some preferring to leave all reference to the electoral register until it emerged normally during the respondent selection procedure: 'I have here the names of the people listed in the electoral register as living at this address, can I check whether they all still live here?'

*Use of explanatory letter.* Interviewers have the option to give the explanatory letter during their initial contact at the address or to leave it later on after they have completed the survey. At 5 per cent of the addresses, the letter was handed over during the initial introduction (mainly by one particular interviewer); at a further 11 per cent of addresses it was given in response to the contact's reaction to the introduction; thus in 16 per cent of the cases it was handed over before the interviewer had established whom to interview.

*Funding of the survey.* In this particular survey, interviewers were not asked to mention the funding of the survey in their initial introduction as it was not considered particularly helpful to do so and contacts were given this information at only 8 per cent of the addresses at this stage. It was of course given in the explanatory letter. In other surveys, the name of the sponsor is often regarded as a very important part of the initial information to be conveyed.

*Additional information given to selected respondents*

When the respondent selection procedure had been completed, the interaction between interviewer and contact entered a new phase: if the contact was not the selected respondent, the interviewer had to negotiate access to that person sometimes entering into quite lengthy discussions about when might be the best time to find them in or to persuade the contact to allow the interviewer to call again to see them.

When the contact turned out to be the selected respondent, the interviewer usually gave some further information though in a quarter of the cases they simply asked for the interview. The main items of information given at this point were:

- how long the interview would take (given to half these cases)

- a further description of the survey (a quarter of cases)
- that answers would be treated in confidence (one fifth of cases).

## When the respondent is not the first contact

When the person selected for interview was not one who helped with the selection procedure, interviewers had to deal with very variable situations and they showed a considerable lack of discipline in doing so: in only a third of these cases did the interviewers give their own name or mention SCPR; in two thirds a description of the survey was given but there were few mentions as to how the address had been selected. Apart from the length of the interview, mentioned to two fifths of these respondents, the items of secondary information were mentioned in a fifth or less of the cases. In a third of the cases the explanatory letter had been left at the previous visit to the address and interviewers tended to refer to this in their initial words to the respondent rather than repeat their basic introduction given to their first contact at the address. Since the respondent had not always read the letter, this seemed to be a poor approach often leading to rather garbled and haphazard presentations of the survey. Interviewer training should clearly make a point of stressing the need to start completely afresh when the selected respondent is first contacted without any assumption that they know what the survey is about.

## What is a 'good' survey introduction?

Is a 'good' survey introduction one that most closely follows the instructions and suggestions from the office or are there other criteria? The lack of adherence to instructions despite the fact that they were recording their introductions suggests that the interviewers' ideas as to what should be put over differ from the accepted wisdom.

We did not expect to find any simple relationship between items of information given and success in obtaining the interview and were therefore not surprised to find none. However, we felt that it should be possible to identify the style and characteristics of a successful survey introduction by comparing the most successful and least successful interviewers. A qualitative appraisal of the general styles of the four most successful interviewers compared with the three least successful (as measured by proportion of eligible respondents who refused to give the interview) suggested that a very brief and succinct introduction is more effective than a longer one that perhaps gives more information. All of the most successful interviewers gave brief introductions in which the items of information were put over simply and economically; they also spoke clearly and coherently with a minimum of 'ums' and 'ahs'. The most successful of all (with 100 per cent overall response rate on the survey) nearly always put over all the required information in remarkably few words:

> 'Hello.  Is this ........ (address)?  My name is ........ and I'm from Social and Community Planning Research.  I'm carrying out a survey on people's social attitudes and your address is one that has been selected at random from the electoral register........'

and she went straight into the selection procedure unless the contact interrupted.

Another very successful interviewer had an equally brief but somewhat less orthodox approach, choosing to emphasise different items of information:

> 'Hello; this is ........ (address)?  My name is ......... and I work for Social and Community Planning Research which is an independent survey organization.  We're doing a survey in this area and they have given me addresses from the electoral roll .......'

In contrast, the least successful interviewers tended to be more wordy and less coherent:

> 'Hello.  Mrs ........?  I'm ......... from Social and Community Planning Research and I want to call on this household on behalf of this company which is an independent research corporation; we're approaching a cross section of the public to ask about attitudes and opinions as to social things that are going on ........' (and she goes into the selection procedure).

The experiment in providing a scripted introduction for some interviewers and asking them to keep as closely to it as possible further supports the hypothesis that a really short and economically worded introduction is the most effective.

## The experiment in scripting interviewers' survey introductions

Fourteen of the total of thirty interviewers working on the survey were asked to use the scripted introduction prepared for them.  The instructions they were given are displayed in figure 5.2.

In addition, there was a long list of suggested answers to common respondent queries or reluctance.

### A prepared script hindered rather than helped

Far from helping interviewers to gain cooperation, asking them to keep to a prepared script seemed to make them less effective: the response rate for interviewers using the script was 59 per cent compared with 76 per cent for those developing their own approach.  This difference is significant at the 5 per cent level on a chi-squared test.

Five of the scripted interviewers also taped their introductions and it was notable that three of these five were the least successful interviewers of the sixteen who recorded their doorstep approaches and none was among the four most successful.

Please read and practise the introduction given below several times before starting work and also again after each of your first few interviews in order to become as familiar as possible with it. Try to keep as closely to the wording as you can comfortably manage while still sounding natural.

WHEN THE DOOR IS ANSWERED
'Good/morning/afternoon/evening: this is ... (address) ... isn't it? I am ... (your name) ... from Social and Community Planning Research. Here is my identity card. We are an independent social research organization and we are approaching a cross section of the public to find out how people feel about a whole range of social issues. This address was selected from the electoral register and I need your help first with a few questions to find whom I should interview.'

GO TO RESPONDENT SELECTION SHEET

WHEN CONTACT HAS BEEN MADE WITH CORRECT RESPONDENT, USE ABOVE INTRODUCTION AGAIN (IF IT WAS NOT THE PERSON WHO ANSWERED THE DOOR) AND ADD:
'This survey is funded by the Economic and Social Research Council; it forms part of an on-going enquiry into the attitudes of the British people towards a number of issues that affect our society. The results of the survey will be helpful to government departments in making decisions about economic and social policies. The information you give will be treated as confidential; your name will never be linked with your answers. The interview shouldn't take more than about 25 minutes.'

**Figure 5.2   Instructions to interviewers using a scripted introduction**

## Adhering to the script is difficult

It was apparent that these interviewers had difficulty in keeping to the script and one made little attempt to do so - and obtained the best results of the five! Although those using the script were more likely to deliver most of the items of information in the first part of the script (the initial introduction) than were the unscripted interviewers, none of the items was delivered to 100 per cent of the contacts (table 5.5). While in some cases this was due to interruption by the contact to indicate a fairly definite lack of interest in taking part, this could not account for such frequent failures to put over the scripted items of information.

**Table 5.5**

**Initial introduction by scripted and unscripted interviews**

(Scripted items of information delivered up to completion of
selection procedure.)

|  | Scripted | Unscripted |
|---|---|---|
| Base: all contacts in each condition | (46) | (90) |
|  | % | % |
| Checked address | 67 | 48 |
| Gave own name | 81 | 99 |
| Mentioned identity card | 43 | 35 |
| Mentioned SCPR | 98 | 100 |
| Independent research organization | 53 | 30 |
| Describes survey topic | 93 | 76 |
| Random sample (Electoral reg. not mentioned) | 19 | 19 |
| Addresses from electoral register | 50 | 44 |

*Why does the script not work?*

There seem to be two reasons why the scripted interviewers were less successful than those who developed their own introductions. One was that the script interfered with the interviewers' spontaneity and flexibility: listening to the tape recordings and reading the transcripts indicated that they were able to deliver the script as long as they were not interrupted; but once they were forced to depart from the script to deal with a question or expression of reluctance to take part, they were unable to pick up the script again or adapt it to the new situation that had developed. Furthermore, the script seemed to inhibit their ability to deal adequately with reluctance; instead of flexibly turning their attention to the essence of the reluctance expressed, they tended to try to counter it with not always appropriate items of information from the script or to try to press on to complete the respondent selection procedure.

The second reason why the script was unsuccessful was that it was not a very good script! Compared with the initial introductions that tended to be used by the most successful interviewers, it contained more information than was necessary and expressed it in too many words. The introduction used by the most successful interviewer provided a model for a clear and economically worded script (apart from her tendency not to mention her identity card).

We should not conclude from this experiment that it is wrong to provide interviewers with a written introduction for a survey. New interviewers in particular say that it is helpful to have an example of how to put the survey over and all can benefit from having a model put before them that indicates how the researcher feels the survey should be presented. But the experiment in scripting the introduction and the comparison of the most and least successful interviewers have demonstrated that the initial statement of business by the interviewer can and should be considerably simpler than researchers might think is the case. Also, interviewers should use it as a guide rather than as a script and not feel bound to pursue it to the last word despite interruptions from the contact.

*But what about 'informed consent'?*

These findings seem to be contrary to the ethical ideal that survey respondents should be properly informed about the nature and purpose of the survey; but all that has been indicated is that the initial statement of business is not the point at which to put over the more detailed information about the survey that the principle of 'informed consent' would require. Some contacts interrupt or respond to the initial introduction with questions or expressions of reluctance which naturally lead the interviewer to give more information but 70 per cent either said nothing significant or simply expressed interest during the part of the interaction that took place before the respondent selection questions were asked.

Nor does it appear that it is appropriate to require interviewers to give a comprehensive list of items of information when they make contact with the selected respondent: the scripted interviewers were given a second section of script which they were asked to deliver after they had established whom they were to interview and had made contact; this script, in addition to giving a slightly fuller description of the survey topic, included four items of information:

- funded by the Economic and Social Research Council;
- the results would be helpful to government departments;
- their information would be treated as confidential;
- the interview would take about 25 minutes.

Although all these items were given more frequently by the scripted interviewers than by the unscripted, only 'length of interview' was mentioned by a majority (60 per cent);[3] 'confidentiality' was mentioned by two fifths and the other two items each by just over a quarter.

The reason that interviewers were unable to deliver the second part of the script with any frequency seemed to be that by this point in the interaction their attention needed to be entirely on the selected person's response so that they could react appropriately to secure the interview. It was thus difficult to revert to the script, especially as some of the information might have already been given in response to questions or expressions of reluctance.

It is clearly not possible to rely on interviewers to put over all the information that the concept of 'informed consent' might require during the necessarily interactive and very variable process of introducing the survey, establishing whom to interview and persuading them to take part. The explanatory letter is designed to fill any informational gaps but is often not given until the end of the interview. Allowing time for someone to read a letter can also break the flow of the interaction and some members of the public may feel under pressure trying to absorb written information in the doorstep situation.

The most appropriate point at which to give fuller and more formal information about the survey would seem to be after consent has been obtained in principle but before the interview starts. The interviewer at this point is moving from the free flowing interaction involved in obtaining the interview to the more structured interaction of the question and answer process. It would be relatively easy at this point to say, 'Before we start, I want to make sure that I have told you all you should know about the survey;' a list of the four or five main points could be actually printed on the questionnaire.

## The advance letter experiment

It was apparent that the knowledge that a household had received an advanced letter affected some interviewers' way of introducing the survey. Since there was no guarantee that the person answering the door had read the letter, the correct approach was considered to be to use the same initial introduction as at addresses not sent a letter and to add at the end 'You may have received a letter about it from us'. Of the sixteen interviewers recording their introductions:

- 3 usually followed the designated approach;
- 4 did not mention the letter unless the contacted person did so first;
- 3 had too few recorded introductions at addresses receiving advanced letters for their approach to be evaluated;
- 6 tended to substitute mention of the letter for the proper introduction: e.g. 'I am ........ from Social and Community Planning Research; you should have received a letter about the survey we are doing.'

If the contacts of this last group of interviewers indicated that they recalled the letter, the interviewer then tended to rely on their memory of it rather than to describe the survey. If the contacts denied knowledge of the letter, the interviewer had then to resume the survey introduction from a rather disadvantageous position.

Table 5.6 indicates the variations in type of introduction received by contacts at addresses that received an advance letter. In half the cases the letter was either not mentioned at all or was mentioned correctly at the end of the initial introduction; but in a fifth of the cases interviewers seriously curtailed their introduction, giving no proper description of the survey in their initial statement.

**Table 5.6**

**Use of reference to advance letter in initial introduction**

| | |
|---|---|
| Base: Addresses to which advance letter sent | (73) |
| | % |
| No mention of letter in initial introduction | 38 |
| Interviewer mentions letter at end of initial introduction | 16 |
| Letter mentioned during a shortened introduction* | 11 |
| No proper description of survey in initial introduction but letter mentioned instead | 22 |
| Contact interrupts initial introduction to mention letter | 13 |

* e.g. 'You may have received a letter saying we are doing a survey about attitudes affecting Britain today.'

## Response to the interviewers' approach

*First response*

The interviewers' initial introductions were almost always designed to lead straight into the respondent selection procedure; the main exception was when they mentioned the advance letter which tended, implicitly or explicitly, to invite a reply from the contacted person.

In around half the cases (table 5.7), the interviewers were able to make their initial introduction and start the respondent selection procedure without any significant interjection from the contacted person (though there may have been social noises such as 'mm-mmm', 'I see' or 'Yes').

A fifth of contacts made neutral or interested comments and only a quarter either asked a question or expressed reluctance to take part at this stage. A small proportion (5 per cent) uttered a definite refusal as their immediate reaction to the initial introduction and a further 2 per cent (from among those who expressed reluctance) went on to refuse to give the necessary information for carrying out the respondent selection procedure.

**Table 5.7**

**First significant response from contact before respondent selection procedure**

| | |
|---|---|
| Base: all taped first contacts at address | (136) |
| | % |
| Definite refusal which was not changed | 5 |
| Reservation or reluctance in the form of a question | 12 |
| Reluctance as a negative statement | 13 |
| Neutral or interested comment | 18 |
| No significant response before selection procedure | 53 |

*Advance letter pre-empts interviewer's skill*

There were nine contacts who refused cooperation before the respondent selection procedure could be carried out; seven of these had received the advance letter and seemed on the basis of it to have already made up their minds to refuse before the interviewer called. However, these must be balanced against ten respondents who expressed a positive interest or immediately welcomed the interviewer because they had received the letter. It is clear that an advance letter to some extent pre-empts the interviewer's skill on the doorstep in that around a fifth of contacts at addresses receiving it had decided how to respond before the interviewer called; very careful consideration therefore needs to be given as to the letter's content; interviewer training also needs to pay attention to ways of helping interviewers to optimize the effect of an advance letter and to avoid stultifying their skill by over reliance on the letter.

*Types of reluctance expressed*

Interviewer training programmes commonly include examples of ways in which the public are thought to express resistance to being interviewed. The tape recordings of doorstep introductions provide a direct picture of the most common sorts of reluctance and their relative frequency.

The definition of reluctance used was extremely broad; it included all verbal expressions of anything except interest or willingness to participate, or completely neutral expressions such as 'mm-mmm' or 'I see', questions about the nature of the survey, the length of the interview etc. were thus classed as reluctance even though they may often have been simple requests for information. Conversely, there may have been occasions when the contact said nothing but was actually feeling suspicious or reluctant to take part. This broad definition is useful, however, since it presents a view of the different reactions with which interviewers had to deal.

From a detailed content analysis, the following categories of reluctance were defined:

1.  *'What is the survey about?'* This category is a general request for further information and includes queries such as 'what is it for?' and 'who is it for?'

2.  *'I'm busy at the moment.'* This is any claim to be busy at the time the interviewer called. The most common were 'I'm in the middle of cooking/ doing the washing etc.' / 'I'm having a meal/about to go out'.

3.  *'I'm not interested.'* Including: 'I can't be bothered' / 'I don't want to know' / 'No thanks'.

4. *Reservations about the nature or the content of the survey.* This category covers cases where there is some suspicion about the survey, for example 'You're not going to ask me any personal questions are you?', as well as instances where people suspect selling.

5. *Length.* This includes any queries or hesitance about the length of the interview.

6. *'I'm too busy in general.'* Unlike category (ii), which was a claim to be busy at that moment, this category covers cases where people say they cannot make any time for the survey, for example, because they are busy working, are going away, or are out every evening.

7. *'Why me?'* This is where people want to know why they in particular should do the survey; it includes such expressions as 'Go next door'/'I'm not the right person for this' and also the question 'Do I have to do it?'

8. *Illness.* This covers those who said that they were unwell/ 'Not feeling too good'/had a 'bad head' etc.

In addition, there were two residual categories:

9. *General reluctance - nonspecific.* This covers any verbal expression by the person which conveys reluctance but which is not an excuse, question or justification. For example: 'Well....', 'I don't really know....', 'Uhm....', and so on.

10. *Others - specific.* These comprise miscellaneous substantive responses given by too few people to form categories; for example: 'I don't know enough', 'I don't agree with doing surveys' and so on.

A category was also provided for those who expressed no reluctance.

Some of the people expressed more than one type of reluctance and multicoding of the categories was permitted. Some repeated the same form of reluctance several times but these are counted only once in this analysis.

Table 5.8 shows the frequency with which the different types of reluctance were met with by the interviewers during their first conversation at the address. At some addresses more than one person may have been spoken to if the first contact did not turn out to be the selected respondent.

One remarkable feature of the table is the high proportion of introductions that met with no reluctance (44 per cent), despite the broad definition of reluctance. Another finding which is perhaps surprising is the small number of people who expressed suspicions of the survey in any way (9 per cent). These two findings are reassuring given the common belief that we are living in a society where people are becoming increasingly afraid of strangers, and also given the nature of the survey (a little known sponsor, no immediate or direct benefit to respondents and so on).

The most common types of reluctance that interviewers have to deal with are requests for more information, claims to be busy at that moment, expressions of lack of interest and nonspecific reluctance such as 'Well, er...'. Clearly, these are the forms of reluctance that interviewer training programmes should address carefully.

**Table 5.8**

**Frequency with which interviewers met the different categories of reluctance**

| Base: All spoken to at first visit to address | (149) |
|---|---|
| | % |
| What is the survey about? | 19 |
| I'm busy at the moment | 17 |
| I'm not interested | 17 |
| Reservations about nature/content | 9 |
| How long will it take? | 9 |
| I'm too busy in general | 6 |
| Why me? | 6 |
| I'm not well | 5 |
| General nonspecific reluctance | 17 |
| Other specific reluctance | 11 |
| No reluctance expressed | 44 |

*Some kinds of reluctance are 'tougher' than others*

How often do people who express a certain kind of reluctance nevertheless agree to be interviewed in the end?

To answer this question it is necessary to look only at the 121 taped conversations with people who were selected respondents (table 5.9). These include contacts who turned out to be the selected respondent and other selected respondents who were finally contacted.

**Table 5.9**

**Frequency of expressing types of reluctance by whether
selected respondent interviewed or not**

|  | Total | Interviewed | Refused | Signif. |
|---|---|---|---|---|
| Base: Selected respondents* | (121) | (96) | (25) | |
|  | % | % | % | |
| What is the survey about? | 17 | 14 | 28 | n.s. |
| I'm busy at the moment | 17 | 9 | 44 | p < .0001 |
| I'm not interested | 15 | 1 | 56 | p < .0001 |
| Reservations about nature/ content | 13 | 9 | 24 | p < .05 |
| How long will it take? | 12 | 14 | 4 | n.s. |
| I'm too busy in general | 5 | - | 20 | p < .0001 |
| Why me? | 9 | 5 | 20 | p < .05 |
| I'm not well | 3 | - | 12 | p < .01 |
| General nonspecific reluctance | 20 | 6 | 64 | p < .0001 |
| Other specific reluctance | 11 | 1 | 40 | p < .0001 |
| No reluctance expressed | 44 | 55 | - | p < .0001 |

* The base is lower than the total number of addresses because some selected respondents were not contacted and in some cases the interviewer omitted to tape record the second visit to the address. Those refusing before the selection procedure are also omitted.

The overall pattern of expressions of reluctance by selected respondents shown in table 5.9 is not significantly different from that encountered in the conversations at the first visit to the addresses. Not surprisingly, considerably more reluctance was expressed by those who refused the interview than by those agreeing to it; three fifths of those agreeing expressed no reluctance at all.

It is interesting to note that general nonspecific reluctance and 'I'm not interested' are each given by over half those refusing the interview whereas questions about the content or length of the survey were relatively less important.

Overall, just over half of those expressing any reluctance finally agreed to be interviewed. Although the numbers mentioning each item of reluctance are small, it is useful to examine the conversion rates for the main types of reluctance (table 5.10). This confirms that 'I'm not interested' and general vague expressions of reluctance indicate serious resistance that is rarely converted. 'Other specific' forms of reluctance are also rarely followed by conversion to an interview. In table 5.10 we have included in this category 'Too busy in general' and 'Illness' which were given by too few people to be shown separately and were never followed by an interview. Those asking questions about length of interview or what the survey was about, on the other hand, were converted in the majority of cases, suggesting these are often simply requests for information; the information received is considered to be satisfactory and the selected person agrees to the interview. It has to be remembered that the interview was relatively short in this study (and often presented by the interviewer as being shorter than it actually was); evidence has already been quoted in Chapter 2 that indicates that longer interviews tend to get lower response rates.

**Table 5.10**

**Proportion of respondents expressing each type of reluctance who agreed to be interviewed**

|  | % agreeing to be interviewed | Bases |
|---|---|---|
| How long will it take? | 92% | (12) |
| What is the survey about? | 61% | (18) |
| Reservations about nature/content | 54% | (13) |
| Why me? | 45% | (9) |
| I'm busy at the moment | 39% | (18) |
| General nonspecific | 24% | (21) |
| Other specific* | 5% | (19) |
| Not interested | 7% | (15) |
| Expressing any reluctance | 56% | (57) |

* Including in this table only, 'Too busy in general' and 'Illness'.

The relatively low conversion rate for 'Busy at the moment' suggests that this form of reluctance is at least in some cases a way of fobbing off the interviewer without having to give an outright refusal though it might also reflect failure on the interviewers' part to make it clear that they could come back another time to do the interview.

## The dynamics of persuasion

Sometimes interviewers entered into chains of interaction with the selected respondents to try to persuade them to take part. In order to understand the dynamics of these interactions and to appraise the success of the interviewers in converting reluctant respondents, the overlap between the different categories of reluctance was examined.

*Multiple expressions of reluctance*

It was notable that those successfully interviewed rarely expressed more than one type of reluctance whereas most of the refusers expressed two or more (table 5.11). Single items of reluctance were mainly questions as to the length of the interview or the comment that they were too busy at the moment (accounting for half these cases), suggesting that these people had more or less acquiesced in their minds provided that the interview could be fitted in with the other demands on their time. The importance of interviewers making it clear that they are willing to come back at a more convenient time if necessary is again highlighted.

**Table 5.11**

**Number of different types of reluctance expressed by
selected respondents**

|  | Total | | Interviewed | | Refused |
|---|---|---|---|---|---|
| Base 1: Selected respondents | (121) | | (96) | | (25) |
| Base 2: Those expressing reluctance | | (68) | | (43) | |
|  | % | | % | | % |
| None | 44 | % | 55 | % | - |
| 1 type | 25 | 44 | 29 | 65 | 8 |
| 2 types | 16 | 26 | 9 | 21 | 36 |
| 3 types | 11 | 19 | 4 | 9 | 36 |
| 4 or more | 4 | 10 | 2 | 5 | 20 |

Conversion rate:

|  | Interviewed | (Base) |
|---|---|---|
| One type of reluctance | 93% | (30) |
| 2 or more types of reluctance | 41% | (37) |

*Indicators of serious reluctance*

The number of items of reluctance expressed can be taken as an indication of the strength of a person's reluctance to be interviewed: over 90 per cent of those offering only one form of reluctance agreed to be interviewed compared with only 41 per cent of those expressing two or more types of reluctance (table 5.11).

What is apparent from studying the variable patterns of overlap of types of reluctance is that the tougher types of reluctance are given on their own relatively rarely; some refusers start with a fairly soft excuse for not doing the interview (such as 'I'm busy just now') and move to a harder line in response to persuasion from the interviewer; others start with general reluctance ('Well, er' etc.) while trying to think up a good reason for refusing. It is very clear that this type of hesitancy indicates strong underlying reluctance to take part and should alert the interviewers to the fact that they are likely to have a problem.

As Goyder (1987) has pointed out, members of the public are not simply passive creatures requiring only the right stimulus to bring about a response that is one of compliance with the interviewer's request. They have wills of their own and enter into a dynamic negotiation with the interviewer. Resistance to being interviewed can be regarded as a continuum: there will always be some determined (at least on the specific occasion) not to be persuaded and others who are pleased to welcome any interviewer; but there is likely to be a fairly large middle group where the interviewers' persuasive skills have a role to play. In this study, just under a third of the selected respondents could be said to fall into this middle group in that they expressed more than one type of reluctance; the interviewers were successful in persuading only two fifths of this group to take part (table 5.11).

To identify the factors that go to make for success in dealing with reluctance, the four most successful interviewers were again compared with the three least successful in terms of refusal rate on the survey, in order to see whether they varied in the strategies they used. Since numbers were small and the material very fluid and variable, the appraisal was mainly qualitative.

### The more successful interviewers are better persuaders

The more successful interviewers to some extent pre-empted resistance by the way they made their initial introduction but the difference between them and the less successful interviewers in the proportion of contacts who expressed no reluctance was not large. Although they met on average with fewer different types of resistance per contact, this may have been because they dealt more effectively with reluctance so that long arguments were avoided. It was certainly not because they encountered only the 'softer' types of reluctance; if anything, they met with fewer questions about the nature of the survey and the length of the interview than did the less successful interviewers, perhaps because they were more efficient at putting over information about the survey when it was relevant to do so.

### There is no one 'right' way to overcome reluctance

The most apparent difference between the two groups of interviewers was that while the less successful ones had a good deal in common with each other, those in the more successful group had distinct styles.

Furthermore, a less successful interviewer could fail attempting to use a strategy that a more successful interviewer found productive.

### Important to address reluctance as it arises

One of the failings of the less successful interviewers was that they tended to be too concerned with the other goals of the introduction (identifying and contacting the selected respondent and, to a lesser extent, putting over facts about the survey) at the expense of dealing with reluctance. This seemed to be a consequence of asking these interviewers to keep to a prepared script. The danger of persisting with these other tasks rather than addressing reluctance as it arises is that it spirals, so that, for example, 'I'm sorry, I'm busy' turns into 'I'm not interested', which is much harder to deal with.

The following example illustrates how one interviewer persisted in attempting to find out whom to interview. (It should be remembered that the transcripts were analyzed in conjunction with the tapes and that some of the 'atmosphere' is lost here).

**Example 1**

Contact breaks in before the end of the initial introduction:

Contact:          'Do you want my wife?'

Interviewer:      'I don't know who I really want! [Giggles] If I could ask you the first few things. Um, how many households live at this address?'

Contact:          'Just the wife and me. Will it take very long, then? I'm going out you see.'

Interviewer:      'It'll take just a few minutes to do this. I've got here a list of the people on the electoral register...'

At this point the interviewer continues with the selection procedure while the contact rapidly becomes more uncooperative. Eventually, the interviewer identifies the selected respondent, who turns out to be the wife:

Contact:          'Well, she's not in.'

Interviewer:      'Isn't she?'

Contact:          'No, I'm sorry.'

Interviewer:      'When is she usually at home?'

Contact:          'Well, I really don't know.'

Interviewer:      'Is she normally available in the day time?'

Contact:          'Well, sometimes she helps me in the market and sometimes she's in and sometimes she's out. You can never pin either of us down really.'

Interviewer:      'Yes, so I can't make a definite appointment then?'

Contact:          'No, I think frankly that you can't.'

Even now the interviewer still persists in trying to discover when the respondent is likely to be available despite the contact's unwillingness to give the information. When the interviewer called again, she was told that the wife had gone away.

It seemed that the less successful interviewers treated the doorstep introduction as a series of logical steps: give information, carry out the respondent selection procedure, contact the respondent and persuade him or her to take part. Since these interviewers did not give priority to addressing and dealing with reluctance, they were disconcerted when something happened to disrupt the sequence.

*Effective strategies*

The more successful interviewers had disparate styles but each of them had identifiable strategies for dealing with reluctance.

The most successful interviewer was confident and matter of fact; she was unperturbed by the selection procedure and countered reluctance with varied but appropriate information or comment. Her usual strategy was to keep answers and explanations succinct: if she sensed too much resistance, she backed off, leaving a leaflet and calling back another day.

In the following example, the interviewer prevents the reluctance from turning into a refusal by retreating, and she manages to obtain the interview on a subsequent visit.

> **Example 2**
>
> Interviewer: 'Could I ask how many households live at this address at the present time?'
>
> Contact: 'I can't be bothered to do that one, I can't really. Do you have to do it?
>
> Interviewer: 'No; would you like to read this letter and I'll leave this leaflet with you and I'll call back when you've read it.'

This style was in marked contrast to the second most successful interviewer, whose strategy was to be persistent, but without pressurizing respondents into feeling they had to do it. While she was as confident as the first interviewer she was more discursive, taking things slowly and replying to respondent's statements with logical, reasoned arguments.

> **Example 3**
>
> Respondent selection procedure done and respondent who was not the first contact is now approached:
>
> Interviewer: 'I'm asking if you would be so kind as to do a survey with me - it's on social attitudes.'
>
> Respondent: 'Well, it depends what you want to know.'
>
> Interviewer: 'Well, it's general opinions, your opinion on certain everyday things, like nuclear missiles.'
>
> Respondent: 'Well, I don't know anything about that.'
>
> Interviewer: 'Do you have an opinion?'
>
> Respondent: 'No, no. I'm not telling you anything about those things. No. So you're wasting your time.'

| Interviewer: | 'Well, there are other things as well ... about schools.' |
| Respondent: | 'Schools I'm not interested in.' |
| Interviewer: | 'The National Health Service...' |
| Respondent: | 'Oh well.' |
| Interviewer: | 'It's just, as I say, if you could spare me the time.' |
| Respondent: | 'Well, I'm washing you know.' |
| Interviewer: | 'Well, could I pop back some other time?' |
| Respondent: | 'No, I don't want you coming back.' |
| Interviewer: | 'Well, could we just start it then - if you don't want to do it that's just fine.' |
| Respondent: | 'Well, go on then and see what you want.' |

Once the interviewer had detected a weakening of resistance she managed to secure the interview. Researchers prefer interviewers not to divulge too much of the content of the questionnaires during the introduction for fear of biassing responses, but this interviewer mentions specific topics and almost starts the interview on the doorstep.

This interviewer was also very adroit at gaining admittance to the house:

**Example 4**

Contact interrupts initial introduction early on:

| Contact: | 'I can hardly walk.' |
| Interviewer: | 'Oh dear yes, you can hardly walk. Just let me step inside, then you can sit down again while I tell you what it's about.' |

Here she empathized with the contact but in a way that contributed to obtaining the interview. The less successful interviewers often seemed to empathize with the reluctance:

'So you really don't want to be bothered?'

'So you haven't got time? OK. Thank you.'

Persistence and empathy are thus two strategies that can be usefully employed but have to be used appropriately and with skill or they can be counterproductive: persistence can become unacceptable and annoying pressure; empathy can validate reluctance and undermine the interviewer's ability to be positive about the survey.

*Close attention and flexibility of reaction*

The more successful interviewers seemed to attend more closely to what was said by the people they contacted, to be more sensitive to the nuances of meaning and to be more flexible in their responses. Compared with the less successful interviewers, they spoke more fluently, gave information more succinctly and appropriately and handled appointment making more tactfully, often using the ploy of leaving the letter and calling again at an unspecified time with some success. They knew when to ease the pressure on the respondent to good effect. They sounded both more relaxed and more confident and were assertive without being aggressive. In contrast, the less successful interviewers were often long winded and repetitive, and persevered compulsively in a way that annoyed the contact. They sometimes seemed to be flustered by expressions of reluctance with the result that they sounded unsure of themselves and thus lacked authority and credibility.

*Emotional pressure*

As a last resort, the less successful interviewers sometimes brought emotional pressure to bear on respondents by indicating that a refusal would be in some way reprehensible because it was hurtful to the interviewer or damaging to the survey:

> 'I'm very disappointed you won't do it.'

> 'If you won't do it, I can't take anyone else, you see, and it's very important we get as many people as possible.'

Although the second example expresses the truth, it does it in a reproachful manner. Making the respondent feel guilty may be ethically questionable and counterproductive.

*Negative and positive aspects of doing a survey*

When the interviewers approach members of the public for an interview, they are asking a stranger for a favour. Brown and Levinson (1978) have usefully codified politeness phenomena in the making of requests, using the concept of 'Face' introduced by Goffman (1967). The term 'Face' is used in the colloquial sense to refer to self image and self esteem.

There are two aspects: 'negative Face', which is the desire to be left in peace and quiet in one's own territory without interference or intrusion, and to have freedom of action; and 'positive Face' which is the desire for approval and for rewarding experiences. In social interactions, people usually cooperate in maintaining each other's 'Face', based on mutual vulnerability. In the survey introduction, the interviewers are working towards the overt goal of trying to obtain the interview while at the same time pursuing the covert goal of maintaining their own and the contacted person's 'Face'.

There is an inherent tension between negative and positive 'Face' needs. The rules of politeness are designed to indicate that each participant in the interaction is aware of the other's need to preserve both aspects of 'Face'. 'Negative' politeness is used to show that the speaker is aware of the other's negative 'Face' needs: it is formal and reassures the person that the request will cause minimum interference. 'Positive' politeness indicates that there will be positive rewards for helping.

In analyzing the tape recorded survey introductions, it was notable that all the interviewers mainly countered reluctance by attempting to minimize the negative 'Face' threats. With remarks such as 'It won't take very long', 'It's strictly confidential', they attempted to reduce intrusiveness and convey reassurance. They rarely indicated that there could be positive rewards to respondents in terms of an enjoyable and interesting experience or an opportunity to contribute to a worthwhile survey through which they could express their views. Only the most successful interviewers seemed to address the positive 'Face' requirements of respondents by indicating that they would find it interesting and also by giving as necessary clear information about the survey.

Although reassurance and the minimizing of intrusiveness are important in the doorstep interaction, the positive aspects of taking part also often need putting if some reluctant people are to be persuaded to give their time to be interviewed. The next chapter examines why people agree to be interviewed and what are the rewards of doing so. This will take us a stage further in identifying the components of doorstep behaviour that lead to a successful outcome.

## Notes

1    Later to become the Joint Centre for Survey Methods. The study was funded by the Economic and Social Research Council under their block funding of the Centre.
2    The survey which provided the opportunity to conduct this study was the face to face interview section of an experiment designed to compare face to face and telephone interviewing. It was funded by the Economic and Social Research Council.
3    It was notable that the scripted interviewers were more likely to say that the interview would take 20 or 30 minutes whereas unscripted interviewers were more 'economical' with the truth saying 15-20 minutes, 10 minutes or 'just a few minutes'.

# 6 Why do people agree to be interviewed?

From the viewpoint of the person approached, there is inevitably a degree of intrusiveness about the request to take part in a survey: the interviewer initiates the interaction, usually without any prior notification, and puts the prospective respondent in the position of having to make a decision.

The rules of politeness governing the making of a request discussed in the last chapter indicate that asking a favour is likely to set up a tension between the desire for self esteem enhancing and rewarding experience and the wish not to be threatened or disturbed. To understand how people reach the decision to agree or to refuse to give an interview a broader theoretical framework is needed. Kahn and Cannell (1957) have usefully applied psychologist Kurt Lewin's 'Field theory of motivation' to the decision to give an interview.

According to field theory, a person's behaviour is the outcome of a process in which a number of factors are weighed up; an individual may have several needs, desires or goals that are relevant to a decision that has to be made, and also beliefs, perceptions, attitudes, values and considerations that provide the background of internal 'information' that comes into play in making the decision. This constellation of factors provides the 'psychological field' which underlies the decision to behave in a particular way.

Some of these factors will be in opposition to each other: for example, the desire to continue to watch a television programme may be in conflict with the desire to know who is at the door; the need to feel safe may be at variance with the need to be liked by the stranger on the door; the goal of getting the housework done may clash with the goal of being helpful to society by participating in the survey. The unpleasant tension brought about by these conflicts will be resolved by weighing up the relative value of the needs, desires and goals, the choices of action available, the difficulties and the psychological cost perceived as being involved in the possible courses of action and so on. The individual will choose a course of action in the light of all these factors and the reasons for the choice become intelligible in so far as we are able to see the decision process from the perspective of the individual making it.

Groves & Cialdini (1991) describe two different styles of processing information that may be used when making decisions; the 'systematic' approach involves an analytical and thorough appraisal of all available information; the 'heuristic' approach uses a short cut analysis that looks for individual prominent features in the situation that have previously been associated with good decisions. They argue that, in the context of deciding whether or not to give an interview, most people will use the heuristic mode. Taking part in a survey is rarely of sufficient importance for the potential respondent to want to review systematically all relevant information; nor are the pressures of the doorstep situation conducive to this type of process. Although some individuals approached may attempt a more systematic analysis of the information given by the interviewer, most will base their decision on one or two features such as the length of the interview or their liking for the interviewer.

The request for an interview is essentially a request for help on a larger project, i.e., the survey. It is a broader scenario than that within which the door to door salesperson works in that it concerns issues beyond those involved in selling; it offers less personal gratification of goals through acquisition (whether it be a new broom, an insurance policy or double glazing) and appeals to more subtle altruistic ways of enhancing self esteem; above all, there is less threat because no financial commitment is asked for from the survey respondent. Theories and research concerning 'helping behaviour' fit well within the overall framework of field theory and are particularly pertinent to explaining why people agree to be interviewed.

## Helping behaviour

There has been a considerable amount of research by social psychologists into why people help or don't help in a given situation, ranging from helping in emergencies or cases of violent crime to answering requests for the time or change for the phone (Piliavin et al., 1969; Tajfel, 1981; Darley and Latane, 1970). Only House and Wolf (1978) seem to have used participation in a survey as a helping task to be investigated.

Certain main themes emerge from the literature that are relevant to the decision to help with a survey:

1. *Perceptions of the person asking for help:* the literature shows that the perceived characteristics, approach and behaviour of the person asking for help can affect response to the request;

2. *Benefits versus costs:* the individual approached weighs up the rewards of helping (including enhancement of self esteem) against the possible costs in time, money, danger, embarrassment, etc.;

3. *Legitimacy of the request:* people are more likely to help in a situation where they perceive the need as legitimate; for example, they are more likely to help if they think someone is ill rather than drunk;

4. *Belief in ability to help:* a factor that inhibits people from helping is that they do not know what to do or do not feel adequate to do what is needed;

5. *Personal responsibility:* someone is more likely to help if they feel that it is their responsibility to do so and no one else's;

6. *Empathy:* an individual may vicariously experience the need of the person asking for help, or the feelings of disappointment, despair or rejection if refused; this feeling is the basis of altruistic behaviour where no personal reward is envisaged beyond the warm glow engendered by it;

7. *Mood and circumstances:* the extent to which an individual helps another is often affected by their mood and circumstances at the time of the request: a person late for an appointment or in a state of emotional distress is unlikely to provide help unless the other's need is perceived as being of greater urgency and importance than their own. Angry people have been found to be more likely than those not angry to refuse a request (DeNicholas, 1987).

## The respondent's decision process

What people say to the interviewer when asked to participate in a survey is not a sufficient basis for understanding why they agree or refuse to give the interview. Although it is useful to know how people express reluctance to take part, what they say indicates only the outcome of a complex decision process and is likely to be tempered by politeness; for example, a person may prefer to give an excuse, 'I'm far too busy', rather than simply to say 'No'.

To find out what goes on in people's minds when they are approached for an interview, depth interviews were arranged with around 30 individuals who had taken part in the SCPR British Social Attitudes Survey in 1986.[1]   Ten interviewers each recruited three of their respondents who were willing for a specially trained depth interviewer to call on them the following day.  This 'double interview' technique was pioneered by Belson (1981) as a way of establishing how respondents interpret the questions they have been asked and how they work out their answers.

Other researchers also interviewed respondents (Kahn and Cannell, 1957; Goyder, 1987; Fowler and Mangione, 1990) but with structured questionnaires and in less detail.

One of the problems of such surveys is that the very people that it would be most enlightening to talk to - those who refuse to be interviewed - slip through the net.  However, Goyder showed that some of those who agreed to his 'Survey on Surveys' had refused other surveys in the past.  Brief interviews with refusers to an SCPR survey also indicated that many had refused because the present time was inconvenient rather than because they definitely did not want to take part (Lievesley, 1986).  There is thus little evidence that there is any sizeable group of people who can be identified as hard core 'survey refusers'; almost anyone might accept or refuse according to how the various factors influencing them are weighed up at the time the request is made.

It was apparent from the depth interviews that a number of factors are taken into account in deciding whether or not to give an interview and are (very rapidly) weighed up through the sort of process indicated by psychological field theory.  Respondents varied both in what factors they considered and how many different factors occurred to them.  While a few made some attempt at a systematic logical appraisal, most used the heuristic approach.  The factors are examined within the seven categories culled from the examination of helping behaviour theory outlined above.

*1.  Perceptions of the interviewer*

Interviewer characteristics, appearance and approach are all factors that can affect the way in which the prospective respondent perceives the request.

*Sex of the interviewer* seems to have relatively little influence.  Research on helping behaviour has shown that people are in some circumstances more willing to help females than males; in survey research it has been found that male interviewers tend to get significantly lower response rates than females, but the significance reduces when differences in level of experience are taken into account.  Fowler and Mangione (1990) report that female interviewers were more likely than males to be perceived as 'friendly'.  We had only one male interviewer whose work was followed up by depth interviewers but all respondents were asked whether the sex of the interviewers would make a difference; most of them said it would not affect them.  Some, however, said that they would feel more wary of a male stranger on the doorstep or that they would feel less relaxed talking to a man.  One man said that he would find it easier to say 'No' to a man.

*Age of interviewer* was rarely mentioned as of any importance though a few said that an older person would be easier to relate to.  It is possible that there is an interactive effect between age of interviewer and age of person approached.

*The way in which the interviewer dresses* is generally agreed to be of some but not major importance.  Most people seemed to feel that casual (though tidy) clothes were preferable to smart or formal wear which they felt salespeople would wear or which would make them feel intimidated. People on the whole seem to want interviewers to be 'one of them'; while one person said, 'An interviewer shouldn't turn up with pink hair', another (a nineteen-year-old punk) said, 'I wouldn't trust an interviewer in a suit'!  It thus seems that interviewers should dress according to the area they are assigned to but should avoid extremes of smartness, casualness or exoticness.

*The way in which the interviewer approaches the prospective respondent* is considered to be extremely important.  People have very definite ideas about the rules governing this sort of interaction and in the main are agreed as to what they are.  Foremost is the requirement  that the interviewer should not be 'pushy'; this kind of intrusive behaviour would be regarded as rude and as giving complete justification for immediate refusal.  It is also important to them that the interviewer should be friendly and cheerful and that information as to what the survey is about and what participation entails should be given clearly and in plain language; speaking too fast to take in what was said without giving a chance for the respondent to ask questions was considered pressurizing. People want to feel that they have a choice as to whether to participate and resist any attempt to make them feel guilty.

### 2.   Benefits and costs

It is clear from the follow up depth interviews that most people approached for an interview do indeed weigh up what they perceive as the positive and negative results of agreeing to help though there is considerable variability between individuals as to what these factors are. Some did not see any particular benefits to themselves in taking part.

The main perceived benefits of taking part in the survey were concerned with the experience of the interview itself:

(i)   *The novelty of the experience and curiosity about it* were frequently mentioned; some had experienced a market research interview or political opinion poll, but none had given a long social research interview; they wanted to know what it was like and thought it would probably be interesting.

(ii)  *The chance of a break in the routine of everyday life* was also perceived as a benefit by some; it provided an excuse to stop doing the household chores for a while.

(iii) *Liking the interviewer* and the opportunity the interview gave for pleasant interaction was for many respondents an important perceived benefit.

(iv)  *The chance to express opinions,* 'to have a say' and to have their views taken into account, was a strong attraction in some cases.

(v)   *The very act of helping* was considered a benefit by some; it gave them a warm glow to feel that they could help the interviewer or make a contribution to the survey. Mowen & Cialdini (1980) found that when interviewers added the words 'it would really help us out' at the end of the request for an interview, refusals decreased by 19 per cent.

The perceived costs of agreeing to the interview in part pertained to the interview itself but also to the wider context:

(i)   *Suspicion of the stranger on the doorstep* emerged as a major initial concern. Although the sense of being at risk might persist, it was interesting that those who had agreed to be interviewed trusted their ability to judge whether the interviewer was genuine or not, reassured for the most part by the presentation of the identity card.

(ii)  *Fear of not being able to get rid of the interviewer* at the end of the interview or if they wanted to stop the interview before its end, or if the interviewer turned out to be trying to sell them something, bothered some respondents. This is a subsidiary aspect of the suspicion of strangers.

(iii) *The time the survey would take* was an obvious cost that had to be weighed up by respondents. The British Social Attitudes interview which they had given the day before had taken about an hour. All these had obviously decided that the time cost was acceptable but evidence has been presented in Chapter 2 that length of interview is a factor affecting response; being 'too busy' was also a frequent form of reluctance given by people asked for an interview in the taped introductions study, though the interview on that survey was only about 25 minutes.

(iv) *That the interview might be an unpleasant experience* was an important consideration for some; a few were concerned that such a long interview on broad social issues could become dull and boring; several were afraid that they would be made to feel inadequate because they didn't know enough about the issues to answer questions properly; some were worried that they would be embarrassed by personal questions. In fact, all those interviewed said that they had enjoyed it and had no regrets about taking part; but Goyder's analysis referred to in Chapter 2 indicated that lack of salience of the survey topic was associated with low response, especially for long interviews.

These fears were sometimes expressed overtly to the interviewer on the doorstep in the form of reservations about the nature or content of the survey or suggestions that the interviewer should find someone else to answer the questions, all of which were difficult for the interviewer to deal with adequately. In addition, they may have been behind the refusers' most common reason for refusal, 'I'm not interested'.

The interviewers' task on the doorstep is to make clear what the benefits of taking part are while minimizing the costs through reassurance and information. It is helpful if they are aware of the range of fears and reservations that may lie behind general unspecified expressions of reluctance such as 'Well...er' and direct statements such as 'I'm not interested', which Goyder equates to 'No'.

## 3. Legitimacy

The people who agreed to the follow up interview had already given an hour long interview; it was therefore not surprising that none of them thought that surveys in general were unacceptable or an invasion of privacy, though one said they could be too personal. However, among refusers in the study of doorstep introductions were some who said that they 'didn't believe in surveys' or, as one put it, that asking survey questions was 'poking your nose into others' affairs'.

Although respondents did not regard carrying out surveys as being an illegitimate activity, there was considerable variation as to whether it was a worthwhile one; quite a few were cynical as to whether surveys did any good, whether findings ever filtered through into policy or whether anyone took any notice of the results. Despite these doubts about the effectiveness of surveys, the majority thought that research should be undertaken to find out what people think and they still liked having a chance to express their views, hoping that it would have an effect.

Most spontaneously made a distinction between market and social research feeling that the latter was more worthwhile; a few actually went so far as to say that they would not take part in a market research survey, but most thought that they would probably find it quite interesting to do so.  A survey among the public on attitudes to market research carried out by the Market Research Society (Bowen, 1979), indicated that there is considerable public good will towards it, that market research is not seen as an invasion of privacy and that it is thought to perform a useful function.  Refusers in the survey were followed up and over half were interviewed using a shortened questionnaire; they were found to have less favourable attitudes to market research but were not strongly negative.

We have already seen that interviewers are sometimes asked to establish their credentials as bona fide interviewers to prove that they are not selling anything and are not potential assailants.  On surveys, especially those among certain minority groups, such as people on state benefit or immigrants, and those on topics pertaining to their way of life, there has been found to be suspicion that the interviewer was a snooper, or that the findings of the survey would in some way be detrimental to them or to people in their community.  Warwick and Lininger (1975) point out that this type of concern is often widespread in developing countries where the right not to disclose information about themselves might be regarded as a crucial aspect of freedom.  The extent to which surveys are regarded as legitimate business is therefore culture specific.

## 4.   Belief in ability to help

Most of those taking part in the depth interview follow up study seemed to have no doubt about their ability to answer questions but some had initially felt that the questions might be too difficult or that they would be expected to have opinions on subjects that they knew little about.  This emerged in some as a fear of being made to feel inadequate and in others as a reluctance to be bothered with the survey.  The interviewers had managed to reassure these respondents but there were a few in the taped introductions study who had refused because they did not feel that they knew enough or felt that they were too old to undertake the interview.

## 5.   Personal responsibility

Respondents did not feel any strong sense of responsibility towards the survey but several admitted to a sense of obligation in that they had been picked for the survey and had been informed that no substitutes could be taken if they refused.  Some felt flattered that they had been selected and that no substitutes could be taken; but others felt that any undue pressure from the interviewer to participate could quickly dissipate this sense of obligation.  Some felt that they ought to do the interview since surveys were useful: 'The statistics have got to come from somewhere'; 'Somebody ought to do it and if it's not going to be me it's going to be someone else - but I didn't feel I *had* to do it'; 'I thought I had a choice but that I *should* do it'.  In other words, they seemed to feel unwilling to be responsible for reducing its effectiveness by being uncooperative. Information about the sample selection process or the rules against substitution, if handled correctly, can subtly enhance this feeling.

## 6. *Empathy*

For several respondents, empathizing with the hopes and fears of the interviewer seemed to be a factor in deciding to do the interview. Some said that they felt sorry for the interviewer, including one who was extremely cynical about the value of surveys. Others empathized with how the interviewer would feel if refused: 'There's nothing worse than everyone saying "No".' Babbie (1973) noted that an eight months pregnant interviewer achieved an above average response rate.

Empathy can cover a very broad spectrum of feeling: an interviewer who projects confidence, interest and warm friendliness is likely to arouse a similar response in the person contacted who will feel a reluctance to damage the interviewer's sense of self esteem by rejection. On the one hand, they feel a sense of disinterested altruism toward the interviewer who is seen as vulnerable; on the other, their own self esteem might suffer if they refused without some strong justification as they would feel guilty of unkindness and selfishness. Goyder calls this 'the psychic wear and tear' of refusal. Several of the depth interview respondents admitted that they would have felt bad if they had refused.

## 7. *Mood and circumstances*

The respondents cited being ill or busy as being the kind of thing that would justify a refusal. Each time interviewers approach an address for the first time, they are entering an unknown situation; the person contacted may be involved in a row or have recently been bereaved; they may be feeling unwell; they may be in the middle of household chores or entertaining a visitor; they may be feeling stressed by the pressure of circumstances. People will not usually admit immediately to a stranger that they are under emotional stress but the claims to be busy at the moment (or in general) and the difficulty of persuading those who made these claims to do the interview may well be an indicator that the interviewer has called at a time of psychological stress rather than at one that is merely inconvenient.

## Goals and motives

It is apparent that people do not all take part in surveys for the same reasons; each, as indicated by field theory, weighs up a number of factors that may be to do with the interviewer, the perceived costs and benefits of taking part, the extent to which they think the survey worthwhile, their belief that they are competent to do it or are obligated to do it, their empathic response to the interviewer, all within the context of how they are feeling and what they are doing at the time.

The main goals that appear to be pursued during the process of deciding whether or not to give the interview can be divided into what we might call 'negative' and 'positive' goals;

*Negative goals*

To preserve themselves from danger or stress

To limit any disruption or intrusiveness

To avoid an unpleasant or embarrassing experience

*Positive goals*

To have a pleasant interactive experience

To have an interesting or novel experience

To take part in a worthwhile endeavour

If their beliefs about surveys in general or this one in particular, or their perceptions of the interviewer lead to greater weight being given to the negative than to the positive goals, they are likely to refuse to participate. There is only one negative goal that works in the interviewer's favour: the desire to avoid the unpleasant feelings that saying 'No' engenders in them; this is really the other side of wanting a pleasant interactive experience.

One of the most important human needs is concerned with the preservation of self esteem; at several points in the discussion of respondents' reasons for helping with the survey the perception of possible threats to self esteem or an opportunity to enhance it through participation in the survey have been pointed out. People want to feel that they are approved of, are liked and are competent. They want to feel that they are participating in a mutually enjoyable and interesting interaction and that the activity is worthwhile. The concept of 'Face' discussed in Chapter 3 is a subsidiary formulation of the concept of self esteem that is particularly relevant to the initial interaction between interviewer and the individual contacted at the address but which needs to be taken further in understanding what motivates people to accept or refuse an interview.

The respondents who were interviewed in the follow up depth study were clearly people for whom the positive goals outweighed the negative. It was apparent, however, that they varied according to whether their sense of self esteem and enjoyment was primarily related to the experience of being interviewed and personal interaction with the interviewer, or to the wider and less personal context of the value and importance of the survey and the chance to have a say. Although both these factors could have an influence on the decision of an individual, one was usually dominant; for the majority, the experience of being interviewed and the interaction with the interviewer were clearly of more importance to them than the value of the survey. These two factors were called respectively 'intrinsic' and 'extrinsic' motivation by Kahn and Cannell (1957). They reported that a mail survey to people who had been interviewed indicated that feelings about the interviewer and the process of being interviewed were favourably rated more frequently than was the nature of the survey itself; the relationship with the interviewer was more important than the subject of the survey to the majority of the sample.

Quotations from two respondents in the depth interviews illustrate the difference between these two viewpoints:

*Intrinsic motivation:*

'I knew it would give me a chance to sit and chat with somebody - to hell with the decorating!'

*Extrinsic motivation:*

'I thought it was about time somebody wrote a book about this country. I just thought it was about time we had a survey of what people thought.'

The empathic response of respondents to the request for an interview reflects the division into intrinsic and extrinsic motivation: there are those whose impulse is to help the interviewer, to respond on a personal level, and there are those who are more concerned to participate in something that may have an impact on society and to have rational reasons for taking part. Some of these repudiated the notion that desire to do the interviewer a favour might be a factor, as though responding on a personal level rather than rationally might make them feel gullible.

Fowler and Mangione's (1990) follow up telephone interviews with respondents to a survey on health issues produced some intriguing results relevant to the interpretation of our findings: interviewers who were rated as particularly friendly by their respondents got significantly fewer refusals than those not so rated; conversely, interviewers whose respondents rated themselves as having fully understood the purposes of the survey tended to get higher refusal rates. This suggests that interviewers who concentrate on putting over the value of the survey and the rational reasons for participation are likely to do less well than those who are primarily concerned to make a friendly and warm impression. Female interviewers were more likely to be perceived as friendly than male interviewers, though the above result still held when the analysis was repeated for female interviewers only. It may be that male interviewers are more likely to feel that they should put a lot of emphasis on the impersonal reasons for participation as a contrast to a typical salesman's approach, or it may be that they are perceived as more sinister and less friendly simply as a result of the greater suspicion attached to male strangers on the doorstep.

**Why do people refuse to be interviewed?**

Analysis of the factors that lead people to agree to be interviewed provides a context in which to consider the more limited data available as to why people refuse the request.

*Calling at an inconvenient time is a reason for many refusals*

The refusers to a survey carried out by the Survey Methods Centre at SCPR for methodological research purposes were followed up and over 80 per cent were contacted and gave some information as to why they refused (Lievesley, 1986). The results are shown in table 6.1 on page 115. Almost a fifth of the refusers gave as their reason that the time was inconvenient;  Goyder (1987) showed a similar proportion of the refusals to his 'Survey on Surveys' for this reason and that 'What you are doing when the interviewer calls' was 'extremely' or 'very important' to 74 per cent of respondents in deciding whether or not to take part.   This underlines the importance of appropriate timing of calls, especially on samples where repeat calls to obtain the interview are not made (such as on quota samples).  It also indicates how essential it is for interviewers working on probability sample surveys to be prepared to call back another time: it is very likely that someone interrupted by an interviewer when deeply engaged in something may answer brusquely that they are 'not interested' or are simply 'too busy' (in general) and are not prepared to discuss the matter further at that time; a further call at another time might find them more receptive.  This is supported by the success of reissuing refusals to another interviewer, and also by an analysis of reasons for refusals assessed by interviewers employed by the Office of Population Censuses and Surveys on the Family Expenditure Survey (FES) and the General Household Survey (GHS), (Nicol, 1988) (see table 6.2 on page 115).  Much effort is put into getting as high a response rate as possible on these important and demanding government sponsored surveys; 'genuinely too busy' emerged as a reason in 12 per cent of the cases on FES and 18 per cent on GHS (compared with 5 per cent of the refusers to the SCPR survey).  None were recorded as refusing because they were too busy at the time the interviewer called.  It is possible that recall interviews with these people might have revealed some who refused because of the inconvenience of the timing of the call but interviewers were evidently at pains to establish that the refusal was not due to this and made many calls to obtain cooperation.

*Dislike of the topic of the survey*

The subject matter of the survey, as presented in the interviewer's introduction, was given as the reason for refusal by 16 per cent of refusers on the SCPR survey; the subject was described as being 'issues of current importance' - a vague and perhaps to some an intimidating subject.  The topic of the survey accounted for only 8 per cent of reasons for not participating in Goyder's 'Survey on Surveys', and interviewers recorded this as the reason for not participating in the General Household Survey in only 9 per cent of the cases. On the Family Expenditure Survey, however, on which it is very much more difficult to obtain cooperation, 22 per cent of refusers were reported to have done so because of the subject matter and 8 per cent because of the record keeping involved. FES collects information on income (generally considered to be a sensitive subject) and requires household members to record expenditure over two weeks (table 6.2). It is therefore a survey that overtly demands a lot of its participants. It was found that fewer reasons for refusal were recorded for FES than for GHS: 1.2 per cent per FES refuser compared with 1.6 per cent per GHS refuser. This suggests that on FES the exceptional subject matter and the record keeping occupied the foreground in people's minds, becoming the overriding objection and excluding other possible objections, whereas GHS refusers referred to a wide range of possible reasons for not doing surveys as they countered the interviewers' efforts to persuade them.

*Non-acceptance of the legitimacy of surveys*

The doubts about the legitimacy or worthwhileness of surveys expressed by those who were interviewed in the depth study were more widespread among the refusers and constituted a major reason for nonparticipation. Differences in coding schemes make comparisons difficult but it seems that on both the SCPR survey and GHS rather more than a quarter of refusals gave as their reason that they did not believe in surveys, that they were a waste of time and money, inaccurate or that nothing happened as a result of them (tables 6.1 and 6.2).

Although such opinions may be rationalizations to back up a disinclination to take part, they indicate an underlying attitude that surveys are not important and do not contribute anything to the public good.

Rejection of the survey because of doubts of its legitimacy took the specific form of not wanting to do a survey for the government in power for over one in ten of GHS refusers. Warwick and Lininger (1975) raise this as a particular problem in some developing countries.

*Fear and nervousness*

The various fears about the consequences of taking part (doubts about ability to perform adequately, worries about confidentiality or intrusiveness, or fears that it might be a sales ploy) featured among the reasons for refusing but not as extensively as one might have expected from the admissions to these feelings among survey respondents who received follow up depth interview. This suggests that these fears are not very strong and that interviewers are fairly adept at allaying them.

*'Can't be bothered'*

People who say they 'can't be bothered' to do the survey or that they are 'not interested' are expressing a subjective reaction unadorned by rationalizations or excuses. Around a fifth of refusers to the SCPR survey and to FES responded in this way and over a third of refusers to GHS.

We can only hypothesize as to what underlies this response to a request to take part in a survey but we know from the study of taped doorstep introductions that interviewers find it difficult to counter. It almost certainly implies that surveys are not regarded as of much importance by these people and that, at least on this occasion, they were not prepared to put themselves out to do it; their self esteem was not seen as being affected by refusing and their desire not to be disturbed or intruded upon or to be exposed to an unknown situation was uppermost.

**Note**

1    This study, including much of the background reading, was carried out by Penny Young as part of the SCPR Survey Methods Centre's programme of research on non-response.

**Table 6.1**

**Reasons for refusal to SCPR survey on Issues of Current Importance
(based on follow-up interviews with refusers - Lievesley, 1986)**

| | | |
|---|---|---|
| Base: | all refusers | 135 |
| | | % |
| Time: | - It was an inconvenient time | 18 |
| | - Too busy to take part in surveys | 5 |
| Topic: | - Disliked the topic of the survey | 16 |
| Legitimacy: | - Surveys are a waste of time and money | 18 |
| | - Never see the results/nothing happens | 6 |
| | - Surveys are inaccurate/don't believe in sampling | 3 |
| Fear: | - Too old/not educated enough | 11 |
| | - Worries about confidentiality/ invasion of privacy | 6 |
| | - Worries about selling under guise of research | 3 |
| Can't be bothered/ not interested | | 18 |
| Refused to give information about refusal | | 10 |
| Not contacted on follow-up | | 8 |

(Percentages add to more than 100 as some gave more than one answer.)

**Table 6.2**

**Reasons for refusal to the General Household and Family Expenditure Surveys
(reasons recorded by interviewers onto a precoded list
at the time of refusal - Nicol, 1988)**

| | | GHS | FES |
|---|---|---|---|
| Base: | all refusers | 1355 | 2446 |
| | | % | % |
| Time: | - Too busy | 18 | 12 |
| Topic: | - Dislike survey matter | 9 | 22 |
| | - Put off by record keeping | - | 8 |
| Legitimacy: | - Doesn't believe in surveys | 29 | 15 |
| | - Anti-government | 13 | 6 |
| Fear: | - Too old | 11 | 6 |
| | - Previous bad experience with surveys | 4 | 2 |
| | - "Not discussing private business" | 4 | 7 |
| | - Doubtful of confidentiality | 2 | 1 |
| | - Suspicious/nervous | 2 | 2 |
| Can't be bothered | | 35 | 20 |
| Others | | 16 | 8 |
| Late contact | | 8 | 4 |

(Percentages add to more than 100 as some gave more than one answer.)

# 7 Interviewer doorstep strategies

The recorded doorstep interchanges between the interviewers and their contacts at the selected addresses reveal a fast moving, free flowing interactive process. The studies described in the last chapter show that members of the public approached for an interview bring a variety of attitudes, evaluations and goals to the interaction. To deal competently with this unfolding situation and to steer it to a successful conclusion requires a high degree of social skill; interviewers must be adept at putting over the benefits of taking part, at allaying suspicion and at finding legitimate persuasive ways of countering reluctance to take part.

Some say that interviewers who are good at obtaining cooperation are 'born and not made', implying that training can have little effect in improving their skill; but this is belied by the fact that experienced interviewers tend to achieve higher response rates than new interviewers (Durbin and Stuart, 1951; Lievesley, 1986; Colombo, 1983; Couper & Groves, 1991). There has been a considerable body of research in social psychology into the nature of social skills and the ways in which they are acquired: it is apparent that the social skills used in interpersonal relations are learned and that, if they are inadequate, new skills can be taught provided that the requirements of the situation can be correctly identified. Although some people who take up interviewing may have already acquired a high degree of relevant social skills through their upbringing and life experience, it is possible for others to learn the required skills through training.

Social skills training techniques have been developed over a number of years and adapted to a variety of interactional situations. (For a brief review of this literature, see Argyle, 1984.) The first essential step is the detailed analysis of the situation in which the skills are needed. The analysis of what happens in the initial interactions between interviewers and the persons contacted and the depth interviews with respondents provide considerable information on the doorstep situation, but we also need to know how interviewers perceive it: we need to know what goals they consider appropriate. To collect this information, group discussions were held, two with interviewers of varying levels of experience, and one with field supervisors. In addition to carrying out interviewing assignments, field supervisors regularly accompany experienced interviewers and also supervise the whole of the first day's work of new interviewers. They were thus able to report on observations of both new and experienced interviewers as well as on their own practices.

## Situational analysis

Argyle et al. (1981) provide a useful structure for the analysis of interactive situations that can be applied to that between interviewer and contact on the doorstep. He identifies eight components of a situation that need to be considered:

1. *Goal structure:* each party in an interactive situation will be pursuing one or more goals; these might include goals concerning one's own well-being (e.g., physical safety); social needs (e.g., acceptance, dominance, self esteem); and task accomplishment (e.g., obtaining the interview). Goals are not always selfish and may be in pursuit of higher order goals.

2. *The rules governing behaviour:* the ways in which people set about achieving the goals of social interaction are governed by their notions as to what sort of behaviour is permissible in the situation. In an interaction between strangers, the rules are largely determined by general consensus; the interaction is likely to be disrupted if the parties have very disparate views as to what the rules are. Rules vary in strength according to the amount of disapproval which follows disregarding them.

3. *The role systems:* each party to an interaction will have a role that is defined by the situation (such as that of 'interviewer' or 'contact') and that will broadly determine the behaviour of each; but the details of the roles develop dynamically and there is likely to be some subtle jockeying for position as the relationship between the participants is negotiated. The relationship may include a number of dimensions such as dominance/submission, friendliness/hostility, cooperation/competitiveness, intensity/superficiality, socio-economic/task orientated roles (Wish et al., 1976).

4. *The repertoire of behavioural elements:* it is necessary to establish the range of behaviour that is (or could be) undertaken by each participant in pursuit of their goals within the framework of the rules governing the situation.

5. *Sequences of episodes:* the moves to achieve some goals may need to occur in a certain order; this may be broadly imposed by the nature of the task but at a more detailed level may be determined by subtle consideration of ways of optimising the route to the goal.

6. *Analysis of stress elements:* each individual in an interaction may have goals that are in conflict with each other (e.g., the goal to persuade the other to do something may conflict with the desire to be liked by that person). The goals of each party may also conflict. These goal conflicts are the main sources of stress, but disparities in interpretation of the rules governing the situation and difficulties in establishing an appropriate role may also cause stress to one or both parties.

7. *Achievement motivation:* the pursuit of goals, especially task orientated goals, may be affected by the intensity of the desire to achieve the goal and also by the degree of optimism or pessimism that exists that the goal can be achieved. Stress factors can increase pessimism and reduce morale.

8. *Cognitive structure:* in order to behave effectively it is necessary to have an appropriate set of concepts about the situation; some understanding of the rules governing the interaction is essential if the relationship is not to break down. It is also important that the behaviour of the other is correctly perceived and interpreted and that attention is given to relevant elements and not to extraneous events. It is then necessary to have an understanding of the repertoire of appropriate and effective behaviour to achieve the desired consequences. A cognitive structure is especially important for teaching social skills as it provides a framework on which to hang the practice of the skill and speeds up learning. A conceptual framework can even enhance and extend the range of the skills of those already gifted by giving them insight into what they do so that they can appraise it objectively.

Using the eight aspects of a social situation defined by Argyle as a framework, a detailed analysis of the interaction between survey interviewer and contacted member of the public was carried out, using the information from the group discussions with interviewers and supervisors, amplified by the understanding already gained from the analysis of the tape recorded introductions and follow-up interviews with respondents.

## 1.    Identifying the goals

The task orientated goals of the interviewer on the doorstep are clear cut: they are to make contact at the address and to gain attention sufficiently to be listened to; to obtain the necessary information for selecting the correct person for interview; to contact the selected person (if not the initial contact) and to persuade them to give an interview.  Subsidiary goals are to establish the legitimacy of the survey and to gain the trust of the potential respondent.  There are certain other subsidiary goals set by the survey organization:  that the respondents should base their consent on genuine information about the purpose of the survey, the sponsor and so on, and that the consent should be willingly given so that they are motivated to answer the questions fully and honestly.

In addition to these task orientated goals, interviewers indicated that they have certain personal goals which reward them and also further the achievement of the task goals:

> (i)    *Social goals:*    these include wanting to be accepted and appreciated and to avoid rejection: 'When you're new, a refusal really casts you down.   When you've more experience, you remember the times you persuaded them'; 'When you see an answering smile, it's probably going to be all right'; 'If you get a good first interview, it sets you up for the day'; 'A broken appointment drags you down more than anything';

> (ii)   *Achievement goals:*    interviewers take a pride in the exercise of skill in persuading the reluctant respondent: 'I quite enjoy the challenge of the person who asks lots of questions and is a bit difficult'; 'If it's a difficult survey, you try even harder on the doorstep';

> (iii)  *Altruistic goals:*    it is important to interviewers to avoid being seen as a threat by the contacted person or as intrusive, and to make the prospect of the interview interesting and pleasant for the respondent. 'Being rather a tall man, I always step well back to make myself appear smaller, especially if it's an older person'; 'I may tell them that I don't need to keep them very long this time - all I need to do is find out who I need to speak to and make an appointment to come and see them'; 'You show an interest in their viewpoint';

The depth interviews with respondents revealed that their goals during the initial contact are to find out what precisely the stranger on the doorstep wants; they also want to preserve their safety, to prevent unwanted intrusion into their space and time, and to avoid loss of self esteem by being taken advantage of; these are the negative goals.  But they also want to have enjoyable encounters and interesting experiences and to participate in worthwhile or rewarding activities. The interviewers and supervisors showed a fairly comprehensive empathic understanding of how the people contacted might be feeling and what their goals in the situation might be.

## 2. The rules governing the doorstep interaction

The doorstep situation is one in which the interviewer approaches the territory of a stranger and makes a request, first for information to select a respondent, secondly for an interview. Social consensus has established rules that apply to each component of the situation: there are rules governing the approach to someone else's territory, rules concerned with the proper way of approaching strangers and rules that apply to the making of requests; these all contribute to establishing the particular set of rules that apply to the complex situation of the survey introduction in order to achieve the goals. It is an asymmetrical situation in which the interviewer has a plan of action whereas the contacted person is in the position of having to decide how to respond. The rules that interviewers must follow that emerged from the group discussions are as follows:

(i) *Say who you are and state your business briefly:* 'The introduction should be very short and clear'; 'You should be relaxed, and say as little as possible; if you say too much it sounds like a sales patter and their eyes glaze over'; 'The first thing you do is say you are doing a *survey*'. 'I sometimes say "I'm not selling anything"'; 'You have to be concise, precise and to the point, and full of enthusiasm - all in a few seconds!'

(ii) *Be polite and respectful at all times, however aggressive or rude the contact is:* 'If they are rude to you, you become even more polite'; 'You want to be rude back but you must never do so'.

(iii) *Be non-threatening and reassuring:* 'The first impression you make is all important - smile and look them in the eye'; 'Always keep a distance; if you are right on top of them, they would be totally intimidated'; 'Be friendly, normal and unaffected'; 'Mentioning that you've told the police often helps'; 'Some of them worry about confidentiality'.

(iv) *Avoid being pushy or intrusive:* 'You mustn't be pushy'; 'If they're doing something, don't insist on doing the interview now'; 'Releasing the pressure by saying you'll leave them a letter and come back another day often reassures them'.

(v) *Respect the contact's territory:* 'Never step over the doorstep unless you're asked'; 'If it's pouring with rain or dark and windy,

I might *ask* if I can step inside the door'; 'With some people you can say "Shall I sit here?" but with others you've got to wait until they invite you to sit down'; 'I'd never ask to use their toilet'.

(vi)  *Be responsive to the situation:* 'If the person is obviously harassed, immediately apologise and offer to come another time'; 'If they open the door only a crack, you know you've got to be very reassuring - perhaps offer to come back when someone else is in'; 'If their eyes shift away, you know they're trying to think of a way to say "no"; I might give them the explanatory letter and come back another time'.

(vii)  *Be likeable and attractive:* 'It's yourself you're selling in the first place'; 'Present yourself as a warm and friendly person'; 'Put yourself over as a nice person - turn on the charm!'; 'If you keep talking you can keep eye to eye and keep smiling; play it by ear and maybe talk about the cat or the garden'; 'It's hard to say no to someone who's admiring your cat!'; 'With some people, it helps if you make them laugh'.

(viii)  *Be positive about the survey:* 'Most people *do* enjoy the interview so you can genuinely say that they'll find it interesting'; 'I say it won't help you directly but it will be used to improve things in general'.

(ix)  *Appeal to the contact's altruism:* 'I sometimes say "I wonder if you can help me"'; 'I ask them to help me with the respondent selection procedure'; 'Most of them like to think they can make a contribution'; 'I think they feel sorry for you when it's freezing cold or wet'.

(x)  *Use only legitimate methods of persuasion; never indicate that the interview is compulsory:* 'An interviewer can't put their foot in the door'; 'You've got to believe in the survey yourself, then you sound sincere'; 'They want to know what's in it for them; even on the most difficult [to sell] survey, you can tell them that they have a chance to give their views'; 'I learnt that I didn't have to be a horrible person to be a successful interviewer; I didn't have to pressurize or trick people'.

(xi)  *Give information that is asked for in terms the contact can understand:* 'A lot never ask any questions; most often they ask how long it's going to take. An hour sounds an awfully long time, so I would say "45 minutes to an hour, it depends on your answers" - but I'd never say 30 minutes when I knew it was nearer an hour'; 'It's very hard to explain about the respondent selection procedure; random sampling doesn't mean a lot to most people'; 'Some of them want to know everything: who's paying for it, who's going to use the results, what good it's going to do'.

The sorts of things that interviewers say indicate an acute awareness of the rules within which they must operate; these rules protect them, at least to some extent, from abuse and help to identify who they are (as distinct, for example, from a salesperson). The members of the public contacted by the interviewers are also bound by the rules of politeness between strangers and interviewers are aware of this: 'Most people don't like to be rude'; 'Once you've got them to smile, it's more difficult for them to say "No".' But because the contacted people are in their own territory and are being asked a favour, they are less constrained by the rules than are the interviewers: 'Some people can't just say "No"; they have to be rude.' The interviewers realise that any infringement of the primary rules of politeness and respect for territory on their part would immediately be seized upon by the contact as a justification for refusing or even for slamming the door. Breaking these rules is also likely to damage their professional reputation as interviewers both in their own eyes and in those of the public. The skill of obtaining agreement to give an interview involves learning how to be persuasive and persistent without breaking these rules.

The eleven rules governing interviewer behaviour on the doorstep reflect an awareness of the goals of the people contacted: not to be endangered or intruded upon, to have enjoyable encounters and experiences and to participate in worthwhile and rewarding activities. Three main themes thus underlie the rules that the interviewers must work within:

- giving reassurance, avoiding threat;

- being positive about the benefits of taking part (including the pleasure of the interaction, the interest of the interview and the value to society of the survey);

- appealing to feelings of altruism (including helping the interviewer and benefitting society/the sponsor).

The first six rules governing interviewer behaviour on the doorstep are all concerned with what Brown and Levinson (1978) called 'negative politeness' which is used to show that the speaker is aware of the other's negative 'Face' needs; it is formal and reassures the person that the request will involve no danger and will cause minimum intrusion.

Rules (vii), (viii) and (ix) are expressions of 'positive politeness'; by their use, the interviewer signals that there will be positive rewards for helping with the survey; they indicate that the interviewer's company will be pleasant, the interview will be interesting and that participating will be a worthwhile activity that will help both the interviewer and the wider society. They are designed to enhance the contact's self esteem, sense of acceptance and general sense of well being.

Rule (x), 'Use only legitimate means of persuasion', and rule (xi), 'Give information that is asked for', relate more to what is considered ethical behaviour in survey research than to the preservation of 'Face', though using only legitimate methods of persuasion enhances the interviewer's sense of self esteem and the giving of information can be used to allay suspicion or to put over the value of the survey.

### 3.    Establishing the roles of interviewer and respondent

Since the doorstep situation is a meeting between strangers, the specific roles in the interaction have to be developed. The interviewers begin this process by their initial introduction of the survey and the establishment of their identity. The way in which this is done is seen as important for the development of an effective role: 'You must know your stuff so that you can speak with complete confidence'; 'I always assume they are going to be delighted to see me'; 'A relaxed and friendly approach, like a neighbour'.

The overarching role that the interviewer wants to establish is that of 'survey interviewer': a professional and impartial collector of important information for a serious and interesting purpose. But initially a subsidiary aspect of that role is as a petitioner making a request. Although the interviewer's role is that of petitioner, the disadvantage of being in this position is offset by two beliefs: one in the social value of the work they are doing, the other that the selected person will enjoy the interview and find it a rewarding experience: 'If you think the survey is worthwhile, it helps you put it over'; 'It all comes down to your enthusiasm and interest in the survey; I've been interested in all the surveys I've worked on'; 'Convey that what they have to say is really important'; 'Say "I think you'll find it interesting" and give them the explanatory letter; that shows your authority'.

The contacted person initially is in the role of granter or refuser of requests and also is in their own territory; the advantage of this position is reduced, however, by the asymmetry of the interaction: the interviewer has specific task objectives, has been trained in the assigned role and has a strategy for pursuing the objectives whereas the contacted person has to appraise both the stranger on the doorstep and the message being put over, and decide whether to cooperate. If the contact agrees to give the respondent selection information, the two participants move into the roles of questioner and answerer; when a respondent has been selected, the interviewer has to move back into the role of petitioner in order to persuade the selected person to take part.

Some interviewers maintained that they used the same initial approach for all types of people encountered, but most modified their role according to their first perceptions, both of the environment and of the contacted person: 'The more affluent keep their affairs to themselves; they're more reticent. They are less easily impressed by the sponsor's name'; 'Middle class people ask more questions and want to be sure they're not wasting their time'; 'You have to be extra reassuring with an elderly person, or someone who only opens the door a crack.'

The interviewers regarded it as essential to keep control of the situation but without appearing to be dominating. The contacted persons were sometimes thought to be trying to seize the initiative as the following interchange illustrates:

*Interviewer 1*

'I had a case recently where a short introduction went over well with the husband who did the grid [i.e., respondent selection procedure]; the wife was chosen. She asked so many questions that it reached a point of no return; it became like a sales patter.'

*Interviewer 2*

'Don't say too much - ever! You could say, "Since you are so interested, can we start the interview?" You've got to be in charge, but without domination.'

If the person contacted is unresponsive, some interviewers find it hard to maintain their role; they feel a compulsion to fill in the silence with further explanation and repetitions and their confidence starts to ebb. What happens in this situation is that the 'petitioner' aspect of their role starts to undermine their grasp of the overarching role of professional survey interviewer. The rules governing ordinary social interaction begin to reassert themselves. One of these is that someone in the 'petitioner' role carries the onus to avoid any gaps in the conversation in order to preserve both their own and the contact's 'Face'. Sometimes a deliberate attempt to undermine the interviewer is attributed to the contact: 'It saps your confidence if you get no feedback; you start talking too fast and saying all the wrong things'; 'It's usually men who do that [i.e., don't respond]; they're trying to be superior'; 'I say, "Are you with me so far?" suggesting that they're being a bit stupid by being silent'. Slipping into the questioner role was generally agreed to be a good way to regain the initiative in the interaction.

It is apparent that some of the dimensions of role definition identified by Wish et al. (1976) operate in the survey introduction; these are dominance/submission, friendliness/hostility, cooperation/competitiveness and socio-emotional/task oriented aspects. The interviewer tries to establish a subtly dominant role while also being charming, relaxed and friendly; this is done by keeping control of the interaction, by a confident manner, by smiling and keeping eye contact, and by establishing their professional status through the use of identity card and introductory letter. The interviewer's role is task orientated rather than socio-emotional whereas the contact's role may have a larger socio-emotional component. The interviewer hopes that the contact will assume a role that is slightly submissive but primarily friendly and cooperative, but it may become competitive for the dominant position, uncooperative or even hostile.

Clark and Pinch (1988) analyze the methods by which market pitchers obtain a sale and some of their conclusions are relevant to the task of the interviewer on the doorstep. They maintain that the social norms (or rules) that operate during an interchange have both constraining and enabling effects: the constraints make it possible to conduct an orderly transaction but also provide the means whereby one party can manage the exchange. By taking advantage of the group norms operating in a situation, one can effectively limit the range of options open to the other. The socially adroit interviewer uses the group norms of politeness between strangers to obtain a hearing; by a friendly, smiling approach, making a joke or admiring the cat, the interviewer uses the norms governing friendly interactions to increase the difficulty of refusing; by giving a clear and succinct account of what is required and moving on quickly to ask the respondent selection questions, the interviewer maintains the initiative in the conversation; by withdrawing before a refusal becomes firm, and returning another time, interviewers keep their own options for action open. Overall, by maintaining a confident and authoritative manner, the interviewer conveys the worthwhileness and importance of the survey, making use of the group norm that discourages people from harming the efforts of others.

## 4.    The repertoire of behavioural elements

It is apparent that there is no one correct way to introduce a survey and interviewers are very aware of the need to tailor their behaviour to meet the requirements of each unique doorstep situation. Groves & Cialdini (1991) hypothesize that skill in tailoring one's approach builds up through experience and is a reason why experienced interviewers tend to get better response rates than the inexperienced. Making interviewers aware during training of the range of behaviour available to them can speed this process. But it is not sufficient simply to have a list of possible ways of acting without also developing the skill to know when a particular form of behaviour is appropriate. Training should not only extend interviewers' repertoire of ways of dealing with questions or reluctance to participate, but also greatly enhance their ability to decipher the verbal and nonverbal clues given by the contacted person as to how they are reacting to the interviewer and the requests being made.

The wide range of behaviour that interviewers can use to achieve their goals has been indicated broadly in the process of defining the rules that have to be followed and the roles to be established; but a more systematic and detailed analysis is necessary to provide the material for interviewer training. The identification of the range of appropriate behaviour emerges in part from the group discussions but also from the analysis of tape recorded doorstep situations and the comparison of interviewers with high and low refusal rates.

Interviewer behaviour has to be adapted to each stage of the survey introduction; the initial contact, the respondent selection and dealing with reluctance each have their appropriate repertoires of behavioural elements that are consistent with the rules that have to be followed and the roles that the interviewer is trying to establish.

The behaviour that interviewers should use is thus identified according to the rules that constrain it or the role that it is designed to establish at each stage of the introductory procedure. The behaviour here described is that appropriate for a social survey requiring a respondent selection procedure. Other types of survey would require some differences of detail but the general principles apply to most face to face surveys.

## (i) Initial contact

*Identify self and state business (rule governing approach of stranger to another's territory):*
- Introduce self and organization for which are working.
- State that are doing a survey and describe its subject and purpose briefly.
- Mention sponsor.
- Explain that need to ask a few questions to find out whom to interview.

*Give impression of confidence and competence (role establishment):*
- Prepare initial introduction and practise it.
- Organize papers in advance.
- Make eye contact.
- Speak clearly and in a relaxed manner.

*Be non-threatening, allay suspicion:*
- Dress appropriately for the area.
- Show identity card and possibly also introductory letter, to establish your own and the survey's legitimacy.
- Stand back from the door.
- Reassure as necessary (e.g., 'I'm not selling anything').
- Relaxed, friendly manner.

*Be polite and respectful:*
- Use formal politeness, avoid overfamiliarity.

*Respect contact's territory:*
- Do not step across the threshold without permission.
- When inside, always remember it is their territory.

*Be likeable and attractive:*
- Smile.
- Be warm, friendly, charming, outgoing.
- If appropriate, comment in friendly manner on garden, cat, etc.

In many cases the contacted person will readily agree to provide the information for carrying out the respondent selection procedure; some, however, will indicate suspicion, doubt or reluctance, either by body language or verbally. The interviewers ignore these signals at their peril. But it is useful, before examining ways of dealing with reluctance, to set out the basic repertoire of behaviour for selecting respondents.

### (ii) Administering respondent selection procedure

The respondent selection procedure is set out in questionnaire format (see Appendix I) and it is stipulated by SCPR that it should be administered as such; the interviewer thus has to establish a change in role by the way in which the procedure is introduced. The range of possible behaviour surrounding the procedure falls within the broad categories of rules set out earlier:

*Reassure contact:*
- Explain that it is necessary to ask a few questions to find out whom to interview.
- Answer any questions about the procedure (eg., how address was selected, why need information about the household).
- Say that the procedure will take only a minute or two.
- Point out that it may not be the contact who is selected.

*Appeal to altruism:*
- Ask contact to help with the procedure of establishing whom to interview.

*Be positive:*
- If selection grid has to be used to select an individual, explain procedure to contact ('This may interest you'; 'It has to be a random procedure').

### (iii) Dealing with reluctance

Expressions of suspicion, doubt or reluctance may occur at any point: during the initial introduction, during the respondent selection procedure, when asking to see the selected respondent (if not the contact) or when asking the selected person to give the interview. Reluctance may be expressed verbally or nonverbally. Whenever and however it occurs, an extended repertoire of behaviour is required by the interviewer.

In order to adapt their approach to the person and the situation as it unfolds, interviewers must observe and accurately interpret what is happening; the rule to 'Be responsive to the situation' thus entails considerable perceptual skill. The social skills model places great emphasis on the importance of accurate perception as a prerequisite for the choice of appropriate behaviour.

*Be responsive to the situation:*
- Be perceptive, observant and imaginative.
- Watch for signs of suspicion or fear (e.g., door opened only a crack, body language indicating fear, aggressiveness indicating suspicion, etc.).
- Observe any cues that now is not a good time to call (e.g., sounds of altercation, children yelling, TV programme, cooking smells, indications that guests are present, etc.).
- Watch for indications of reluctance to take part (e.g., breaking eye contact, looking over shoulder, rigidity, backing away, starting to close the door, etc.).
- Listen both to what the contact says and how it is said (e.g., 'Well...er...um' probably indicates reluctance, 'I'm not interested' may be based on fear and suspicion).

*Be flexible in approach:*
- Adapt to the situation in order to maintain the professional role.
- Answer specific expressions of reluctance or suspicion directly.
- Modify approach according to the type of person contacted.
- Be prepared to change tack (e.g., withdraw, make a joke, offer introductory letter).
- Maintain or regain the initiative by asking a question.

The appropriate response to the indicators of reluctance will include one or more of the following categories of behaviour which extend rather than replace those appropriate at the initial contact or during the respondent selection procedure:

*Give reassurance:*
- Acknowledge the other party's anxieties or suspicions (e.g., 'I can understand why you feel that way').
- Be prepared to withdraw and return another day, avoid intrusiveness.
- Stress complete confidentiality of information.
- Say police have been informed.
- Have a relaxed, friendly manner; don't pressurize or try to force the other to surrender.
- Use introductory letter to establish bona fides.

- Answer questions or give unsolicited information as appropriate (e.g., how long interview will take, how name and/or address were obtained, how survey is funded, how results will be used).

*Use legitimate means of persuasion:*
- Explain that have to select people at random and cannot take a substitute.
- Say that everyone's views are important, however little they know.
- Answer questions in a straightforward manner.

*Be positive about the survey:*
- Smile, be charming and polite so that contact feels they would enjoy being interviewed.
- Say that most people have found the interview enjoyable and interesting.
- Explain the purpose of the survey more fully, indicating that it is important and worthwhile.
- Say that their views are important; everyone's views matter, not just those of the well informed.
- Say that it is a chance for them to have their say, make a contribution.

*Appeal to altruism:*
- Point out that the survey will help others, will contribute to the good of society, etc.
- The success of the survey depends on people like them being willing to help (e.g., 'It's easy to get the views of those who are not busy; if we don't take busy people, your views won't be represented; taking substitutes is not allowed so we will have to do with one less if you don't take part').

This analysis identifies the main categories of behaviour that interviewers should have in their repertoire; resourceful and experienced interviewers can become virtuosos in their application, using many variations on these main themes. The purpose of this analysis is to provide a basis for teaching an initial repertoire to new interviewers on which they can build. As indicated, a great deal can be conveyed by body language, facial expressions and the way in which contact is established and maintained.


## 5.   Sequence of episodes

The pursuit of the goals and the rules of politeness governing interactions between strangers and the making of requests impose a broad sequence that must be followed:

- the interviewers must first introduce themselves and state their business;

- they must establish whom to interview before asking for an interview;

Within any part of the interaction:

- the interviewers must answer any questions they are asked (though they should avoid being drawn into a prolonged question and answer session);

- the interviewer must deal with the specific forms of reluctance or suspicion indicated rather than ignore them;

- the contact must answer the respondent selection procedure questions once agreement to do this has been given.

Beyond these simple sequence rules, there is no indication from the analysis of taped doorstep situations that giving particular information earlier rather than later in the process has any effect in obtaining the interview. If anything, too much information early on was counter productive, as was demonstrated by the success of interviewers who used brief introductions.

The discussion with supervisors raised the question as to whether the initial introduction taught in the training schools at that time and stipulated in the project instructions for each survey presented the best sequence. Interviewers are instructed to:

- check that they are at the correct address;

- give their name, say their are working for Social and Community Planning Research and show their identity card;

- say that they are doing a survey on .... (topic) .... for .... (sponsor)... to .... (purpose) ...;

- say that they want to interview one person at the address and that they need to ask a few questions to establish who this is.

Some supervisors thought this overcumbersome and preferred a more flexible approach; some suggestions were:

- only check the address first if there is any doubt about it, otherwise do so after initial introduction of survey;

- don't give name and show identity card until invited into the house;

- just say a 'social research organization'; 'Social and Community Planning Research' is confusing, especially if there is a university research team and a funding sponsor to be mentioned;

- break up the initial introduction with a joke or a question: 'I say "I'm an interviewer from Social and Community Planning Research - phew, that's a mouthful, isn't it?"'; 'I say, "Have you ever heard of us?" They haven't, of course, but it makes them answer you.'

Their aim was to put over themselves and the main message about the survey with the minimum of extra verbiage or confusing information. They agreed, however, that only experienced interviewers should be allowed such flexibility; new interviewers should be taught a set procedure so that they would remember important points such as checking the address and showing their identity card. How much flexibility should be allowed even to experienced interviewers over such matters as when they show their identity card or whether they give the name of the research organization or not is matter for management policy decision. What is interesting here is the fact that experienced interviewers find that management policy hampers their efforts to put over the survey on initial contact.

## 6.    Analysis of stress elements

Social interaction of any sort may engender stress in one or both participants; the uncertainties inherent in any encounter between strangers and the tensions involved in making or receiving a request render the initial encounter between survey interviewer and potential respondent particularly prone to be stressful.

The kinds of stress that may be experienced by the person contacted for an interview have been examined in Chapter 6; they express the conflict between positive and negative 'Face' requirements: the desire to be liked and approved of may be at variance with the fear of being threatened or intruded upon. Some people find it hard to refuse a request without justifying it by exaggerating the sense of intrusion in order to give them an excuse to be angry. The analysis of the interviewers' goals in the interaction and the rules governing pursuit of those goals indicates that interviewers are aware of the potentially stressful effect that their approach for an interview may have on the person contacted and are at pains to minimize it.

Interviewers themselves may also experience stress: to many, the initial approach to an address and the attempt to obtain cooperation are the most difficult parts of the whole interviewing process. They often feel nervous as they ring the bell; they feel uncertain about their reception and fear rejection, even abuse, which can result in a sense of loss of 'Face' and self esteem. New interviewers may feel generally anxious until experience gives them confidence, but all interviewers may feel uncertain about approaching some kinds of address: 'You sort of psyche yourself up before you knock'; 'My heart sinks when I see an entryphone; they find it so much easier to say "No" when they can't see you'; 'Houses or flats with big dogs - I always think they're suspicious of strangers'.

Another source of stress for the interviewer is the conflict between the task of persuading and the need to avoid pressurizing. Any form of reluctance can cause the interviewer some feelings of stress and a refusal can seriously damage the interviewer's sense of self esteem and confidence: 'I have to remind myself of all the nice people I've met who haven't refused'; 'Some days you meet two or three refusals in a row - then you might as well go home!'

Ploys by the contacted person that undermine the role the interviewer needs to adopt (such as asking a lot of questions, making disparaging comments about survey research or using an aggressive manner) can reduce interviewers' confidence and cause feelings of stress.

Training and experience can play a large part in maintaining interviewers' confidence by ensuring that they have a wide repertoire of behaviour to deal with every aspect of the doorstep situation, especially with the more common forms of reluctance and with the tactics that members of the public might adopt. They need to understand the stress that the contacted person may feel and to view the evasive or aggressive behaviour that it might generate with a certain amount of professional detachment. Kahn and Cannell (1957) indicate the importance of overtly acknowledging the contacted person's fears or reservations by comments such as 'I understand why you might feel like that', before going on to attempt to counteract them. This is called 'active listening' and is discussed as a technique for countering expressions of reluctance in Chapter 8.

Interviewers also need to understand and accept their own vulnerability, in particular the way in which their morale can be damaged by an abusive refusal or by a series of unsuccessful approaches. Many interviewers are aware that they are less successful if they are feeling unwell or stressed by other events in their lives and advise avoiding interviewing on these days. Experienced interviewers also develop ways of restoring their morale if it is damaged by their encounters with members of the public: 'Stop and have a cup of tea'; 'Go home and start again tomorrow'; 'I remember the times when I *have* persuaded someone who was harassed or rude to take part'; 'Saying "I can see this isn't a good time" and withdrawing definitely pays off'; 'Withdraw before you get an outright refusal because they lose face if they change their mind'.

Making new interviewers aware of the stress they may feel but also teaching them positive morale boosting techniques is important. To know that even the most experienced interviewer sometimes gets refusals and abuse is helpful. The supervisor or field controller can also provide essential support by keeping in regular touch, listening to their tales of woe and suggesting practical ways of dealing with the situation more effectively.

## 7.    Achievement motivation

One of the objects of interviewer training is to impart an idea of realistic response rate objectives and to convey the belief that these can be achieved. The motivation to achieve as good a response rate as possible may be partly monetary as pay is often linked to success, but it is also a matter of professional pride. This can be fostered by encouragement and feedback from field controllers. As has been indicated in section 6 above, success in persuading people to take part is affected by morale, which is in turn enhanced by success in obtaining interviews and reduced by refusals and broken appointments. Interviewers also say that over-long interviews, ones that are difficult for respondents or that use repetitive questioning forms reduce their confidence in their ability to persuade people to take part because they feel they can no longer honestly say that the interview is enjoyable. Butcher (1986) reports that on pretests for the National Travel Survey, response was increased from 58 per cent to 75 per cent as a result of changes to the design that altered interviewers' perceptions of their task; these included relaxing rules that applied to only a small minority of respondents (so the changes made very little actual difference to the task), reducing the demands on the respondents' time (though not on the interviewers') and giving interviewers more information about the purpose of the survey and the reasons for asking each question. Nelson (1988) suggests that it is particularly important for interviewers to understand the purpose of and need for complex and ambitious surveys if they are to achieve satisfactory levels of response. Rosenthal (1979) has shown that anxious people are more likely to overestimate the signs of rejection than the less anxious who are more accurate decoders of verbal and nonverbal signals. Crespi (1945) has shown that interviewer cheating behaviour is more often the result of low morale than of basic dishonesty.

Field management experience also indicates that over emphasis on obtaining interviews rather than on the quality of the information can lead to cheating. Interviewers also say that pressure of work (too large an assignment, too many assignments and tight deadlines) and low pay for the amount of work involved affect the extent to which they are able or willing to make extra effort to obtain interviews. Good field management is therefore an essential part of keeping up morale and of motivating interviewers to try to achieve high response rates while keeping a balance with the requirements of other aspects of the work. Initial training can only lay the groundwork for this.

## 8.   Cognitive structure

The detailed analysis of the doorstep situation undertaken here provides the basis for developing a cognitive structure that is appropriate to present to new interviewers.  A cognitive structure presents a framework within which the learning of the social skill can be organized.  It provides a rationale that enables trainees to make sense of the learning process and to apply their own initiative in the development of their skill.  The repertoire of elements thus becomes an organized set of possible courses of action rather than a long and possibly confusing list of items.

The conceptual framework that interviewers need as the foundation for their expertise consists of a relatively small number of basic principles:

  (i)   There is a need for preliminary preparation and study of the survey materials in order to be familiar with the procedures, to be able to answer questions or to give information and to feel confident.

 (ii)   The initial introduction should be brief and should incorporate certain prescribed items of information and behaviour.

(iii)   How interviewers present themselves initially is a very important part of gaining cooperation (e.g., smile, make eye contact, dress appropriately, be warm and friendly).

 (iv)   Accurate observation of the contacted person, the way the door is opened, the visual, auditory and olfactory clues from the dwelling is essential.  This should be linked to an imaginative awareness of the variety of different possible situations and moods that the contacted person may be in when the interviewer calls and the stress that the request for an interview may generate.

  (v)   To pre-empt or to answer verbal or nonverbal expressions of reluctance, there are three main strategies to use:

  - Be reassuring and avoid being threatening;

  - Be positive about the benefits of taking part;

  - Appeal to altruism, including indicating the social value of the survey and/or asking for help in carrying it out.

 (vi)   Reluctance or refusal to participate often arises from the current situation or mood of the contacted or selected person; coming back another time will often secure the interview, even after a refusal.

(vii)    There is no one right way to introduce a survey; an individual and flexible approach within the rules laid down is likely to be most effective. There are, however, limits to what is permissible.

(viii)    Interviewers may occasionally experience stress caused by refusals, especially if abusive. There are ways of minimizing this that can be learned.

## Social skills training applied to the doorstep situation

Some interviewers are naturally skilled in obtaining cooperation, others achieve a level of skill through experience; but without training they are likely to have little awareness of the principles on which their skill is based. By adopting a social skills approach in training, the naturally gifted have a chance to gain insight into the nature of their expertise and to enhance it; for those less gifted, the process of reaching an acceptable level of proficiency can be shortened and standards in general raised. What is more, supervisors trained in this way would be more effective in helping interviewers to polish their skills in the field.

A number of specific techniques have been developed for teaching the skills necessary to achieve social goals and some of them are particularly applicable to training interviewers in the asymmetrical, task oriented social situation of the survey introduction. Some of the teaching techniques used in adult education are also appropriate for interviewer training. Both social skills training and adult education are essentially practical and interactive processes. How they can be incorporated into an interviewer training session is discussed in the next chapter.

# 8 Training to get high response rates

## Selecting potentially good interviewers

The argument in Chapter 7 has been that the doorstep skills required to persuade people to participate in surveys can be taught using a social skill training approach. However, it is clear that new interviewers vary considerably in the level of appropriate social skills that they have developed during the course of their lives. Training in doorstep techniques is more likely to be effective if the trainee can build on a foundation of relevant social competence, particularly in view of the limited amount of time usually available for interviewer training.

To what extent can interviewers who are likely to be good at gaining cooperation be selected at the recruitment stage? Interviewing is a multi-skilled activity, requiring the ability not only to put over the survey and persuade the reluctant respondent but also to read the questions as worded, to record the answers accurately and to keep accurate records; interviewers are also required to have the virtues of honesty, self discipline and courage. All of these aspects are important and must be taken into account in the recruitment interview; the recruiter must have a systematic approach and an assessment form to complete at the end.

Applicants should be sent an application form in advance to collect basic information on age, sex, family or job commitments, previous experience, availability for interviewing work and distance prepared to travel; this provides a basis for discussion during the recruitment interview in which the applicant's social skills can be observed. It is also appropriate to ask the applicant to conduct a dummy interview, with the recruiter acting as respondent; this enables the recruiter to make some assessment of any claims to have previous interviewing experience and of the applicant's ability to read questions and to record responses accurately; how the applicant copes simultaneously with a task and with the need to maintain a good personal relationship can be observed.

No research has conclusively shown that any particular interviewer demographic characteristics are associated with good response rates, or with any other aspect of the interviewer's task. There is some evidence that men initially get higher refusal rates than women (Fowler & Mangione, 1990) but this difference tends to disappear with experience. Some studies suggest that interviewers in the middle years are more successful than younger or older interviewers, the 'middle years' being variously 40-50 (Lievesley, 1986) or 25-45 (Hansen & Marks, 1958), but in the main it seems to be an advantage to have a fieldforce that is not homogeneous in terms of characteristics as some interviewers are more successful with certain types of respondent than others: some feel quite confident approaching well-to-do houses or business and professional people, whereas others feel daunted by this type of work but may be very successful in suburban estates or poorer areas; some may have the right touch for gaining the participation of elderly people while others may be more successful with the young. The most valuable interviewers are those who have a chameleon quality of adapting to every sort of area and every type of respondent.

Fowler & Mangione (1990) made telephone calls to respondents on an experimental survey and asked each of them to rate the interviewer who called on them for such qualities as friendliness, how relaxed the interviewer was, how professional, and how interested in the research: there was a marked intercorrelation between ratings on these variables and all were associated with refusal rate but only the perceived friendliness of the interviewer reached statistical significance. The female interviewers were more likely to be voted as friendly than the males. If respondents' ratings of the interviewer show a significant relationship with the interviewer's ability in general to gain cooperation, it can probably be asserted with some confidence that the recruiter's rating of applicants would be equally valid. The ratings could be extended to include those attributes that were indicated by respondents in our depth interviews as influencing them in deciding whether or not to give the interview and that interviewers themselves felt were important. Applicants could usefully be rated on the following dimensions:

- Friendliness
- 'Charm' (defined as social grace or how much the recruiter liked the applicant)
- Confidence
- Dominance/submissiveness (extreme dominance would be related to 'pushiness'; a middle position would be the preferred one)
- Likely to get on with most people/limited in suitability

-       Interest in the work
-       Appearance and dress:  too formal for general appeal/an acceptable balance/too informal or exotic.

In addition to identifying those likely to get few refusals, it is necessary to try to spot those who are likely to have low noncontact rates: availability and willingness to work during the evenings and at weekends have been shown to be an important prerequisite for reducing noncontacts (Lievesley, 1986;  Swires-Hennessey & Drake, 1992).

Formal ratings by recruiters on these dimensions would systematize the intuitive assessments that are usually made during the recruitment interview, and provide the basis for an appraisal of the extent to which such ratings are predictive of good response rates.  As discussed in Chapter 1, there is often a dearth of applicants for interviewing work and recruiters have to accept people whom they judge not to be wholly suitable in order to cover the sample.  This may be unfortunate as regards the quality of the interviewing work but provides a good opportunity to undertake much needed research to validate the selection criteria that would be applied in more fortunate times.

## General principles of training

Interviewer training has improved considerably over the last twenty-five years as the emphasis on standardized interviewing procedures has increased.  In Britain, most major survey organizations give three days of training to those who have no previous interviewing experience, this being a requirement for membership of the Market Research Society's Interviewer Quality Control Scheme.  Sometimes, large numbers of interviewers have to be recruited for a survey being carried out in one area;  as there will be little prospect of these interviewers being required again in the near future, their training can be specific to the survey to be carried out.  Unless the survey is very complex, they can often be adequately trained within two days.

In all the training courses, the emphasis tends to be on questionnaire administration, with relatively little time devoted to the problems of gaining cooperation.  In a study of the effects of length of interviewer training, Fowler & Mangione (1990) found that there was a major increase in quality of interviewing behaviour when trainees were given two days' rather than one day's training, but very little was gained when the training was increased to five or ten days.  It would therefore seem that, in a three day training course, more time could be devoted to gaining cooperation than is usually the case without sacrificing the quality of the interviewing itself.

Effective learning is more likely to take place if a number of different teaching modes are employed;  while written and verbal explanations of instructions have a part to play, long lectures and long reading sessions should be avoided; it is essential that these are broken up into sections which are augmented by other methods that involve the trainee in active participation; these other methods include written exercises, discussion, demonstration followed by critical appraisal, and role playing practice.

In Britain, most training courses take place entirely in a central location to which the trainees travel; but some organizations, notably OPCS Social Survey Division and SCPR, are developing home study packages to cover part of the training. This saves on costs, which can be quite considerable if trainees have to travel far to the central location and perhaps be put up overnight; but cost is not the only consideration; some parts of the interviewer's task can be more quickly and effectively learned by individual study than in a group. In the United States and Australia, where distances make centralized training prohibitively expensive, elaborate packages involving home study, written exercises, telephone interviews with the supervisor and tape recordings of dummy interviews with members of the public have been devised by the main government or academic survey institutions.

*Ongoing training*

There is a limit to what can be effectively learned without experience of the reality of practical work in the field. It is only by knocking on doors and trying to persuade a member of the public to take part in the survey that the significance of what has been taught is fully realised and any gaps in knowledge become apparent. For this reason, OPCS Social Survey Division ask newly trained interviewers to carry out a small dummy assignment of interviews with members of the public; most other organizations arrange for each new interviewer to be accompanied by a supervisor on their first day out in the field. In this way, trainees build on their training and begin the process of gaining experience based on a sound foundation.

Further one day training courses also play a very useful role: SCPR invites interviewers who have completed two or three assignments reasonably satisfactorily, and who can thus be judged as being likely to continue as interviewers, to attend an additional training day as a prerequisite for being appointed to the interviewing panel proper (and moving into a higher pay bracket). This provides an important opportunity for them to discuss their experiences as well as to extend their expertise. It also improves morale and provides an incentive to improve. Occasional remedial classes are also held for interviewers whose interviewing skills are good but whose response rates are poor.

Through these measures and through supervision and monitoring of their work, interviewer training becomes an ongoing process that interacts with their growing experience.

**Content of basic training**

The basic training in contacting the public, selecting respondents and persuading them to take part in the survey has to cover:

> *How to organize the time in the interviewing areas:* the best days and times to make contact and to get interviews; grouping addresses and planning a route; optimizing the chances of finding the 'not at homes'; appointment making and keeping; the first visit to the area and contacting the police (if required). Keeping costs down by good organization of time and by avoiding unnecessary visits to the area.

> *The basics of sampling methods and respondent selection procedures:* the main different kinds of sample used by the organization and why; the requirements for interviewing a named respondent, all residents in a household, or for selecting a respondent at random.

> *The definitions needed to identify the correct person(s) to interview:* the main ones are the definition of a 'household', 'residence' at an address, 'householder' and 'economic activity' status.

> *Introducing the survey and persuading:* including the initial introduction; carrying out the respondent selection procedure; asking for the interview; dealing with reluctance.

> *Interviewer morale:* coping with refusals and noncontacts; contact with the supervisor and with other field staff.

> *Record keeping:* recording time and date of all calls at an address; record of outcome at address; information on noncontacts and refusers; pay and expenses claims and any other administrative matters.

*The interviewers' manual*

All major survey organizations have an interviewers' manual which forms an integral part of their training and also, perhaps more importantly, provides a reference source to which interviewers can refer to refresh their memories or to deal with problems. OPCS Social Survey Division's 'Handbook for Interviewers' (McCrossan, 1991) and the SCPR 'Interviewers' Manual' (1984a) are quite large booklets covering all aspects of the interviewer's work in some detail and are designed primarily as reference works rather than as training aids: though parts are used in training, they are too long for a trainee interviewer to read and take in at a sitting.

*Home study*

Home study can make a very effective contribution to the training process provided that it is organized in such a way as to demand active learning and output from the trainee. The SCPR home study pack includes the Interviewers' Manual, a Training Handbook and a tape recording of demonstration interviews.

> *The Interviewer's Manual:* this is accompanied by an instruction sheet which directs the trainee to read only certain sections and to read each section before tackling the specific point of the home study package to which it relates.

> *The Training Handbook:* the purpose of this handbook is to teach the trainees the main definitions used in respondent selection procedures or in the household demographics section of a questionnaire, to familiarize them with the main respondent selection procedure used and to get them used to finding their way around the 'Definitions' section of the Interviewers' Manual. It consists of three sections: establishing household status and residence at the address; identifying the economic position of people in the household; and the most frequently used respondent selection procedure. Each section comprises three cases of varying difficulty for the trainee to sort out, the answers being given on the following page; these are followed by a number of exercises to which the answers are not given and which the trainee has to solve by referring to the Interviewers' Manual. The completed handbooks are returned to the training officer for marking. They have proved most valuable in teaching the definitions ahead of the group training session and enabling the trainer to appraise a recruit's ability to read and apply the manual; they also provide material for follow up work in the group training session.

> *The tape recording of demonstration interviews:* the purpose of the tape recording is mainly to introduce trainees to the basics of conducting the interview and to provide a model of how a trained professional interviewer works; but the opportunity is also taken to demonstrate the survey introduction and the administration of the most commonly used respondent selection procedure. For the interview on the first side of the cassette, a completed questionnaire is provided and the interview is interrupted at intervals for 'voice over' explanation; for the interview on the second side of the cassette, a blank questionnaire is provided and the trainee has to record the answers from the tape, thus employing the principle of active involvement of the trainee in the learning process.

*The group training session*

Group training sessions are more effective if the numbers are fairly small (e.g., six to twelve) to allow for maximum participation. In the face to face teaching situation, the learning that has taken place during the home study is tested and extended: it is tested by the well known adult education technique for small group training sessions in which the trainer throws out questions from time to time for the trainees to answer; it is extended through practising those parts of the interviewer's task which make use of what has been learned: for example, when practising the doorstep introduction, the trainee has to use the definitions and apply the respondent selection procedure that were learned during the home study. As these have to be applied while also trying to build a friendly relationship with the contacted person, it is important that the interviewer is thoroughly familiar with them.

The training session also covers those aspects not dealt with or only touched on briefly during the home study day. Aspects of the task of gaining cooperation not dealt with in the SCPR home study day include organizing one's time in the interviewing area, route planning, reducing noncontacts, and record keeping. These can be taught through demonstration, and with the aid of blackboard, flip charts or an overhead projector; any forms that are regularly employed for these procedures on surveys are used during the training course. The trainees will have to put what they learn about these tasks into practice on their first survey and their competence should be assessed by the supervisor who accompanies them on their first day's work. The supervisor should also give them further advice and instruction if needed.

Introducing the survey, administering the respondent selection procedure and dealing with reluctance to participate are touched on only briefly in the home study day, by demonstration in the tape recorded interviews. A major (and often neglected) function of the face to face training session should be to ensure that interviewers go out into the field confident that they can deal adequately with the doorstep situation. Social skills theory and training techniques provide an effective approach for teaching the skills involved.

## Social skills training techniques

The basics of a social skills approach were set out in Chapter 7 in which the nature of the social skills required in the process of contacting the public, introducing the survey, selecting the respondent and persuading them to participate were analyzed. The approach involves the application of a variety of teaching and learning techniques within a structured framework and should contain the following components.

1. *Breaking down the situation into its component parts*

The goals, rules and appropriate ways of behaving change as the doorstep situation develops; it is therefore necessary in training to deal separately with the different phases of the interaction and then to build them into a whole.  The different phases are:

- the initial speech to the person who opens the door;
- establishing whom to interview and asking for the interview;
- answering questions and dealing with reluctance and refusal.

2. *Teaching the conceptual framework*

Analysis of the cognitive structure underyling doorstep behaviour provides the conceptual framework within which the learning of the social skills involved can be organized.  The insight and understanding that this framework gives provide a rationale that enables trainees to make sense of the learning process and to apply their own initiative to the development of their skill.  It is unfolded during the course of the training through a variety of techniques:

(a)     *Short periods of direct explanation of some procedures,* for example, the use of the identity card and explanatory letter, the administration of the respondent selection procedure.

(b)     *Analysis and discussion of general principles* through explanation and through question and answer sessions.

(c)     *Repetition* is used to highlight recurring themes such as the three main ways of obtaining cooperation:  being reassuring, being positive about the benefits of taking part, appealing to altruism.

(d)     *Handouts:*  as the basic principles are unfolded step by step during the training, written summaries setting these out in clear and concise terms are handed out.  This process introduces trainees to concepts that may have been unfamiliar such as the role of perceptual skill in interpreting the situation so that they can make an appropriate response.  The handouts encapsulate what has been taught in a form that can be taken away and used as an ongoing aide memoire.

3. *Modelling*

With the aid of an assistant the trainer should demonstrate good, indifferent and poor examples of the doorstep interaction which trainees then evaluate in discussion;  this encourages trainees to use their critical faculties and to identify some of the details of behaviour that comprise the skill of contacting a person and introducing the survey. Modelling of ideal behaviour also conveys an impression of the skill as a whole so that trainees can learn by empathic identification and imitation. It is particularly important for conveying body language aspects of the skill.

4. *Imaginative exercises*

Trainees should be asked to project themselves into a variety of situations and to imagine how they might be perceived in them; this exercise sharpens up their ability to interpret the reactions of those they approach. For example, trainees might be asked to think back to a specific time the previous evening and to recall what they themselves were doing and how they would have reacted to being contacted by an interviewer. This leads on to trainees being asked to think of a number of other possible situations that might be happening behind the doors on which they are about to knock and what clues they might pick up both before and after the door is opened. The possible feelings of a number of different types of people in different situations are then explored (e.g., an old lady living alone, a businessman just home from a difficult day at the office) and trainees are asked to suggest what verbal and nonverbal clues might indicate fear, annoyance, trust, friendliness, etc.

These exercises help to make trainees more aware of the variety of different situations that might exist in people's homes and of the different reactions they might meet. Importantly, it introduces trainees to the concept of perceptual skill and teaches them to be aware of the nonverbal signs that experienced interviewers respond to.

5. *Role playing and feedback*

Role playing is a key social skills training technique. In this context, it requires trainees to practise the doorstep procedure in as realistic a way as possible. A role playing session should be incorporated into each phase of the training course: making the initial introduction, establishing whom to interview and dealing with reluctance. The role playing should be followed by feedback.

Feedback should come not only from trainers but from fellow trainees who learn both from each other's mistakes and through thinking about what alternative behaviour might have been effective. In this way, their repertoire of behaviour is extended. Feedback is an important component of social skills training.

Self criticism is also regarded as useful and the use of tape recorders and video cameras is recommended if resources allow.

Role playing exercises should be designed in advance of the training session to provide trainees with progressively more challenging situations. In much of the role playing work, the trainer or assistant act as the contacted person in order to present a series of pre-prepared situations. However, reverse role playing, where the trainee plays the part of the contact, is also used as this helps to extend the trainees' understanding of contacted people's reactions, sharpens their perceptions and encourages a detached view of the interaction process.

Through the modelling and role playing parts of the training course, the trainees practise dealing with the various ways in which reluctance is expressed and help each other to acquire an appropriate repertoire of responses. Although it is helpful to give interviewers examples of useful tactics for countering some of the most common ways in which reluctance is expressed (as illustrated in Appendix II, Handout 6, p.221), their developing skill should be founded on a grasp of the main underlying strategies available to them:

(i)   that there are three main ways of dealing with reluctance:

- giving reassurance,
- being positive about the benefits of taking part,
- appealing to feelings of altruism;

(ii)  that withdrawing before reluctance becomes a firm refusal and returning another day often wins the interview;

(iii) that reluctance can only be dealt with appropriately if interviewers pick up the nonverbal clues through observation of and listening carefully to the contacted person;

(iv)  that the reluctance expressed should be addressed directly and succinctly, with appropriate information; long explanations and multiple arguments should be avoided.

Kahn & Cannell (1957) have pointed out the importance of listening carefully and then indicating overtly that one has heard and understood the prospective respondent's reservations or reluctance. The Michigan University Survey Research Center trains its interviewers in a technique they call 'active listening' (Guenzel et al., 1983). This involves listening carefully to the expression of reluctance, then rephrasing it and reflecting it back, followed by some information designed to counter the reluctance. For example:

Respondent:      'I'm too busy.'

Interviewer:      'I appreciate that you are very busy but the survey is important. It's easy to get the views of people who aren't busy and we really need to have the views of people like you to ensure that the results are unbiased.'

The interviewer may guess at the real reasons behind the expression of reluctance and address their remarks to that, for example:

Respondent:      'I'm not interested.'

Interviewer:     'I can understand that it might not seem like a very interesting survey but it covers a wide range of important subjects and most people have enjoyed having a say. There are no right or wrong answers and no special knowledge is required.'

If the interviewer has guessed wrongly, the respondent may well counter with the true reason, giving the interviewer another chance to put over persuasive information. Groves & Cialdini (1991) have argued that, when reluctance is expressed, it is advantageous to the interviewer to keep the exchange going in the expectation that the respondent will sooner or later provide an opportunity for the interviewer to put over a persuasive argument. The recordings of the doorstep interactions indicate that interviewers need a very high level of skill to manage a long interchange successfully.

## 6. *Motivating and building morale*

Self esteem and expectations of success are important factors in developing good social skills. Interviewers' self esteem and expectations can have a marked effect on their response rates; steps should be taken to enhance these throughout the training session but especially at the beginning and end. The first section of the session introduces the concept of response rate, showing how to calculate it, indicating what sort of levels could be expected and would win approval from field management. Empathic understanding of the new interviewer's feelings of anxiety on approaching the house of a stranger to ask for an interview should be shown by the trainer and assurances given that most people will be pleased to see them, will readily agree to take part, will enjoy the interview, will be pleasant, friendly and interested. The ways in which interviewing can satisfy trainees' personal goals are thus indicated.

At the end of the training session, these messages are reiterated; in addition, there should be the opportunity for discussion of the stressful experiences that they might undergo and how to deal with them and restore their morale.

In Appendix II is an outline for a face to face training module that uses all of these techniques; it is based on the understanding of the process of obtaining cooperation gained from the tape recorded interchanges, the depth interviews with respondents and the discussions with interviewers. It is designed as a basic introductory module lasting about two hours since time in interviewing training courses is usually at a premium. Clearly, longer spent on it, especially in role playing, would bring benefits.

## Training course requirements

The proper organization of a training course is a major undertaking that requires a considerable amount of preparation. Not only does its content have to be determined but the appropriate techniques for each part of it have to be selected; these often involve the preparation of documents that, in addition to the interviewers' manual, may include: sets of exercises such as the SCPR Training Handbook; respondent selection and other forms, the completion of which have to be learned; questionnaires to be used in trial interviews; and handouts that summarize the main points conveyed by each section of the training course. These should all be clearly headed, so that the interviewer can remember what they applied to afterwards, and a pocket folder provided in which they can be stored.

Doorstep introductions for demonstration purposes and a number of graded examples of doorstep situations also need to be prepared in advance, ranging from one where the contacted person is cooperative and where the respondent selection procedure is simple, to ones where different and progressively more difficult complications are introduced at each phase of the process. In order to standardize the training received by each interviewer as much as possible, these examples and exercises should not be left to the discretion of the training officers but set out in advance.

The value of other teaching aids should also be considered: the use of a blackboard, flip charts or an overhead projector would clearly be helpful for putting over some of the information and instructions to be conveyed. Tape recorders can also play a very useful role in that the trainees can appraise their own performance which develops their capacity for self criticism. Video, if available, can obviously take this process a stage further and be particularly valuable in helping to train interviewers' perceptual skills in interpreting body language.

One problem with the use of role playing techniques is that the participants can be rather self conscious. By making the process initially into a game in which the trainer overacts and caricatures the role they are playing, much cathartic laughter can occur and the trainees become more able to throw themselves into the roles they are asked to play; they begin, thus, to feel their way into and become familiar with the role of friendly but professionally competent and confident interviewer working on an interesting and worthwhile survey. Being comfortable in this role is an important part of maintaining good morale.

It is, of course, essential that those who carry out the training of interviewers should themselves be trained in the principles and procedures involved. Their training usually starts with them assisting at training sessions, discussion of and practice in the techniques used, and then moving to conducting training sessions under supervision. In order to ensure uniformity, all trainers should be monitored from time to time and seminars should be held with training officers at which procedures and methods are reviewed, discussed and, if necessary, revised. Feedback should also be sought from trainees from time to time. In this way, training methods develop and improve, and are updated as survey procedures change.

## The project briefing

Most social surveys involving random sampling are preceded by a day long interviewer briefing session, usually conducted by the researcher responsible for the project. Many of the principles that apply to basic training also apply to the project briefing: there should be a minimum of verbal exposition and a maximum of active participation; samples of the documents to be used on the survey should be provided and completed in the process of carrying out examples; the examples used for interviewers to learn and practice the procedures should be prepared in advance so that they are standard at each briefing session; the examples should progress from simple to more complicated ones.

Briefing sessions are ideally fairly small (not more than about twenty interviewers) so that everyone's participation can be ensured and observation made of how well each interviewer is coping with the task of absorbing the information. Although the researcher will usually conduct the briefing, there should be trained field personnel present whose job it is to overlook what each interviewer is doing and to watch for signs of incomprehension.

Written instructions should also be supplied to interviewers, to be read after the briefing and to be a source of reference when problems or unusual situations are met with.

The written instructions should contain information on the background to the survey and an example of how to introduce it on the doorstep. Following the appraisal of what makes a good introduction set out in Chapter 5, this example of an introduction should be as brief as possible. Additional information that interviewers can give as necessary should also be set out. There might well be a requirement that some of this information should be given after the introduction and respondent selection procedure but before the interview itself starts so that those participating in the survey are properly informed of its purpose and who it is sponsored by before giving their final consent.

Some organizations attempt to improve the efficiency of the briefing day by sending out the instructions and the questionnaire in advance. Experience has shown that this can sometimes be counterproductive: confronted with these documents without verbal preparation, some interviewers feel overwhelmed by the apparent complexity of this task and withdraw from the survey; unless the interviewers are set particular tasks, such as reading a particular part of the instructions and answering a short questionnaire about procedures, or carrying out a dummy interview with a friend or relative, it is often found that some interviewers fail to undertake the home preparation properly; thus at the briefing the researcher is faced with a situation in which some interviewers are prepared as desired while others are not.

One of the functions of the briefing is to convey to interviewers a sense of the importance and worthwhileness of the survey and thus how essential it is that all aspects of their work are carried out well. Evidence has already been presented that interviewers' attitudes towards the survey can affect the response rate they get: if they feel it is important and worthwhile, they will be more sincere and convincing in putting it over to prospective respondents and more persistent in tracking down those difficult to contact. The briefing can make a significant contribution to interviewer morale by helping them to feel part of a team that includes the researcher as well as field personnel and other interviewers. It is thus essential that it is well conducted. Feedback from interviewers collected anonymously and accepted by researchers with humility can help to make the briefing session an efficient and rewarding instrument of training.


## Supervision and monitoring

Some prospective interviewers drop out during the training as they discover that interviewing is more demanding than they had realised. For those that complete the training, morale and enthusiasm are usually high. Their first venture into the field can sometimes be a rude awakening. Continuing contact with interviewers in the field is vital to maintain good morale. Valerie McGregor, Field Consultant, considers poor morale to be due to lack of support from field management and to be a major reason for the loss of interviewers, especially in the major conurbations: in a short article, 'The Lady Vanishes' (MRS Newsletter, February 1989), she concludes from informal discussions with interviewers who resigned that among the main factors are poor pay for the work required and poor conditions, notably lack of contact with field management and lack of feedback about the quality of their work so that they have little sense of achievement. She sees commercial pressures on field management teams as being largely to blame. Hall & Katryniak (1990) found that among reasons for leaving the fieldforce were a sense of isolation from other interviewers, from supervisors and from head office and little feeling of being part of a team; they did not feel supported or appreciated.

Newly trained interviewers clearly need a considerable amount of support during their first couple of assignments to keep up their morale and to help them develop their expertise. SCPR's policy is for a supervisor to accompany them on their first day in the field on their first assignment and for them to be accompanied again at some point during their second assignment. During their first assignment, their supervisor should be in frequent telephone contact to encourage and advise.

More experienced interviewers also need to be regularly supervised; the convention adopted by most organizations and the standard set by the Market Research Society Interviewer Quality Control Scheme is for every interviewer to be accompanied at six monthly intervals. The purpose of supervision is to ensure that interviewers do not start to deviate from the required procedures as they gain experience and confidence, and to help them with any problems they may have; it also provides an opportunity for the interviewer to ask questions, discuss problems and air any discontents. Supervisors thus have an important role as intermediaries between the interviewers and office based field management.

Supervisors play an important part in the ongoing training of new interviewers as well as in maintaining the standards of experienced interviewers; it is therefore important that they too should be properly trained in their role. Supervisors are selected from the more experienced and able interviewers so they already have a high level of personal skill in all aspects of the interviewer's task; but this does not guarantee that they will be good at teaching these skills to others.

In some organizations, those who train new interviewers are also those who supervise their work, but in most large organizations there is a two tier system whereby recruitment and training is carried out by regional managers (also variously called regional supervisors or regional field controllers) and the bulk of supervision is carried out by a second tier who combine their supervisory work with interviewing. Some organizations, notably OPCS Social Survey Division, have a specialist team who carry out recruitment and training, including the training of supervisors. Supervisors should also be accompanied in the field from time to time (usually once a year) to ensure that their own work has not deteriorated and to give them a chance to discuss supervisory problems with a more senior person.

Supervisors should also be provided with a manual that sets out their duties and explains the objects of supervision and the procedures to be followed (see SCPR Field Supervisors' Manual, 1984b). Their training should consist of a day's session, individually or with other newly appointed supervisors, that goes through all aspects of the role and allows ample time for discussion, especially of their training role and the task of appraising an interviewer's work and completing the report form.

Their skills in helping the interviewers that they accompany to become more expert can be enhanced by sitting in on and assisting at the interviewers' training sessions, especially by taking part in the role playing exercises.

The supervisor's training should include delineating their responsibility for ensuring interviewing standards by making clear what discretion they have to arrange a second accompaniment with an interviewer whose work they judge to be below standard or, indeed, to take away assignments from someone they regard as unsatisfactory.

The regional field managers also have a very important function in maintaining morale, ensuring good response rates and seeing fieldwork is completed on schedule by regular telephone contact with their interviewers. Fieldwork on random sample surveys is usually spread over four to six weeks to allow time to contact those away or ill; during this period, the regional field managers should contact each member of their team working on the survey every week. In order to fulfil this function adequately, it is essential that they receive from head office weekly progress figures for each interviewer; these should show the number of addresses assigned and the number dealt with, and numbers of achieved interviews, refusals, noncontacts and other nonresponse.

The weekly conversations with the interviewers working on the survey would include discussion of progress and any problems in obtaining cooperation; the relatively inexperienced interviewers and any with poor response rates would be invited to discuss various aspects of their experience and to enlarge on any refusals or difficulties in making contact that they have encountered; in particular, their ability and willingness to visit their area in the evening or at weekends would be checked; if the area is regarded as unsafe, arrangements might be made for someone to accompany the interviewer or for part of the assignment to be taken over by a male interviewer.

Any interviewers who are falling behind schedule would be asked about their prospects for completing the assignment on time and a judgement made as to whether some of their addresses should be passed to another interviewer. The supervisor would learn quickly if an interviewer had fallen sick or has family problems that may make completion of the assignment on time difficult. An interviewer who struggles to complete an assignment while unwell or in the midst of a family crisis is not likely to be persistent in trying to obtain cooperation or in tracking down the person who is out a lot.

It also has to be recognized that interviewers may be working on more than one survey at a time and may need help in deciding priorities. This may be difficult if the interviewer is working simultaneously for more than one organization.

It is also important that those who appear to be doing well are congratulated; the opportunity can be taken to explore the possibility of their taking on further addresses to help those behind schedule or having personal difficulties, or, at the end of the fieldwork period, to take a reissued assignment of refusals and noncontacts in a final attempt to improve the response rate.

Through these conversations, the importance of good response and high standards of interviewing are kept in the forefront of interviewers' minds, a sympathetic ear is given to their problems and difficulties, and swift remedial action can be taken when necessary. Interviewers feel they have someone to turn to if they need help or support and head office have ongoing information about progress and early notification of problems through this process of regular two way communication.

## CAPI

Computer Assisted Personal Interviewing (CAPI) is becoming firmly established as a mode of data collection, especially for ongoing and repeated social surveys. Interviewers using a CAPI system have to learn how to operate a laptop computer which they take with them to the interview instead of a paper and pen questionnaire; they ask the questions in the normal way but key the answers into the computer.

It has been found that a high proportion of interviewers already experienced in administering complex questionnaires, can adapt to using a computerized questionnaire with suitable training. Although no experimentation has been done, it has been reported that interviewers using CAPI have an increased sense of professionalism. There is no indication that the public is more resistant to being interviewed with the aid of a computer; indeed, it seems that response rates may even be a little higher, due partly, perhaps, to the effect of increased self esteem on interviewer morale. Some respondents, also, may be impressed by the use of a computer and more willing to cooperate as a result.

# 9 Gaining cooperation on telephone surveys

## An expanding mode of data collection

An analysis of the processes and problems of gaining cooperation in surveys would be incomplete without some consideration of the specific requirements of telephone interviewing which is increasingly favoured for both market and social research. Its use is already widespread in the United States where it has become the most commonly used mode for conducting structured market research interviews (Frankel, 1989). It is expected to develop to a similar level in Canada, Britain,[1] other western European countries and in the Antipodes over the coming decade as telephone coverage spreads to all sectors of the population.

The factors that have given impetus to the development of telephone interviewing have not only been those connected with wider telephone ownership and the relative cheapness of the method; they include the worsening problem of obtaining interviews in inner city areas or of finding interviewers prepared to work in places where they feel their safety may be threatened. These are often areas where telephone penetration is lowest, but the poor response obtained by face to face interviewers is thought by many researchers to severely reduce any advantages that face to face interviewing might have.

Telephone interviewing has been used extensively for many years for surveys among employers and managers at their place of work; usually these were (and sometimes still are) conducted by interviewers from their own homes. The growth of telephone interviewing during the 1970s and early 1980s led to the setting up of centralized telephone interviewing installations for both business and population surveys, a development that has revolutionized telephone interviewing. Dedicated telephone interviewing facilities allow for stricter control and closer supervision of interviewer behaviour than is possible with from-home telephone surveys or with face to face interviewing. They also make it considerably easier for researchers and survey sponsors to be more closely involved in the interviewing phase of their surveys; the result has been increased research interest in response problems and data quality.

Spurred by the growing interest in its adaptation to social research in the United States, there has been a considerable amount of methodological research on telephone interviewing during the past decade. It has done much to identify the special problems of gaining cooperation and the particular interviewing skills required so that telephone interviewing techniques have greatly improved since the early days and the differences in results from those obtained by face to face interviewing have largely disappeared.

*Advantages and limitations*

In addition to the tighter control of the interview process made possible by centralized telephone installations, an advantage of telephone surveys is that they can be carried out more quickly than face to face surveys, especially when Computer Assisted Telephone Interviewing (CATI) is used. In a CATI survey, the interviewer works at a computer terminal instead of with a paper questionnaire; the questions come up on the screen and the interviewer keys in the answers. Any routing dependent on the answer given is carried out automatically by the computer and the next appropriate question appears on the screen. With CATI, response rates and results can be available very quickly; however, the costs of programming the questionnaire onto the computer preclude its use except for very large or ongoing surveys, preferably with short and simple questionnaires.

Telephone surveys are also generally cheaper than face to face interviewing surveys. The cost advantage is more noticeable in the United States where special telephone lines at concessionary rates are available and where random sampling for face to face interviewing is relatively complex and expensive. In Britain the situation is reversed; long distance telephone calls are relatively expensive and random sampling for telephone surveys is also more problematic than for face to face surveys.

Telephone surveys have their limitations; visual aids cannot be used to help put over questions and answer categories; the interviewer is deprived of all the visual cues that give information on the respondent's reaction and also of the opportunity to communicate verbally by smiling, eye contact etc. Nonresponse is usually 5-10 per cent higher on telephone than on comparable face to face surveys.

Although telephone interviewing was initially regarded as appropriate only for very short questionnaires, it has been found that 20-30 minute interviews are acceptable both for business and general population surveys.

*Are the answers different?*

A major question that had to be answered before telephone interviewing could be generally accepted was whether mode of interviewing affected the answers given. Findings both in the United States and in Britain indicate that differences are small (Groves & Kahn, 1979; Sykes & Collins, 1987). Respondents tend to give briefer answers to open questions on the telephone and there are some mode effects on answers to sensitive questions: people are more reticent on the telephone to questions about personal finances but are less likely to give socially acceptable answers to questions concerned with social prejudices. There is also evidence that people are more willing to disclose medical problems over the telephone. It therefore cannot be taken for granted that face to face interviewing always gives more accurate information.

## Access to the public by telephone

The appraisals of the comparability of answers have been made on strictly comparable samples. But can telephone interviewing yield as good a coverage of the population as face to face surveys?

Not all households have telephones, even in the most affluent societies, there are sections of the population inaccessible to a telephone approach. Furthermore, growing numbers of people prefer not to have their numbers listed in directories, causing problems in drawing representative samples of telephone owners. These factors affect the applicability and design of telephone surveys.

*Telephone penetration*

In Sweden and Canada, almost every household has a telephone and in the United States coverage in 1986 was about 93 per cent (Trewin & Lee, 1988). In Britain, estimates for 1990 based on the OPCS General Household Survey and Omnibus Survey, were that about 88 per cent of households and about 90 per cent of adults had a private telephone (Deepchand & Thomas, 1992).

Although the proportion of households without a telephone in affluent countries may appear trivial, it can be significant for survey research; telephone ownership is lower among the young, single person households and among the less affluent, especially among the unemployed, those in rented accommodation, those without cars and among ethnic minorities. For many social research surveys, the sector of the population inaccessible by telephone is of particular importance, such as people with special needs or in areas covered by social programmes, and their loss from the sample may lead to significant bias. The answer is either to use face to face interviewing or to adopt a mixed mode approach, using the telephone where possible and interviewing those without telephones face to face.

Market research surveys, on the other hand, are often less concerned with those whose purchasing power is minimal; many surveys are directed at particular groups (e.g., car owners or house buyers); others cover a restricted population by excluding (for example) those 65 years or over and/or those in socio-economic grade E (dependent on state benefits). It often makes good marketing sense to confine the research to the broad sector of the population within which the market is likely to lie. Telephone surveys can thus provide a perfectly adequate basis for many market research studies.

*Unlisted numbers*

Telephone numbers may be unlisted in the directories for a variety of reasons: because the person does not want to be listed, because it is a new installation or because someone has moved. The proportion of telephone numbers that are ex-directory varies from country to country. In Britain, British Telecom are reported as saying that 25 per cent of numbers are unlisted and in the United States the figure is similar (Foreman & Collins, 1991). Results from the OPCS surveys cited above indicate that, of the 90 per cent of adults who are in telephone-owning households, just over three-quarters said that their number was not listed in the directory. The cumulative effect is that only 69 per cent of adults had their number in the directory (Deepchand & Thomas, op.cit.).

The characteristics of those with unlisted numbers in part compound the effects of non-coverage: they tend to be young and less affluent. There are also compensating differences in that unlisted numbers tend to be in urban areas whereas telephone ownership is lower in rural areas (Collins & Sykes, 1987; Trewin & Lee, op.cit.). Deepchand & Thomas (1992) show that a sample based on directory listed telephone numbers would over represent home owners and the affluent; single person households, young women and the unemployed would be under represented.

*Sampling approaches*

For market research telephone surveys, the sample is usually drawn from telephone directories on the basis that coverage is sufficient for their purpose. The problem of unlisted numbers is sometimes addressed by the use of 'Directory Plus-One' dialling. This method starts by selecting a sample of numbers from the directories but in every case the number dialled is one higher than that selected from the directory; the resulting sample then covers both listed and unlisted numbers. Although this method goes some way towards covering ex-directory people, its efficiency cannot be calculated as there is no information available on the variability of the incidence of ex-directory numbers in different areas of the country (Foreman & Collins, op.cit.).

In the United States, samples of telephone owners are obtained by the use of Random Digit Dialling (RDD),[2] an approach that covers unlisted numbers. Telephone numbers are randomly generated by computer; since business numbers and unallocated numbers form a large proportion of these but tend to be clustered, a two stage procedure is adopted: at the first stage the selected numbers are dialled; usually about 25 per cent of them are found to be for residential addresses. Each of the successfully contacted numbers is taken to represent a block of 100 numbers. At the second stage, additional numbers within the same block are randomly generated and dialled until a predetermined number of residential addresses (say, five or ten) has been successfully contacted. Around 65 per cent of the second stage numbers are found to be for residential addresses.

There are several problems that have militated against the use of RDD in Britain; one is the unstandardized telephone numbering system which enormously complicates an RDD approach; another is the lack of readily available up to date detailed information about the numbering system. An experiment by Foreman & Collins (op.cit.) indicated that the use of blocks of 100 numbers may not be appropriate in the UK where clustering of types of numbers seems to take place in smaller groups. They concluded that more experimental work needed to be done to adapt the method for UK use and that it was unlikely to be adopted by market research companies as long as the emphasis for telephone research is on speed and cheapness.

For social reasearch in the UK, the recommended solution to the problem of nonaccessibility by telephone due to nonownership and to ex-directory numbers is to use a dual mode approach (Collins & Sykes, 1987). A sample of addresses is selected from the electoral register and the names of all electors are recorded; the names and addresses are submitted to the British Telecom retrieval service for the supply of telephone number for those they have listed in their directories (which are revised daily). Telephone numbers can be obtained in this way for around 60 per cent of the names, leaving 40 per cent to be interviewed face to face, the respondent selection procedures being as described in Chapter 2. The OPCS Labour Force Survey has also used PAF samples in this way: the addresses were traced in the electoral registers to find a name, which was then looked up in the telephone directory. Only 40 per cent of the addresses selected were covered in this process, leaving 60 per cent to be covered by face to face interviewing. It was estimated that a small cost saving was achieved compared with 100 per cent coverage by face to face interviewing. The response rate for the telephone interviews was only marginally lower than for the face to face interviews.

The success of a dual mode approach depends on there being no mode effects on the answers obtained; Sykes & Collins (1987) demonstrated that differences in answers were minimal and conclude that it provides a viable compromise when other factors justify a telephone survey. Since at least 40 per cent of the sample remain to be interviewed face to face, cost savings are unlikely to be remarkable and may be nonexistent: a dual mode approach also necessitates considerable additional design and management effort. Furthermore, the telephone is inappropriate for the long and complex interviews necessary in much social research. It is thus not surprising that the main application of telephone interviewing to social research problems in Britain has been in follow-up interviews with those previously interviewed face to face. The OPCS Labour Force Survey currently uses this method as it has now become a rolling quarterly survey in which each respondent is interviewed five times: the first interview is conducted face to face but the four subsequent interviews are conducted by telephone among those who have one and are willing to be interviewed on it.

### Response to telephone surveys

The problems of obtaining cooperation over the telephone are similar to those on face to face surveys: the salience or sensitivity of the topic and the length of the questionnaire affect response in the same sort of way. Comparing response rates of telephone and face to face surveys is not always easy, primarily because numbers dialled but not answered remain in an ambiguous position: it is not known whether the address is ineligible (e.g., empty or a business), whether it is a noncontact or even, in the US, whether it is an unissued number. In face to face surveys, it is usually possible to obtain some information about the address, either by observation or enquiry next door, and to categorize the noncontacts into those who are away, sick or simply out. However, from experiments where the sampling method, population covered, survey topic and questionnaire length are all kept constant, it seems that response to telephone surveys is less good than for face to face (Groves & Kahn, 1979; Collins et al., 1988). The difference seems to be of the order of at least 5 per cent and sometimes nearer 10 per cent in controlled experiments in both the United States and Britain.

As on face to face surveys, response is higher on telephone surveys when the topic is of direct interest to those approached and when any adult can answer the questions rather than using a respondent selection procedure (Cannell et al., 1987). A longer interview (40 minutes compared with 20 minutes) has been found to get a lower response rate (Collins & Sykes, 1987); response to the 20 minutes interview was 59 per cent but dropped to 48 per cent for the 40 minutes interview, mainly due to increased refusal. There is some indication that the more the survey characteristics favour a high response rate, the smaller the difference in response between the telephone and face to face approach.

Two factors are exacerbating the difficulties of gaining cooperation on telephone surveys in the United States and are likely to cause increasing problems in other countries: one of these is the 'absolute explosion of telemarketing that uses the guise of a survey to screen prospects, or to grab their listening attention' (Honomichl, 1989). The other is the rapid development of ownership of telephone answering devices as cheaper machines become available. Honomichl quotes a study that indicated that 25 per cent of US households had one in 1986 and that in about half the cases it was used to screen all incoming calls.

*Who are the nonrespondents?*

A survey conducted only by telephone can be subject to bias due to lack of telephone penetration, unlisted numbers and/or limitations in the available sampling facilities. It is necessary also to assess the extent to which nonresponse compounds the bias from noncoverage to a greater extent than in face to face surveys.

As with face to face surveys, nonresponse to telephone surveys tends to be higher among the elderly and those in the lower educational categories. In the United States, these biases have been found to be greater on telephone surveys (Groves & Kahn, 1979; Cannell et al., 1981 and 1987); telephone penetration, on the other hand, is lower among the young. A telephone survey would thus tend to under represent both the younger and older age groups. However, it is interesting to note that this finding was not upheld in a British study that compared characteristics of nonresponders to telephone and face to face interviewing on four different experimental surveys (Collins et al., 1988). This may be due to differences between Britain and the United States in attitudes to the use of the telephone or in the characteristics of the elderly who have telephones.

In face to face interviews, it is commonly found that nonresponse is higher in inner city areas than in other types of area. On telephone surveys, the difference in response between large urban and other areas is less marked; furthermore, it seems that telephone surveys get better response than face to face among people who live in urban apartments and other sorts of accommodation with a common lockable entrance. These are the types of dwellings that commonly have entryphones and other security systems that make access very difficult for face to face interviewers (Groves & Kahn, 1979).

Collins et al. (op.cit.) point to another possible way in which the sample achieved over the telephone may be less biased than that obtained on a face to face survey: in a comparison of samples of telephone owners achieved by telephone and face to face methods in terms of eight characteristics, only two showed significant differences; those interviewed by telephone contained a higher proportion of people in paid work and also of people whose partner was in paid work, and a lower proportion of nonworking homemakers or people whose partner was a nonworking homemaker. This suggests that telephone interview samples contain a higher proportion of working couples, a group that tends to be somewhat under represented in face to face surveys.

The conclusion seems to be that any particular bias in telephone surveys, compared to face to face surveys, is likely to arise from lack of access by telephone to a cross section of the public rather than from differences in response. Bias arising from nonresponse tends to be similar in kind to that on face to face surveys; in some respects, a telephone survey may suffer from less response bias than a face to face survey, but the differences in sample characteristics attributable to mode of interviewing are small and unlikely to affect the findings.

### Categories of nonresponse

Typically, noncontact rates are considerably lower than refusal rates on telephone surveys and are often lower than on face to face surveys because it is relatively cheap and easy to make many attempts by redialling the number. The difference between response rates is therefore mainly due to higher rates of refusal to cooperate on telephone surveys.

Other sources of nonresponse may also be slightly higher for telephone surveys; the hard of hearing, the frail elderly and those with language problems may all be more likely to declare themselves incapable of being interviewed by telephone than face to face, with which it is easier for other members of the household to help them. The lower response to telephone surveys indicates a need to pay considerable attention to all factors that can be shown to increase response.

## Minimizing noncontacts

Noncontact rates are only lower on telephone surveys when full advantage is taken of the method's flexibility and relative cheapness. Much methodological research has been designed to identify the optimum number and pattern of calls to achieve a satisfactorily low noncontact rate at an economic cost.

### Length of fieldwork period

As with face to face surveys, short fieldwork periods tend to result in higher noncontact rates; Seebold (1988) found that extending the fieldwork period on the US National Crime Survey from two to four weeks led to a 3 per cent increase in response; the noncontact rate was reduced by 6 per cent and the refusal rate increased by 3 per cent, indicating that those who have to be dialled many times are more likely to refuse when finally contacted than are those contacted after only one or two calls.

*Number of calls*

It is difficult to establish any clear rule as to how many diallings should be made to try to obtain an answer: RDD samples present special problems because of the high proportion of ineligible numbers generated: Groves & Kahn (1979) found that up to ten calls were necessary to identify 93 per cent of working household numbers. On social surveys where an appraisal of response rates is important, at least this level of success in identifying eligible households is necessary; in other types of survey, the requirements may be less stringent.

Samples drawn from listings such as the electoral register do not have the same problems of ineligible numbers as RDD samples. The number of calls required to be made is therefore more dependent on decisions as to what is acceptable on each survey. Collins et al. (1988) found that up to seven calls produced an acceptable noncontact rate on a Survey of Attitudes to Alcohol carried out in conjunction with OPCS (table 9.1). One of the advantages of centralized telephone interviewing is that it is a simple matter to keep records of the number of attempts made on each number, to re-present numbers for additional attempts and to make the decision before the end of fieldwork to increase the number of attempts if the noncontact rate threatens to be unacceptably high.

**Table 9.1**

**Percentage of noncontacts by number of calls**
**(Survey of Attitudes towards Alcohol)**

| Call no. | Noncontacts* |
|----------|--------------|
|          | %            |
| 1        | 30           |
| 2        | 22           |
| 3        | 16           |
| 4        | 12           |
| 5        | 9            |
| 6        | 7            |
| 7        | 5            |

* Includes 'Rang but no answer' and 'Selected person out'.

*Call pattern*

The number of calls required to make contact can be reduced considerably by making the calls at times when people are likely to be at home. The research into the most favourable times for making contact on face to face surveys described in Chapter 4 is equally relevant to telephone interviewing. The best times for making contact on general population samples were shown to be:

- Weekday evenings, after 4.30pm but especially after 6.30pm
- Saturday evenings, after 4.30pm
- Sunday mornings, before 2.00pm
- Sunday evenings, after 6.30pm.

Clearly, different patterns would be optimum for other sorts of sample: in telephone market research studies targeted at housewives, weekday mornings have been found to be a good time to contact nonworking housewives; in a very large consumer tracking study using an RDD sample in which the interview could be taken with any adult, male or female, it was found that noncontacts at first call were actually higher after 5.00pm and at weekends. Although the differences were statistically significant, they were not sufficiently large to outweigh other considerations such as cost of calls and interviewer payment rates (Kerin & Peterson, 1983).

Cost savings will be optimized if the first calls are made at times most likely to be successful for the type of population being sampled. The rules attaching to face to face interviewers that subsequent calls should be made on a different day and at a different time are also applicable to telephone surveys. In particular, those not contacted after three or four calls should be dialled at the weekend or on weekdays during the day, to pick up those on shift work who are out during the evenings; confining all calls to the times shown by research as most likely to result in contact is not a good policy. Further calls might be made at the end of the fieldwork period to catch those who have been away from home. Telephone surveys require more calls on more and different days to achieve noncontact rates similar to those on face to face surveys (Groves & Kahn, 1979). The reason for this is probably the lack of information about an address which a face to face interviewer can often obtain.

The exception to the above rules is when noncontact is due to the number being engaged; these should be redialled within a few minutes to take advantage of the likelihood that a busy line indicates someone is at home.

Even with a centralized telephone interviewing facility, the management of additional calls is complex and needs careful organization. With CATI systems, the parameters can be built into the program but for other systems it forms an important part of the supervisor's role; computerized sample management is helpful.

*Number of rings*

Allowing the telephone to ring for a long time before concluding that there is no one there to answer it is clearly wasteful of interviewers' time when it is quick and easy to dial again later. Research directed at establishing an appropriate ring policy indicates that most calls are answered within quite a few rings: Smead & Wilcox (1980) found that 97 per cent of answered calls with a consumer panel were answered in less than five rings; Sykes & Hoinville (1985) found that 90 per cent of answered calls were answered within seven rings. Although a policy of restricting the number of rings increases the number of calls required to make contact, it has been found to be a more economical way to use interviewers' time.

## Reducing refusals

Whereas it is relatively easy to reduce the rate of noncontacts on telephone survey, refusals are often higher than on face to face surveys. Only a small proportion of refusals seems to be due to dislike of the mode; Collins et al. (1988) found in follow-up interviews among refusers that 8 per cent gave reasons to do with the mode such as being tired of unsolicited calls, objecting to telephone surveys or disliking talking on the telephone; 5 per cent said that 25 minutes was too long an interview, but in other respects the reasons given for refusing were the same as those given in the face to face survey.

It is commonly found that refusals in telephone surveys tend to occur earlier in the interaction than is the case with face to face interviewing. Collins et al. (op.cit.) found that a third of refusals occurred before the respondent selection procedure could be carried out to establish whom to interview; a further 22 per cent refused on behalf of the selected person; less than half of the refusals came from the selected person. This is in sharp contrast to the comparable face to face surveys in the experiments (table 9.2).

**Table 9.2**

**When refusals occur**

|                    | Telephone | Face to face |
|--------------------|-----------|--------------|
|                    | %         | %            |
| Before selection   | 34        | 12           |
| By proxy           | 22        | 29           |
| By selected person | 44        | 69           |

It appears that face to face contact with a person gives the interviewer more scope for prolonging the interaction, providing an opportunity for some of the ploys described in Chapters 7 and 8, such as smiling and maintaining eye contact, admiring the cat, and so on. It may be, however, that a number of people who are going to refuse anyway, find it easier to do so immediately over the telephone than face to face because the rules of politeness governing telephone interactions are less stringent.

A number of tactics for increasing cooperation on telephone surveys have been investigated; several of these have not proved helpful. There is no significant relationship between time of day or day of week of the contact and whether or not an interview was agreed to. Nor have experimental manipulations of the content of the survey introduction had any effect. Groves & Magilavy (1981) describe a 'foot-in-the-door' experiment; 'foot-in-the-door' techniques are based on the theory that it is easier to get someone to cooperate on a larger task if they have already helped with a smaller one. In their experiment, two questions and the name of the person contacted were asked at an initial call; the interview proper was requested at a second call. They concluded that the method did not obtain a better overall response rate than the usual approach and was no substitute for a follow-up of refusals by another interviewer.

There are some field management tactics that have been found to reduce refusals.

### Advance letters

It is not possible to send advance letters to members of RDD samples, but in surveys where the addresses of the sample are known there is evidence that an advance letter improves response: Dillman et al. (1976) found that refusal rates were 6 per cent lower when an advance letter was sent; Collins et al. (1988) also obtained higher response with an advance letter in two experimental studies though the effect on refusals was not statistically significant. As with face to face surveys, an advance letter changes the situation with which the interviewer has to deal, pre-empting to some extent their persuasive role; although on balance an advance letter does more good than harm, there is some evidence that those who make up their mind not to participate on the basis of the advance letter refuse before the respondents selection procedure and in a way that leaves no room for the interviewer to be persuasive.

### Making appointments

The tactic of withdrawing when a refusal seems about to happen and making another attempt later, recommended to face to face interviewers, also seems to be appropriate on the telephone. In the Survey of Attitudes towards Alcohol, interviewers were instructed to try to make arrangements to call again at a more convenient time when a contacted person seemed reluctant but had not refused: 81 per cent of the addresses at which appointments were made resulted in an interview at a later time, compared with 58 per cent of addresses where appointments were not made (Collins et al., op.cit.). This is in keeping with the finding for face to face surveys, that much refusal to participate arises because the time at which the approach is made is inconvenient. A quick indication on the part of the interviewer that they can call back another time can often prevent reluctance from becoming a refusal.

*Shortening the respondent selection procedure*

Face to face interviewers often feel that carrying out the selection procedure to select one adult at random for interview causes a hiatus in the process of persuasion; over the telephone it is even harder to maintain the sort of interaction that will lead to cooperation. Groves & Kahn (1979) conducted experiments with two alternative methods; one involved asking how many adults lived at the address and how many were female; the respondent was then selected on the basis of gender and relative age (e.g., 'the youngest female', 'the second eldest male'). The second method selected the person in the household who last celebrated a birthday. The methods were found to lead to somewhat improved response rates but both were less efficient than the usual full listing approach in producing a strict probability sample. They are therefore only used on surveys that are likely to have particular problems in gaining cooperation where errors from nonresponse are likely to outweigh those from noncoverage.

Asking for information about other members of the household at the beginning of the interview is similarly felt by interviewers to have a bad effect on the development of a cooperative interaction. In a study in which any adult could answer the questions, Monsees & Massey (1979) experimented with the position of demographic questions about household members: for half the sample these questions came first followed by questions about the telephone answerer; in the other, the order of these two blocks of questions was reversed. Higher response rates were obtained when the household questions were placed after the personal questions to the telephone answerer.

*Reissuing refusals*

Most telephone survey organizations make a further call to refusers to try to persuade them to take part, a procedure that is less restricted by cost considerations than in face to face interviewing. Usually numbers are reassigned to interviewers known to get high levels of response. In the United States, organizations report that between 25 and 40 per cent of refusals are converted but Collins et al. (1988) obtained only a 13 per cent conversion rate on the Attitudes to Alcohol Survey, perhaps because they were working with a relatively inexperienced interviewing team.

As with face to face interviews, conversion is related to the 'hardness' or 'softness' of the original refusal and usually some selection is made of numbers for reissue based on the details of the refusal recorded: Collins et al. (op.cit.) did not reissue those who refused by phone or letter to the advance letter, those who expressed strong objections and threatened to complain, those who said they disliked surveys in general and the elderly or those clearly worried about the call. Conversions seemed to be easiest when the selected person had not previously been spoken to (either not contacted or the subject of a proxy refusal), when it was an older person who required a clearer explanation of the survey, and when the original reason for refusal referred to the situation at the time of the request ('too busy/tired/not well').

## Interviewer qualities

As with face to face interviewers, there is considerable variability in refusal rates between interviewers on telephone surveys. It is relatively easy on telephone surveys to randomize the allocation of numbers between interviewers so that area effects are eliminated, allowing the interviewer effects on response to be examined. It is reported that the University of Michigan Survey Research Center obtains interviews with about 84 per cent of those contacted, but that the 10 per cent of interviewers with the poorest response rates have rates of less than 65 per cent while the top 10 per cent of interviewers may have no refusals at all. Even grater variation is reported by Statistics Sweden (Groves & Lyberg, 1988). Comparisons over time showed that response rates achieved by individual interviewers from survey to survey were remarkably consistent (Oksenberg & Cannell, 1988). This leads to consideration of the rather harsh policy of dismissing interviewers who show consistently high refusal rates; Eastlack & Assael, (1966) found that it was possible to reduce refusal rates on a market survey from around 30 per cent in the first three months to 12 per cent in the remaining seven months by weeding out the poorest interviewers. However, this is an expensive policy, to be adopted only if better selection and training fail to solve the problem.

As with face to face interviewers, experienced telephone interviewers tend to get lower refusal rates than those new to the work, suggesting that the required skills can be learned (though there might be a certain amount of self weeding by less successful interviewers). Some studies have suggested that women obtain better response rates than men, but the differences disappear when the (on average) longer experience of women interviewers is taken into account (Groves & Fultz, 1985). No other interviewer characteristics have been found to be associated with refusal rates.

Oksenberg & Cannell (1988) undertook an investigation to try to establish whether there were particular vocal characteristics that led to some interviewers getting much better response rates than others, and this research is worth describing at some length.

They found that refusals tended to occur very early in the exchange, often during the first few sentences of the interviewer's introduction. By standardizing the introduction they demonstrated that variations in refusal rate were not due to what was said but how it was said. The next step was to tape record an example of each interviewer's initial introductory sentences on the telephone (i.e., before the contacted person replied) and to subject it to paralinguistic analysis. This process was carried out for three groups of interviewers; one consisted of US Census Bureau telephone interviewers working on the National Crime Survey; the other two groups were Survey Research Center interviewers working on the Consumer Attitudes Survey; these two groups included only interviewers with especially high or especially low refusal rates.

A team of four specially trained listeners rated each interviewer's performance on a number of physical characteristics of the voice: average pitch, variation in pitch, loudness, rate of speaking and the extent to which the pronunciation was standard (i.e., similar to that of national radio announcers). Acoustic equipment was also used to provide physical measures that equated to average pitch, variation in pitch and rate of speaking; measures of intonal contours of certain key words were also obtained.

A study of previous research on paralinguistics had indicated that people's impressions of and attitudes to other people are strongly influenced by vocal characteristics. The trained listeners were therefore also asked to rate each interviewer on some personal qualities: how confident, competent, friendly and interested in the task they sounded, and also how pleasant the voice was to listen to.

Agreement among the raters was good for the physical characteristics and adequate for all the other evaluations except how pleasant the voice was to listen to. Correlations between listeners' ratings and the acoustic measures of pitch and rate of speaking were also good.

A number of extremely interesting relationships between success rate and voice characteristics was found; interviewers who achieved low refusal rates tended to:

- speak rapidly,
- speak loudly,
- use standard American pronounciation,
- sound competent,
- sound confident.

Intercorrelations indicated that speaking rapidly, loudly and using standard pronunciation create an impression of competence and confidence. Having a particularly low pitched voice and little variation in pitch was found to be associated with high refusals. It was also found that the better interviewers tended to use a falling tone on the key words that occurred early in the introduction; these were 'Hello', their own name, and the word 'Bureau' in the name of the organization. The authors point out that falling tones at the ends of words are considered to be appropriate for declarative statements and rising tones for questions. They suggest that using a rising tone on these key words might give an impression of diffidence.

These findings provide strong pointers to the style that interviewers should adopt on the telephone and parallels the findings for face to face surveys that interviewers should make a positive approach; putting the emphasis on being ingratiating, non-threatening and friendly is not particularly successful. The more forceful interviewers were perceived as being as friendly as the less forceful. The authors point out that these findings are consistent with research that indicates that a forceful manner is a characteristic of those able to lead and influence others.

It would be valuable to attempt to replicate the Oksenberg & Cannell study in other countries as the interpretation created by particular vocal characteristics may be specific to a particular culture, accent or language. It must also be born in mind that it is possible to speak too fast and too loudly; the interviewers that took part in this study had already been selected and trained according to certain criteria considered appropriate for the conduct of telephone interviewing, one of which was speaking slowly. The optimum speed and loudness of speech needs to be established for each country.

## Selection, training and management of telephone interviewers

As with face to face surveys, telephone interviewing of samples of the general public requires interviewers to work mainly in the evenings and at weekends. In the United States, the fact that the country covers three time zones enables work in centralized telephone units to be spread throughout the day, but in Britain the work on weekdays is often concentrated in the late afternoon and evening. The earlier part of the day might be filled with surveys among non-working housewives or with businesses. Except for those units that are designed to deal mainly with continuous surveys, workloads are likely to fluctuate considerably. A flexible interviewing force is required with members available to cover a wide range of times and prepared to accept irregular engagements for work.

Usually telephone interviewers are hourly paid members of a panel; those experienced in manning such units recommend that the panel should be two to three times the number of work stations in the unit; thus if there are fifty work stations, a panel of 100-150 interviewers would be required (Pile, 1991).

Interviewers are offered work on an assignment basis (though they may work on more than one survey at a time) and are engaged to come to the unit at particular times of the day and on particular days of the week, perhaps being asked to work five shifts of four or five hours in a week.

The location of a centralized telephone survey unit is important; although easy access to it for the researchers enables them to be more closely involved with the data collection phase of their research than is possible with face to face surveys, for it to be sited within a good catchment area from which interviewers can be recruited is a greater priority.

*Selection*

Since no particular characteristics are associated with being good at gaining cooperation on telephone surveys, selection has largely been concerned with ascertaining that the applicant is available at the times when shifts are run and with an intuitive appraisal of other aspects of suitability.  It is recognized that vocal characteristics are particularly important and that personal appearance and facial expression have no part to play.  It is also realized that how a person sounds on a telephone cannot always be judged by hearing them speak face to face.  Some units therefore ask applicants to telephone the recruiter in the first place so that an appraisal can be made.  The work of Oksenberg & Cannell, (1988) gives some very useful pointers as to how this appraisal can be made more systematic.  It suggests that a person's speech should be evaluated in terms of speed, loudness, closeness to a standard accent and the impression given of confidence and competence.  It must be remembered that the interviewers studied in this research, however, had already been through a selection procedure which applied certain criteria and had probably rejected those whose speech lacked clarity, who spoke too fast, or were inarticulate.  Common sense would suggest the addition of these criteria.

*Training*

It is clear from the success of speech and drama classes that voice characteristics and speech patterns can be changed by training.  Training programmes could well adapt some of the techniques used in these institutions to enhance the vocal skills of those selected for telephone interviewing.

Two full days training are reckoned to be necessary and it is helpful if the telephone equipment used permits call between extensions so that trainees can conduct dummy interviews with the trainer and with each other.  It is also easy to obtain names and addresses from telephone directories to use as training samples.

Training for gaining cooperation on telephone surveys should cover:

- the initial introduction,

- dealing with reluctance,

- follow-up calls to keep appointments or to find an uncontacted selected respondent,

- follow-up calls to try to persuade those who refused or expressed reluctance, at an earlier call.

For the initial introduction, interviewers can be provided with a script (or can write their own) which they can use without the problem of trying to maintain eye contact at the same time. However, a script is purely to give confidence and to ensure that the introduction is kept brief and simple, not to act as an inhibiting straitjacket. Tape recordings can be used so that interviewers can listen to models of the correct way to introduce the survey, using a forceful manner, speaking relatively fast and loudly and with a falling rather than a rising inflection on key words. They can also listen to their own and each other's recordings and develop a critical ear. Plenty of practice with feedback is an essential part of training.

In training telephone interviewers to deal with reluctance, much of the social skills approach discussed in Chapter 8 can be adopted. Collins et al. (1988) found that the less good telephone interviewers seemed to cope as well as the better interviewers until faced with expressions of reluctance, whereupon they tended to lose confidence and be unprepared to deal with the problem; they gave in easily rather than backing off, leaving the option to call again open.

Since there are no visual clues on the telephone, the interviewer needs to be trained to listen very carefully for the response of the person who answers the telephone, to be aware of the range of possible situations at the other end of the line and that it is necessary to respond quickly: a person contacted by telephone can get rid of the interviewer very rapidly by replacing the receiver, and is less inhibited about doing so than when confronted with a physical body smiling on the doorstep. The interviewer needs to judge very quickly whether the person concerned is elderly and perhaps needs a slower and simpler explanation of the survey, or whether they are in the middle of something and should be contacted again later.

To deal confidently and competently with the varying responses, the interviewers need to learn a range of possible tactics: as with face to face interviewers, these can be grouped under a few organizing principles:

> Be positive about the benefits of taking part.
> Give reassurance and information.
> Appeal to altruism.
> Use the 'active listening' technique.
> Be flexible and be prepared to back off and call again.

Advantage can be taken of the interviewer's invisibility to provide memory aids. New interviewers in particular find it useful to have to hand the equivalent of the handouts suggested for face to face trainees. When the telephone interviewing stations are situated in small booths, there is usually wall space to which these can be pinned.

Training should be an ongoing process; in a centralized telephone unit, it is easy to organize supervision and further short training seminars to deal with specific aspects of the work. It is usually advisable to allow new interviewers to develop some expertise and confidence before involving them in recall work, especially calling back on refusers. This can well be the subject of an additional training session.

## Supervision

It is recommended that there should be one supervisor for every 10 to 15 interviewers working on a shift (Pile, 1991). The equipment should allow the supervisor to cut in and overhear an interview without an audible click, though both the interviewer and the respondent should be made aware that this may happen.

Supervisors need to be supplied with regular information on interviewers' performance, especially their refusal rates, a fairly simple matter with a computerized system. Intensive supervision and further training can be organized for any interviewer found to have a problem. Interviewers who fail to respond to further training may have to be dropped.

## Morale

It has been found that interviewers' expectations as to whether or not a telephone survey is going to get a high refusal rate have a greater effect than seems to be the case in a face to face survey (Singer et al., 1983). Training can do much to give interviewers confidence in their ability to obtain cooperation and to instil a positive attitude: the advice of the Survey Research Center at the University of Michigan to the interviewers is:

> Self-confidence comes from being well-prepared. Approach each person who answers the 'phone as if he were friendly and interested. You may assume that if he isn't, it is because he is not yet informed about why you are calling.
>
> (Guenzel et al., 1983)

The supervisors also play an important part in keeping up the morale of interviewers and in helping to raise the expectations of those with relatively poor response rates; this can be quite as important as their management role.

Good working conditions, a time and a place in which to relax from the pressures of what can be very intensive work, appropriate rates of pay, helpful and interested feedback on their performances and ready assistance with problems all play a part in maintaining interviewers' positive attitudes towards the demands of the task they have to undertake.

The researchers can also contribute by being present at shifts and by taking an interest in the details of the problems of gaining cooperation and in carrying out the interview. Centralized telephone interviewing facilities can do much to improve collaboration between the researcher and the interviewing team leading to improved understanding of each other's problems.  They also provide the opportunity for interviewers to discuss various approaches and techniques of persuasion with each other.


## The future

It seems certain that the use of telephone interviewing will continue to grow in industrialized countries as telephone penetration expands, though perhaps not at the rate expected in the mid 1980s.  Applications in market research are already extensive and are likely to increase, in part because the costs of telephone surveys may become more competitive as the capital outlay in setting up a centralized unit is recovered and face to face interviewing becomes more expensive.

In Britain, social research applications are likely to remain mainly in the sphere of research among employees, businesses and institutions, and for follow-up interviews on longitudinal studies, often employing a mixed mode approach.  As telephone penetration spreads, and if some of the difficulties in drawing efficient probability samples are solved, then both market and social research by telephone will increase.

The flexibility and speed of centralized, especially computerized facilities, the absence of the need for samples to be clustered geographically (except in mixed mode surveys) and the limitations in questionnaire length lead to a different approach to survey research that may be reflected in new applications.  In face to face surveys, the cost of making contact means it is more economical to have a relatively long interview, at least up to about 40 minutes; conversely, on the telephone longer interviews inhibit response but making contact is relatively cheap.  Sponsors and researchers are therefore beginning to think in terms of more focused surveys with shorter and simpler questionnaires, bearing in mind that visual aids cannot be used to help with the administration of complex questions.  Such surveys may have advantages over the face to face mode for certain kinds of sensitive subjects and for certain sorts of sample.

Large face to face surveys in market and social research can provide a basis for drawing samples of telephone owners, either to represent the population as a whole or special samples of people with certain characteristics, behaviour or experience, as described by Hahlo (1992).  The viability of this approach will increase enormously as telephone ownership becomes more widespread.

**Notes**

1   The 1990 Report from the Association of Market Survey Organizations (AMSO), which includes the top 30 or so market research organizations in Britain, indicates that 17 per cent of their revenue comes from telephone research, compared with 55 per cent from face to face interviewing.
2   For a more detailed description and evaluation of Random Digit Dialling sampling techniques, see 'Section B: Sampling for Telephone Surveys' in Groves et al. (1988).

# 10 Other types of survey

## Introduction

Survey research is an extremely flexible tool that has application to a wide range of different problems and information needs. The previous chapters have focused mainly on surveys designed to cover samples of the general public interviewed at home. In this final chapter the special problems and requirements of some other types of survey are briefly examined. The objective is not to be comprehensive but to increase awareness of the issues that have to be considered for different types of survey in order to optimize response rates.

Given that an adequate sampling method can be devised to cover the target population, there remain three stages to the process of obtaining the interview: locating and contacting the sampled units, selecting or identifying respondents, and persuading them to give the interview. In preparing for fieldwork, each of these stages needs to be considered with a view to identifying possible problems that could affect response; the role of piloting and feasibility studies in identifying response problems and helping to test out solutions should not be overlooked.

### Locating and contacting sampled units

The 'sampled unit' might be a named person, or it might be an identified location, such as a residential address, a business or workplace, a farm, an institution or a geographically defined interviewing point. Problems may arise in trying to find or identify the sampled unit, such as a farm or the correct establishment of a company or institution; or they may arise in trying to make contact; for example a named person may be protected by carers or secretaries. 'Gatekeepers', as such people are usually called, can cause difficulties on many types of survey: when interviews are required in schools, whether with teachers or pupils, not only does the permission of the head teacher have to be sought, but of the local authority or school governors as well. Similarly, interviews in hospitals or other caring institution sometimes require authorization at more than one level. Such processes can add considerably to the interviewer's task and to the time needed for the fieldwork.

### Selecting or identifying the respondent

In some types of survey, the interviewers have to carry out secondary sampling procedures to make a random selection of individuals to interview; this may entail some kind of listing and ordering of people (e.g., residents in an institution). The procedures would entail the same principles as are used in drawing a sample of the general population (as described in Chapter 2). When the sampled unit is a location, such as a point by the roadside, in a shopping mall or an employment office, the interviewer is likely to have special instructions for selecting a cross section of people. To select a true random sample in such conditions may be quite difficult in some situations and would require a feasibility study.

Sometimes the person to be interviewed is one who fulfils a particular function. Identifying appropriate management personnel in business, commerce and industry can require both tact and knowledge about management structures and responsibilities.

### Persuading

It is the researcher's responsibility to ensure that the task that the respondent is being asked to perform in answering the questions is not too burdensome, either in terms of the time taken or the information required; that it is not likely to be alarming or threatening; and that it is appropriate to the situation in which the interview will take place. Piloting is necessary to ascertain that the interviewer is not being asked to do the impossible in trying to obtain interviews in particular situations and on particular topics, and to explore how the survey can best be presented.

## Longitudinal surveys

Some studies entail interviewing the same sample of people several times in order to measure changes or to track developments over time. The technique is frequently used to evaluate the long term effects of social programmes. Sometimes people are recruited to be members of a panel over a period of time (perhaps one or two years), during which they might be asked to give a number of interviews. Panels are used in market and social research to track changes in attitudes or behaviour over time; these might be to evaluate the effects of marketing or social programmes or simply to plot trends without the results being subject to sampling error.

Cohort studies are another type of longitudinal survey. The cohort members are selected with reference to an event at a particular point in time; for example, SCPR has carried out two year cohort studies of men who became unemployed during a particular period, and three year studies of young people who left school at the end of particular terms to enter the labour market. Both types of cohort were concerned with employment issues.

Longitudinal studies sponsored by government agencies are very common in the US; NORC has been involved in a number of these over the years and have summarised the fruits of their experience (Jones et al., 1986).

A good response rate is very important on longitudinal surveys as nonresponse becomes cumulative over the course of the study; a survey comprising three or four waves may be reduced to a response rate of less than 50 per cent (i.e., calculated as a proportion of the original sample) by the final wave unless special steps are taken. The contention of Jones et al. is that measures that improve response on single wave surveys may be inappropriate on longitudinal surveys whereas there are a number of other tools to maintain response that may be applicable. The points that they stress are:

(i)     Interviewers should have special training and should be rebriefed before each wave so that they understand the special requirements of longitudinal studies and are well informed and well motivated. Feedback of results of earlier waves to interviewers increases their interest and motivation.

(ii)    The highest possible response is important at the first wave; noncontacts and refusals should be reduced to the minimum by full use of such tactics as sending advance letters, making many calls at the addresses of those hard to contact, reissuing noncontacts and refusals to other interviewers, sending letters to noncontacts and refusers, and so on.

(iii)   Incentive payments may have a role to play at the initial interview but must be used only with caution: at the first wave a small payment can legitimize requests to prepare material in advance of the interview such as looking up records. A small advance payment to all sample members, at the first interview, not contingent an agreement to continue, has been found helpful as it indicates a recognition of the fact that giving information can be burdensome. But entrepreneurial respondents such as solicitors or consultants may try to bargain for payment nearer their usual 'fee'. Incentive payments at all waves have been found to reduce data quality. Jones et al. say that incentive payments should never be the main reason for cooperating.

(iv)  The loss at second and later waves is usually due more to failure to locate than to refusals. To optimize response at subsequent waves, the interviewer at the first wave should record all information that may be of help in locating the respondent's address and in calling at an appropriate time.

(v)  Some respondents will move house between one wave and the next: the interviewer at the first wave should provide a card that can be returned by the respondent giving the new address should this happen, and also collect the name and address of a close relative who could be contacted if the respondent is found to have moved without notification.

(vi)  The same interviewer should as far as possible interview the same respondents at each wave so that rapport and familiarity are built up.

(vii)  The interviewers should be provided with any information that might be of help in locating respondents and also a record of their response on previous waves.

(viii)  At third and subsequent waves, the interviewers should give priority to contacting respondents who have already cooperated fully as their data is likely to be more valuable than that of people whose participation has already been sporadic. Whether or not panel members who have missed more than one round of interviewing should be dropped is a matter to be decided with reference to the analysis objectives of each study.

(ix)  Respondents should be sent a letter before each wave to remind them that another interview is due. Their interest and involvement can be increased by sending them some results of earlier waves, providing there is no danger of such information affecting answers at subsequent interviews.

The US Bureau of the Census report that they have had considerable success in converting those who refuse at the second or subsequent waves of a longitudinal survey by sending a letter followed by a call from another interviewer, usually a very experienced field supervisor (Nelson and Bowie, 1988).

The longer the time between interviews, the greater the loss from noncontacts at each wave and the more important it is to employ the practices described above. Some long term cohort studies present particular problems. For example, the British National Child Development Study started with a cohort of all babies born during one week in March 1958. Data were collected at birth from the parents and the children were followed through infancy and childhood through the Health Visitor system. In 1981, when the cohort had reached the age of 23, a major effort was made to find and interview them. The cohort members had last been contacted at the age of 16. To try to trace the members of this young and highly mobile group, use was made of last known addresses of parents, of information received in response to an annual birthday card asking for address changes to be notified and, when all else failed, reference was made to National Health Service Records. The vast majority were successfully traced (87 per cent) and 90 per cent of those traced gave an interview (78 per cent of those traced).

## Workplace surveys

The term 'workplace surveys' is used here to identify a wide range of different types of enquiry in which respondents are interviewed at their place of work. The sampled unit is likely to be an enterprise (e.g., a business or organization) or, for large enterprises, an establishment at a particular location. Respondents may be of two types: the first type is selected by virtue of their function and responsibilities (e.g., personnel management, office equipment buying) or by virtue of their office (e.g., Trade Union representative); the object of study is the enterprise or establishment and the practices and policies in operation there. Respondents in the second type of survey are employees (or subsets of employees) who are interviewed about their own experiences and attitudes.

### Surveys about the workplace

Market research extended its sphere of operations to include manufacturers and businesses as consumers in a major way during the 1950s and 1960s when the postwar boom in the development of electronic office equipment resulted in a highly competitive situation. Originally called 'industrial' marketing research, it is now usually referred to as 'business-to-business' marketing research (or 'business research' in brief). This is something of a misnomer as it often covers public sector establishments as well as those in the private sector.

The specialized nature of the survey topics, the difficulties of persuading senior executives to give interviews and the problems of drawing adequate samples of enterprises or establishments, required the development of a particular expertise, and this provided a climate conducive to the growth of a number of dedicated industrial (or business) market research agencies. In Britain, most of these are members of the Industrial Market Research Association (IMRA) which acts as an umbrella organization that set standards, issues publications and provides a forum for discussion.

In the early days, business research interviewing was often carried out by a specialist in a particular subject, using a mainly qualitative approach. This type of research still has its uses and is essential in markets dominated by a few very large industrial buyers; but as the demands for 'harder' data have increased and the directories that could be used as sampling frames have improved, larger scale quantitative surveys have become the norm. There remains, however, a requirement for a particularly high calibre of interviewer, able to approach senior executives and trained in the basics of business organization. Such interviewing tends to be expensive when conducted face to face and, since the 1960s, more and more business research has been carried out by telephone.

During the last twenty years, government departments and other official bodies have increasingly found the need to conduct research among enterprises and organizations on such issues as employment, industrial relations, the administration and effectiveness of government training schemes, and equal opportunities. The majority of government sponsored workplace surveys use face to face interviewing, but a growing proportion are conducted by telephone or by a combination of the two modes.

*Sampling on workplace surveys*

Business and public sector enterprises and establishments vary enormously in size; 73 per cent of workplaces have under 10 employees and another 15 per cent have 11-24 employees. At one end of the spectrum are sole traders, self employed individuals and small, often family, businesses such as independent shops; at the other end are major companies with many establishments scattered about the country, holding companies with many subsidiaries and giant multinationals and public sector organizations such as local authorities, hospitals, and so on. The first step in any sample design is to define what sorts of enterprises are to be included, whether the sampling unit is to be at the enterprise or the establishment level, and what range of workplaces (in terms of numbers of employees) is to be covered. Much research is confined to workplaces with twenty-five or more employees. These constitute only 12 per cent of the total but cover 70 per cent of all employees.

In Britain, much business marketing research uses a form of quota sampling: lists of businesses of various sizes and types are drawn either from business directories such as Kompass or from a frame known as 'Connections in Business' derived from British Telecom's Yellow Pages database. Quotas within the required categories are set by reference to data derived from these frames or from the Department of Employment's Census of Employment. Interviewing continues until the required numbers in each category have been achieved; those refusing to cooperate are replaced.[1] 'Connections in Business' can be used as a basis for random sampling and is thus used for some public sector workplace surveys.

Government sponsored samples are sometimes drawn from the Department of Employment's Census of Employment database; this covers all establishments and includes information on number of employees and category in the Standard Industrial Classification (SIC) system; it excludes the self employed and sole traders. However, use of the Census of Employment is restricted and many public sector research funders, including some government departments, are denied access.

## Choice of mode

Telephone is often the preferred mode for workplace surveys. Apart from its relative cheapness and speed, busy executives would often rather deal with the survey quickly over the telephone than make an appointment to see the interviewer later. Despite the busyness of the sample members, it has been found possible to carry out telephone interviews up to half an hour in length. If the questionnaire is long and complex, as is often the case with government sponsored surveys, then a face to face interview is necessary.

Sometimes both modes are used, each for a different part of the survey: a short screening interview might be conducted by telephone with face to face follow-up interviews at establishments with certain characteristics or practices; or management interviews might be conducted by telephone but employee interviews face to face, as was the case in a study of the Industrial Tribunal system carried out by SCPR.

Both telephone and face to face interviews might be preceded by a mailed-out datasheet; business executives usually like to know in advance what factual information is going to be required by the interviewer so that they can assemble it ready for the interview.

## Contacting establishments

Whatever mode is adopted for the interview, initial contact is likely to be sought by telephone. Unless this phase of the operation is handled separately by a telephone interviewing team, face to face interviewers need also to have a high level of telephone interviewing skill. It is essential that they sound confident, authoritative and knowledgeable about the way enterprises and establishments are organized so that they are able to penetrate the protective screen put up by secretaries.

Special attention should be given to the description of the survey and its purpose so that it can be conveyed quickly and efficiently. There may need to be some adaptation of this introduction according to the size and type of establishment being contacted.

Advanced letters are usually thought to be helpful in gaining cooperation, but some researchers consider them to be effective only when the target respondent is high in the management structure. On the other hand, some researchers feel that often an advance letter simply provides an opportunity for reasons for nonparticipation to be prepared (Smith, 1991).

## Identifying respondents

Identifying and contacting the appropriate person to be interviewed in an establishment for the purposes of the particular survey is often the most demanding part of the interviewer's role; it requires tact and patience as well as some knowledge of the way in which establishments of that type are likely to be organized. The appropriate person is usually defined in terms of function within the organization, but job names are often of little help. What is required is the person or persons with both the correct level of responsibility for action and knowledge about what actually happens. Funders of business research sometimes think that the more senior the respondent the better, but very senior people in large enterprises often have responsibility for policy but not its everyday application.

Quite often it is found that the ground covered by the survey refers to responsibilities that are shared by more than one person; in particular, the person who implements the decision (e.g., to purchase a piece of equipment or to pursue a particular employee relations policy) may play a relatively minor role in the decision.[2]  There may be further complications in enterprises with many branches or subsidiaries with responsibilities being split between head office and subsidiaries. The researcher needs to establish a strategy for dealing with such eventualities which may require information to be collected from more than one person, not necessarily in the same location. In the series of Workplace Industrial Relations Surveys, conducted by SCPR for the Department of Employment and other organizations, special procedures and a special team of interviewers had to be set up to contact appropriate people at the head offices of enterprises with subsidiaries or multiple establishments (Millward et al., 1992).

It can take many telephone calls to identify and make contact with the appropriate person to interview, whether for a telephone interview or to make an appointment for a face to face interview.

Interviewers should not leave messages about the purpose of their call with intermediaries as they can easily be misunderstood or give an opportunity for a prepared refusal (Smith, op.cit.).

The time allowed for fieldwork on this type of complex survey has to be sufficient for the necessary letters to be exchanged and for appointments to be made with people who may not only be busy but away from their office for extended periods. On a large survey, fieldwork may well take two or three months.

*Gaining cooperation*

In persuading the selected respondents to take part in the survey, the interviewer on a workplace survey has the advantage that the subject matter is usually of direct relevance to the person's work; however, some business people are over-researched, especially those responsible for buying office equipment, and resent the approach of yet another interviewer. In some organizations, it is established policy that permission to take part has to be sought from the head office, involving the delay of a two stage process.

As with general population surveys, the introduction should be as brief as is compatible with giving a good reason for participating and should lead quickly into the first questions. When an appointment for the interview has not been made in advance, especially on telephone surveys, interviewers should be sensitive to signs that the respondent is busy and under pressure; being prepared to call back another time can often save the interview.

A great deal of patience and tenacity are often required to obtain and complete the interview: appointments are frequently broken due to the demands of the respondent's job, which inevitably has higher priority than the interview. Similarly an interview that could in the right circumstances be completed in 30 minutes may take 90 minutes due to interruptions, especially phone calls. Telephone interviews are at least largely free from the latter.

Keeping records of all that happens in the efforts to obtain cooperation is very important: reissuing both noncontacts and refusals to another interviewer of proven ability can be very effective in raising response rates. This process can be more efficiently and economically carried out if the second interviewer has details of who has already been spoken to and what information has been obtained.

Response rates on workplace surveys can vary as widely as those among the general population but are in general no worse. Marketing surveys among the most over researched business people may be as low as 50-60 per cent but on the majority of studies response is usually around 70 per cent. Government sponsored surveys often do rather better: on the Workplace Industrial Relations Survey (Millward et al., 1992), the overall response from the sampled establishments was 83 per cent; where a Trade Union representative was eligible to be interviewed, almost 80 per cent of them agreed to give the interview.

*Interviewer selection and training*

Some specialist business survey agencies build up a dedicated fieldforce that conducts only workplace surveys both for telephone and face to face interviewing. But many non-specialist research agencies use the same interviewers for both general population and workplace surveys. Quite a few interviewers who perform well on surveys among the public turn out to be rather poor at gaining the cooperation of business managers; they feel intimidated by the secretaries and don't know what sort of question to ask to identify the correct persons for interview. As a result, they do not enjoy this type of work and may opt not to do it. With experience and good training, many can, however, develop the necessary confidence and expertise.

Interviewers selected to form a specialized telephone business interviewing panel are quite likely to have had no previous experience of interviewing, though they might have desirable experience of how businesses operate. The voice qualities and manner of speech identified by Oksenberg and Cannell (1988) as being predictive of good response on telephone surveys among the general population are possibly even more important on workplace surveys: it is essential that the interviewer is clear and articulate, sounds confident and competent, and is assertive without being over-pressurizing.

Interviewers selected for large scale face to face workplace surveys, whether from a general survey fieldforce or for a dedicated business interviewing panel, are likely to have had previous experience of interviewing members of the public; certainly such experience provides a very useful foundation on which to build the specific expertise required to tackle some of the more complex workplace surveys. The requirements are rather more stringent than for telephone interviewers since face to face interviewers need to combine the ability to obtain information and gain cooperation over the telephone with the qualities of the good face to face interviewer.

It is important that face to face interviewers should look as well as sound professional; they should dress rather more formally than is necessary for interviews with the pubic, though there is no need for excessive smartness. Actual age is less important than a mature and responsible appearance. Interviewers need to be able to keep their poise, patience and courteousness in the face of broken appointments, interruptions and indications that their time and the survey are regarded as of little importance by the respondent.

A dedicated business telephone interviewing team may need only a short briefing on many surveys. Their basic training should have covered the structure and organization of businesses of different sizes and kinds and many of the surveys will be very simple. More complex face to face surveys using interviewers from a general fieldforce require extensive and thorough briefing in which considerable attention is given to the processes and problems of identifying the appropriate person(s) to interview and gaining their cooperation. The Workplace Industrial Relations Surveys already referred to required two day briefings because they covered a wide range of different types of establishments and also interviews with both management and Trade Union representatives.

One of the advantages of using centralized telephone interviewing facilities is that supervision can be very close; interviewers who have a problem in identifying whom to interview at an establishment can ask for immediate guidance. Adequate supervisory support for face to face interviewers on workplace surveys is essential, entailing not only accompaniment in the field but someone available on the phone to answer queries and to help deal with problems. It is rare for completely new interviewers to be engaged on a face to face workplace survey (unless they have been selected because they have relevant non-interviewing experience); but it is sometimes forgotten that an otherwise experienced interviewer may not have previously done this type of work and should be treated in some respects as a new interviewer.

*Employee surveys*

This type of workplace survey is where respondents are selected not because they fulfil a particular function but by virtue of the fact that they are an employee, working on a particular type of job or at a particular organization. Included here are surveys on behalf of management among their own employees, job satisfaction studies, surveys among people on government training courses, and so on. The sampling problems and methods are the same as described above.

Dealings with management on this type of workplace survey are confined to those necessary to set up the survey and to select and contact the employees. It is often desirable for the interviewer not to be identified with the management and for the confidentiality of the information to be stressed. Less formal clothes and a more friendly approach may be appropriate.

When the sample of employees is drawn from just one firm (or a small number of firms), the fact that those who have been interviewed may discuss the content of the questionnaire with those not yet interviewed has to be borne in mind; such discussion can affect both response rate and quality of the information. It is usually desirable in such circumstances to complete the fieldwork as quickly as possible.

## Elites and professionals

Some surveys are conducted among people selected as 'elites' who represent those in particular positions in society. Favourite targets are those defined as 'opinion leaders'; these may include media professionals, politicians, Trade Union leaders, leaders of pressure groups, church leaders, etc. who have a high media profile. There is likely to be no directory or list of such people to be used as a sampling frame; the 'population' to be sampled has to be defined and listed specially for the survey and is unlikely to be complete.

Many surveys are conducted among people chosen because of their profession, such as general practitioners, university or school teachers, solicitors, nurses and so on. Some form of professional listing or directory is usually available from which the sample can be drawn.

The interviewing of both elites and professionals may be conducted either by telephone or face to face, depending on the length and complexity of the interview. The location for the interview is very often the person's place of work but may be their home or some other neutral place.

The response to surveys among elites and professionals varies considerably according to the relevance of the purpose of the survey to their specific concerns; surveys among professionals to do specifically with their work can obtain response rates well over 80 per cent. Those among opinion leaders who do not see the survey as providing them with a particularly useful forum can be below 50 per cent.

The highly educated respondents in this type of survey usually expect to have a chance to express their particular views; very structured questionnaires that do not allow sufficient opportunity for them to respond in their own words can be unpopular and lead to aborted interviews. This has an adverse effect on interviewer morale and affects the response rate.

The same interviewer qualities are required for surveys among elites and professionals as are necessary for workplace surveys among managers. Some interviewers find interviewing professionals the more challenging; respondents are often highly specialized in their profession and (sometimes deliberately) make no allowance for the interviewer's lack of knowledge on their subject, even though specialist knowledge may not be necessary for the conduct of the interview. Occasionally, specialist knowledge is required to conduct the interview satisfactorily; in these cases, interviewers with the necessary background or qualifications have to be recruited and trained.

## Surveys among elderly and disabled people

The growing number of people in the older age groups and the relative affluence of some of them due to such factors as the increase in occupational pension schemes, has led to their becoming a prospective market for goods and services tailored to their needs. However, the 'elderly' as a specific target market group is usually defined as 'those aged 55 or over'; such a group includes many still working and the market research interest is in the relatively active and well to do sector of the age group. Interviewing samples of the elderly thus defined is not materially different from interviewing a general population sample which will usually include a proportion of older people.

There is, however, a considerable amount of social research among elderly people. Some social research surveys cover all those of pensionable age and are designed to address such issues as the requirements for provision of special housing or social services to the elderly, or to assess the quality of their lives in terms of social contacts, activities, etc. The surveys cover such ground as housing, family and financial circumstances, their health, their ability to look after themselves, whether or not they receive benefits or services, and their attitudes to their life and circumstances.

Other surveys among elderly people are concerned particularly with the needs of the frail elderly and those with mental or physical impairment. The sample sometimes includes those in homes for the aged or geriatric hospitals.

The proportion of those with mental or physical disability is much higher among elderly people than it is in the general population; they are also more likely to suffer from multiple disabilities. Surveys among disabled people are thus likely to include a high proportion who are elderly: on the other hand, the problems and needs of younger disabled persons are often different from those of older people. There is a very wide range of extent and type of disability. Much research is focused on the needs of specific groups, such as those with learning difficulties or mobility problems; some is concerned with specific types of need such as housing adaptations, transport or employment.

*Sampling* [3]

Samples for some focused studies of elderly or disabled people can be selected from the lists of those receiving particular services or benefits; but to obtain a representative sample of all those living in their own homes usually requires a preliminary large scale screening survey to identify people for a later interview (Hunt, 1978). In Britain, a government directive in the 1970s laid down that local authorities should compile registers of people in need to aid them in the planning of provision of housing and services. This led to a number of local surveys involving a first stage screening of a large number of addresses; in many cases this stage was carried out by post.

In surveys that include those living in hospitals and special homes there are often problems in developing an adequate sampling frame of institutions, especially if the private sector is to be included. There is then a second sampling stage to select individuals within the institutions.

*Problems and expectations*

On surveys among elderly or disabled people, there will be some who are unable to give an interview; the decision has to be taken as to whether someone else involved in the person's care can give a proxy interview. Often it is decided that only certain information can validly be given by proxy; either a special shorter questionnaire is provided for this purpose or the interview is confined to certain sections of the questionnaire omitting, for example, the attitude questions. If no proxy is available, then the interview is lost and has to be categorized as nonresponse due to inability to give the interview.

Another problem on surveys among elderly and disabled people is a higher incidence of partial interviews. Sometimes it only becomes apparent during the interview that the respondent is too confused to give a valid interview. Confusion sometimes comes and goes and the interviewer may be able to form a judgement that some questions have been correctly answered and others not, or that the interview with the respondent should be terminated and replaced with a proxy interview if an appropriate person is available.

Respondent fatigue can be another reason for partial interviews. The questionnaires for focused studies among elderly and disabled people are often rather long; the interviewer needs to be sensitive to signs of tiredness or stress (which may lead to confusion) and to be prepared to let the respondent take a break and perhaps have a hot drink. It may even be necessary to come back another day to finish the interview.

This said, problems of confusion, disability or fatigue must not be exaggerated. The majority of elderly and disabled people, including those of advanced years, are quite capable of giving an interview. In an Australian survey of elderly people in Sydney living in their own homes, 89 per cent completed the full interview, 5 per cent completed a shorter version and the remaining 6 per cent were proxy interviews. Among those aged 80 or over, 65 per cent were noted by the interviewers as showing no signs of confusion or memory problems and a further 20 per cent showed only a little (Gibson and Aitkenhead, 1982).

In a survey among elderly people either being supported in their own homes or living in institutions, less than 10 per cent of those in their own homes could not be interviewed in person; however, about two thirds of those living in homes for the elderly and almost all those in geriatric hospitals had to be interviewed by proxy (Morton-Williams, 1979).

Although provision should be made for sample members who are not able to give the interview or who tire easily, and consideration should be given to the fact that hearing may be slightly impaired, interviewers must guard against an assumption that all elderly or disabled people will have problems in hearing, remembering or understanding. A study of interviewer effects on answers to two surveys found that there were stronger effects among the older respondents; this suggests that interviewers have a tendency either to adapt the questions to 'suit' the respondent or to interpret the answers without probing adequately (Collins, 1982/83).

*Making contact*

In general, it is easier to make contact with elderly and disabled sample members who live at home than with other sampled populations because relatively few have jobs. However, interviewers are often surprised to find that quite a large proportion are out a great deal, shopping, visiting friends or family, attending clubs or pursuing hobbies.

When making contact, it must be recognized that elderly and disabled people who are alone in their homes may feel particularly vulnerable and suspicious of strangers at the door. If the contacted person is alone, the interviewer may need to leave the explanatory letter and come back another time when the respondent can arrange for someone else to be present. Saying that the police know about the survey can give added reassurance.

Sample members who are not alone may be protected by the person who cares for them. Carers often have to be convinced of the value of the survey before they will even consider allowing an interview. They are also often prone to underestimate both the ability and willingness of their charge to be interviewed. Interviewers need to be reassuring and accommodating, but to stress the importance of the survey and the need to be able to speak to the sampled person.

When the sampled person lives in sheltered accommodation or in an institution, the interviewer has first to obtain the consent of the person in charge. Usually a special letter for them is required which should be sent in advance to those in charge of institutions.

When agreement in principle has been obtained to interview one or more persons in an institution, the person responsible for the day to day care of the sample member may still raise objections, claiming that the person is too unwell or likely to be distressed by the interview.

Elderly and disabled people tend to be more prone to illness and their illnesses tend to last longer than is the case with other groups; sufficient time therefore needs to be allowed for fieldwork to reduce noncontacts due to illness to an acceptable level.

*Gaining cooperation*

It was indicated in Chapter 2 that, on general population surveys, refusals to be interviewed tended to be higher among the elderly; but surveys specifically concerned with elderly or disabled people and addressing issues of particular relevance to them usually obtain very good response rates. A survey carried out in the Clackmannan district of Scotland covered elderly people living in their own homes, in homes for the elderly and in hospitals; 89 per cent of those living at home and 93 per cent of those in homes for the elderly agreed to be interviewed; 72 per cent of those in hospitals were interviewed, which was in fact 95 per cent of those who were not too ill to be interviewed (Fernando, 1977). Once the sample members realize that the interviewer poses no threat, they often welcome the chance to talk to someone about their circumstances and experiences; they are usually less pressurized because most of them are not working and thus more readily give the time to be interviewed.

Interviewers should be particularly careful to give their initial introduction clearly and slowly enough to be heard properly; speaking too fast can be confusing and daunting and can arouse suspicion. It can also lead to misunderstandings. Sometimes, even though the interviewer may have tried to be clear and unambiguous, the respondent forms the impression that the visitor is from the Social Services Department of the local authority and expects the interview to result in specific action. Respondents may become anxious that the information they are being asked for might affect their benefits. This fear can also arise after the interviewer has left. The explanatory letter left with respondents should pay attention to these points and should always give a number to call for further information. It is a fairly frequent occurrence that a relative returning home after an interview has taken place becomes angry and suspicious on behalf of the elderly or disabled person and needs to be able to reassure themselves about the bona fides of the interviewer and the purpose of survey. Sometimes they claim that the interviewer left the respondent in a distressed state - often to the surprise of the interviewer who was quite likely under the impression that the interview had gone well and that the respondent was quite happy at the end of it. It is possible that some respondents may hide the fact that they are distressed by the interview, but it is more likely that they start to become anxious after the interviewer has left. They may even feel worried that the relative who cares for them will be angry because they agreed to give the interview.

*Interviewer requirements*

Interviewers do not need special training for interviewing elderly or disabled people though they need careful briefing on the demands of a particular survey, especially if those in institutions are included. If measures of physical or mental ability and memory are included, there will need to be training in their administration.

Commonsense suggest that interviewers whose style and dress emphasise the generation gap should be avoided, but any well trained and experienced interviewer can gain the cooperation of elderly and disabled people and carry out a satisfactory interview. It should be stressed that they should expect sample members to be able to cope fully with the question-and-answer process, though they should, of course, be alert to the possibility that this may not be the case. They should be prepared to slow down and to repeat what they have said if necessary and should on no account adapt the questions or fail to probe an ambiguous answer as this can lead to them inadvertently affecting the results.

Interviewers need to be aware that the subject matter of a survey can sometimes cause distress to elderly or disabled respondents, especially if the interview touches on family members, bereavement or loneliness. A sympathetic ear and the patience to allow the respondent to digress a little and talk about the matter is usually all that is required. For the same reason, interviewers should not be in a hurry to leave as soon as the interview is finished in order to ensure that the respondent is not left in an upset state. Because many respondents are pleased to have contact with someone and are not pressurized for time, elderly people in particular may be prone to digress. There are thus a number of factors which lead to greater variability of interview length than is the case in general population surveys.

It is sometimes difficult for the interviewer to obtain privacy for the interview, whether from spouse or carer; occasionally the presence of someone else is a condition for giving the interview. The presence of another should be noted as it might affect the respondent's frankness in their answers to certain questions.

Interviews with some elderly or disabled people can be very tiring for the interviewers as they try to keep to the questioning procedures and control digressions. This taken in conjunction with the much greater variability in the time needed to carry out the interview, should be reflected in the number of interviews per day that interviewers are expected to achieve.

Sometimes, the conditions in which elderly or disabled people live and their mental state cause great distress to interviewers who very much want to do something to help. It is a service both to the interviewer and the respondent to provide a form for interviewers to complete that can be sent either to the respondent's general practitioner or to Social Services. Respondents' permission should, however, always be sought and their wishes respected.

## Ethnic minority surveys

Research studies focused on ethnic minorities are virtually all funded by the public sector. There are two main types of issues addressed by survey research: those to do with experiences of racial discrimination and attitudes towards the wider society, and those to do with their position within society in terms of housing, jobs, income etc. The former cover what are likely to be very emotive subjects whereas the latter are designed to collect mainly factual information.

Some surveys are primarily concerned with racism as related to skin colour and are confined, in Britain, to those from the Caribbean, the African and Indian subcontinents and adjacent areas; others include additional major ethnic subgroups such as Greeks, Turks, Chinese and those from Northern Ireland or the Irish Republic.

### Identifying members of ethnic minorities

As immigrant communities become established over generations and intermarry with other groups, the problem of identifying members of ethnic minorities become more difficult. Questions about country of birth, for example, became less and less reliable as ethnic identifiers. Furthermore, the attempt to identify members of ethnic minorities sometimes arouses hostility: OPCS decided to drop questions about ethnic origin from the 1981 Census because of objections from pressure groups, even though actual question tests had gone reasonably well. The purpose in collecting the information was to provide a basis for assessing whether certain of their needs (such as for housing) were being met to the same degree as those of other sections of the population, but some members of ethnic groups considered that the data could be misused to their disadvantage.

In 1991, after much consultation with ethnic community leaders during the pre-census period and a certain amount of pretesting, it was decided to include two questions in the Census; the first asked for the country of birth for residents of the address; the second asked for a simple self definition of ethnic group: a number of precoded ethnic groups were listed with space for further description for those who did not feel themselves to be adequately covered. This information can be used to identify areas in the country with a particularly high density of ethnic minority people in general or in terms of particular subgroups.

The Census is the only standard and systematic source of information that is available to help design national samples of ethnic minority people. Therefore, to obtain a representative sample, it is necessary first to carry out a screening survey of a large number of addresses.[4] Some surveys among ethnic minorities are confined to areas where they are concentrated. Whereas it is often feasible to carry out a postal screening survey to find a sample of elderly or disabled people, screening operations to find members of ethnic minorities need to be carried out face to face: response to a postal questionnaire would be likely to be low among the very groups it was designed to identify due to suspicion about the purpose of the survey.

*Interviewer requirements*

Screening surveys can be carried out by a general fieldforce but, for the interview proper, the question arises as to whether the interviewer should belong to the same ethnic group as the respondent. Much of the research on this issue has been carried out in the United States where the effects of white and black interviewers on survey results have been compared.

The findings have indicated that race of interviewer can affect the answers to attitude questions that are specifically concerned with racial issues (Hyman et al., 1954; Athey et al., 1960; Williams, 1968; Hatchett and Schuman, 1976). Effects are particularly marked on questions to do with militant protest and hostility towards whites, views on which are less strongly expressed to white interviewers (Schuman and Converse, 1971). No significant differences were found in response rates achieved by black and white interviewers. The applicability of the US experience to ethnic surveys in Britain, and the nature of the problems peculiar to Britain, are discussed in Jowell and Airey (1975).

Ethnic matching of interviewers with respondents is thus advisable on certain sorts of attitude survey - not only for interviewing members of ethnic minorities; on general population surveys concerned with racial issues answers of whites to racial attitude questions have also been found to be affected by race of interviewer (Athey et al., 1960).

On surveys among ethnic minorities that are not concerned with racial attitudes, the main problem for interviewers is that of language: in the US, many Hispanics do not speak good English; in Britain, the language spoken at home by Asian families might be one of several common on the Indian subcontinent. In some subcultures the women mix little with those outside their community and may have little opportunity to learn English. Language matching of respondent and interviewer is therefore needed.

During the screening interview, the most comfortable language for each person eligible for the main survey should be established. A team of interviewers should be recruited to meet the requirements in each geographical area. Fortunately, many Asians speak more than one Asian language fluently.

The interviewers have to be trained in basic interviewer technique as well as in the requirements of the particular survey. Versions of the explanatory letter, sample introductions and questionnaires have to be provided in all the main languages. In training sessions, ample time should be allowed for discussions of strategies, tactics and skills necessary to obtain good response rates as the trainees may have useful information about the problems likely to be met with in trying to obtain cooperation from particular subgroups. For example, there may be particular times of the day or days of the week related to religious practices when it is inadvisable to call; there may be problems in making contact with women sample members or in interviewing them in private. In some cases, it may be necessary for the interviewer to be of the same sex as the respondent.

Organizing fieldwork on surveys requiring language matching can be complex and often involves interviewers working in overlapping areas, or being prepared to travel to cover isolated addresses.

### People on the move

A number of surveys are carried out among people on the move, usually either to do with the journey itself or to do with the destination of the journey. These usually involve some sort of 'flow sampling' procedure such as was briefly described in Chapter 3, though sometimes quota sampling methods are used.

Research to help plan road development schemes or to assess public transport needs frequently require motorist to be stopped and questioned as to the origin and destination of their journey, how often they make this particular journey and possibly also why they are travelling by car rather than by other means. To carry out such a survey requires the help of the police to actually stop the cars and to provide space on the road for the motorists to park while they are interviewed. As motorists are often in a hurry and resent any delay to their journey, the questionnaire has to be very short; interviewers usually wear special 'day-glo' jackets or sashes to prevent accidents; they need to be very clear, brisk and efficient in explaining why the motorist has been stopped and in asking the questions.

Similar surveys may take place on public transport, at railway stations or airports either to ask about the journey itself, the facilities provided or, as in the OPCS International Passenger Survey, to obtain information on the purposes of overseas travel, where people have travelled to, length of stay abroad, amount spent overseas, and so on. Some people in these situations will be simply waiting and will be pleased to give an interview; others may be in a hurry and less willing to stop for an interview; people can also change from waiting mode to moving mode as flights are called, trains arrive or gates opened for embarkation. Again questionnaires have to be short to cover all eventualities. The requirement is sometimes less stringent on homeward journeys from overseas. Interviewers need to be able to establish their authority quickly and assertively and to move as speedily as possible into asking the questions.

Surveys on use of, and attitudes to, leisure facilities, such as museums, sports complexes, zoos, parks or areas of countryside, may require interviews with visitors as they enter or leave the place. There is less likelihood that the people approached for interview in these situations will be pressed for time but nonetheless questionnaires should be no longer than fifteen minutes unless it is possible to take the respondents to a place where they can sit down.

Other types of survey require samples of people using particular services such as benefit offices or job centres, or attending doctors' surgeries. Sometimes, the purpose will be only to collect names and addresses and to ask permission to visit the person at home in order to interview them. If the interview is to be carried out at the time they are contacted, there may be problems in gaining cooperation: on the one hand, if they are asked for an interview while waiting, they may feel that they are going to lose their place in the cue and have an extra long wait; on the other, if the interview is requested after their case has been dealt with, their compliance might be affected by how long they had to wait to be attended to and even by how they felt their case was treated. Such interviews also need to be restricted to about fifteen minutes and should always take place in private, which requires provision of a room for that purpose.

When the interview has to be conducted in private in these situations, it is usually necessary to have at least two interviewers on duty, one to conduct the sampling operation and one or more to carry out the interviews, otherwise it is impossible to ensure that a random sample has been obtained.

## Surveys on sensitive topics

Many surveys include questions that might be considered by respondents to be over-personal, embarrassing or threatening to their self esteem. Questions on income usually meet with some refusal to answer, varying in degree according to the type of question and context; socially taboo subjects such as sexual behaviour commonly get about 5 per cent of respondents refusing to answer questions on them; Bradburn, Sudman & Associates (1979) showed that there tends to be over-reporting of socially approved behaviour and experiences and under-reporting of those that meet with social disapproval.  They also found that there was more refusal to answer personal or threatening questions when someone else was present at the interview; young adults being interviewed in the presence of a parent were the most reticent.  In a survey among teenage boys on whether they had committed crimes of theft, Belson (1975) went to great lengths to provide a neutral interviewing venue away from the respondent's home.

Sensitive questions that form only part of a questionnaire need not be referred to during the introduction to the survey unless they constitute the main focus for the research.  Experience and commonsense indicate that they should not be positioned right at the beginning of the interview, before a certain amount of trust has been built up between interviewer and respondent; nor should they be right at the end, using what Warwick and Lininger (1975) describe as the 'hit-and-run' technique, as this can leave the respondent angry and less inclined to give information in the future.  They should be positioned within a context of other, non-threatening, questions that lead sensibly on to the sensitive questions and the interviewer should explain the need for the information.

### Mode of interview

There is no one best mode of interview for surveys that contain sensitive questions or for surveys on sensitive topics.  Groves and Kahn (1979) found respondents to be more reticent about their income and some other sensitive topics over the telephone than face to face, but a number of other researchers have found that telephone interviewing obtained somewhat more valid answers (Henson, Roth and Cannell, 1974; Rogers, 1976; Bradburn et al., 1979; Sykes and Collins, 1987; McQueen, 1989). Bradburn et al. (op.cit.) obtained better cooperation over the telephone to a survey on drunken driving (among those charged with the offence) but better cooperation face to face on bankruptcy (among a sample of people recently declared bankrupt).  If other factors, such as a short questionnaire, indicate that a telephone could be a viable mode for the survey, then the indications are that the data will certainly be no less valid than it would be from a face to face interview.

A major survey of British Sexual Attitudes and Lifestyles, carried out by SCPR, required an interview of 40 to 60 minutes; face to face interviewing was therefore used (Wellings et al., 1990). The questionnaire included a number of potentially embarrassing questions about sexual behaviour and experience, including questions on behaviour that carries a certain amount of social disapproval. These were presented in a self completion booklet. There were different versions for men and women and the booklet was presented to the respondent at an appropriate point during the interview. The respondent completed it and immediately placed it in a sealed envelope labelled 'Confidential' and identified only by a number. For some sensitive attitude questions (which were in the face to face interview section), the answers were presented on cards and respondents had only to pick out the letter against the answer of their choice. Techniques such as these can do much to reduce embarrassment for both interviewer and respondent.

## Gaining cooperation

Surveys on sensitive subjects tend to get higher refusal rates than general population surveys on other topics; response is usually 60 to 68 per cent rather than 70 to 80 per cent. Response to the British Sexual Attitudes and Lifestyle survey was 63 per cent. This may be compared with a response rate of around 72 per cent on the annual British Social Attitudes Surveys.[5] The two surveys had interviews of similar length and the samples were drawn in the same way from the small users Postcode Address File.

The Sexual Attitudes and Lifestyle Survey covered only those aged 16 to 59; refusals were slightly higher among men aged 45 to 59 than amongst other groups.

Two years of development work preceded fieldwork on this study in order to optimize its acceptance and validity. It started with qualitative work to explore sexual attitudes, the language that people used to talk about their views, experiences and behaviour, the type of language respondents would like the interviewer to use, what parts of the information given to respondents about the purpose of the survey were most important in deciding to give the interview and what subjects they felt most uncomfortable discussing. This was followed by several small scale pilots to develop and test the questionnaire and finally by a feasibility study with an achieved sample of around 1,000.

It emerged from the development work that a prime requirement was that the interviewer should have a non-judgemental approach; other researchers have shown that interviewers who feel embarrassed to ask for cooperation and who expect people to refuse or to give face-saving erroneous answers are likely to produce the effects they expect (Bradburn et al., 1979). Being non-judgemental was more important than interviewer characteristics such as age and gender (Wellings et al., 1990).

For surveys on sensitive topics, assurances of the confidentiality of the information given are particularly important. Those selected for interview also need to have an understanding as to why the information is needed.

Establishing the credentials of the funders and researchers also plays a useful role in gaining cooperation. In the Sexual Attitudes and Lifestyles Survey, the need for the data to help combat the AIDS epidemic and to safeguard our children and future generations was the most compelling reason for taking part. That there had never been a British survey on this topic was also a factor. For some sample members, it was reassuring to tell them in advance that the most personal questions would be put to them in a confidential booklet that they would seal in an envelope without its being seen by the interviewer.

As with all surveys, the initial introduction to the person first contacted should be kept short, unless that person demands more information at that point. When the person to be interviewed has been identified, more information should be given to ensure they understand the nature of the survey. It is generally agreed that a straightforward honest description of the survey works best; any attempt to deceive when trying to obtain cooperation is likely to backfire during the interview. A survey by SCPR in the London Borough of Hackney on the take up of state benefits required detailed information on household income in order to identify people eligible for but not receiving benefit. Interviewers explained to respondents that the information was needed in order to establish whether they might be able to claim benefits they were not at present receiving. It was made clear that the survey organization could not grant benefits but would tell respondents whether they appeared, from the information given, to be eligible. The response rate was 71 per cent in the kind of inner city area that would normally yield a much lower response rate.

Special attention to the content of the explanatory letter to be given to respondents is particularly necessary when the subject is a sensitive one. Sometimes it is helpful to provide additional informational leaflets about the survey, its purpose, intended uses and its funding. It is generally agreed that letters should not be sent in advance as this would be likely to generate a large number of refusals both in advance by letter or telephone and to the interviewer. The content of the letter and any additional leaflets should be evaluated during the development work.

*Interviewer requirements*

Mature and experienced interviewers should where possible be used on this type of survey; but the main requirement is that the interviewers should not feel embarrassed or diffident about describing the purpose of the survey or asking the questions. Any such feelings are likely to be picked up by the respondent. When SCPR were setting up the Sexual Attitudes and Lifestyle Survey, it was found that some quite experienced interviewers did not feel capable of working on it; others maintained that it was the most interesting and rewarding survey they had undertaken. The more experienced interviewers on the survey obtained higher response rates than the less experienced.

It is essential that interviewers understand why the information is required and maintain a matter-of-fact, confident and professional manner. The respondents will usually take their cue from the interviewer and respond in a similar matter-of-fact way. Interviewers need to be very thoroughly briefed and to practise introducing the survey and asking the questions. The discussions, demonstrations and role playing practice at the briefing can do much to defuse any embarrassment that even confident interviewers may feel.

## Development work

The need for adequate development work has been a constant theme throughout this book. No apologies are offered for returning to it in the final words.

Adequate development work is particularly essential for the more unusual types of survey described in this chapter, and for none more so than surveys on sensitive topics.

In addition to attention to the content of the questionnaire and ways of wording and presenting the questions, the development work should include discussions with both interviewers and respondents to establish how best to introduce the survey and gain cooperation. The enormous fund of basic practical knowledge that experienced interviewers build up should be tapped; they should be treated as part of the research team and asked to collect what information they can about reasons for accepting or refusing the interview. They can contribute many useful ideas for the design of the questionnaire and the organization of the survey.

## Notes

1   For further reading on sampling methods in business-to-business marketing research, see Sutherland (1991) and McIntosh (1970 & 1975).
2   See Smith & Bard (1989) and Smith & Dexter (1991) for a review of problems in classifying business respondents and in identifying the decision making units in businesses.
3   Hoinville (1983) usefully reviews the methods and problems of drawing samples of the elderly. It also has relevance for designing samples of disabled people.
4   The problems of sampling ethnic minority groups and experiments in ways of doing so are discussed in Brown and Ritchie (1984).
5   For comparative purposes, the response rate of the Sexual Attitudes and Lifestyle Survey has been calculated in the same way as that of the British Social Attitudes Surveys. The former, however, is based on a PAF sample whereas the sample of the latter was drawn from the electoral register. PAF based samples tend to get slightly lower response rates than those from the electoral register. Johnson et al. (1992) have presented the response rate for the Sexual Attitudes Survey on various bases which provide slightly higher participation rates.

# Appendix I
# Address record form

The example of an Address Record Form given here is the standard SCPR form used for samples drawn from the Postcode Address (small users) File (PAF). It incorporates a procedure for the random selection of one adult for interview from the issued address. The first page presents a grid on which the interviewer records the details of each call at the address with a space for notes at the bottom. This helps the interviewer to organise calls and also enables checks to be made that, where necessary, at least four calls on different days and at different times have been made, including evening or weekend calls.

The selection of an individual for interview entails first establishing how many households there are at the address; if more than one, one is selected by the random procedure set out. The procedure is then repeated, with appropriate modification, to select one adult. The form is set out in questionnaire style and interviewers are trained to use it as such.

At the top of the front page of the form are two labels: the address label and the 'selection' label. The 'selection' label contains two rows of figures: the upper one runs from two to nine and refers to the number of people eligible to be included in the sample who live at the address. (If there was only one person, he or she would be asked for the interview.) The second row of figures is a computer generated set equivalent to one row in the selection grid described in Chapter 3. It will vary from address to address. The interviewer lists all eligible people at the address in alphabetical order of first name (see question 13) which has the effect of ordering them from 1 - $n$; reference is then made to the 'selection' label to identify the person to be asked to give the interview. Referring to the example given on the form, if there were four eligible adults in the household, the person listed as Number 3 at question 13 would be the one selected. No substitution for this person is allowed.

The final outcome of the interviewer's attempts to obtain the interview are recorded on the last page of the form.

Head Office: 35 NORTHAMPTON SQUARE,    Field and DP Office: BRENTWOOD, ESSEX
LONDON EC1V 0AX Telephone 071-250 1866    Northern Field Office: DARLINGTON, CO. DURHAM

**ADDRESS RECORD FORM (ARF)**

ADDRESS                          SELECTION LABEL

|  |  |
|--|--|

Ser.No. 01-04
Card 01 05-06
Field area 07
Sample point 08-10

14 Riverside Road
Bath
BA2 0SH

No. in household
2  3  4  5  6  7  8  9
Selected person no:
2  1  3  2  4  7  6  5

Telephone
number:

Interviewer Name ...                    ... and No.                        11-14

CALLS RECORD (Note all personal visits, even if no reply)          TNC 15-16

| VISIT NUMBER | 01 | 02 | 03 | 04 | 05 | 06 | 07 | 08 | 09 | 10 | 11 | 12 |
|---|---|---|---|---|---|---|---|---|---|---|---|---|
| TIME OF DAY: | | | | | | | | | | | | |
| Up to noon | 1 | 1 | 1 | 1 | 1 | 1 | 1 | 1 | 1 | 1 | 1 | 1 |
| 1201-1400 | 2 | 2 | 2 | 2 | 2 | 2 | 2 | 2 | 2 | 2 | 2 | 2 |
| 1401-1700 | 3 | 3 | 3 | 3 | 3 | 3 | 3 | 3 | 3 | 3 | 3 | 3 |
| 1701-1900 | 4 | 4 | 4 | 4 | 4 | 4 | 4 | 4 | 4 | 4 | 4 | 4 |
| 1900 or later | 5 | 5 | 5 | 5 | 5 | 5 | 5 | 5 | 5 | 5 | 5 | 5 |

DATE:
i)   Day (Mon = 1, Tues = 2 etc)

ii)  Date

iii) Month

EXACT TIME OF CALL

NOTES

ALWAYS RETURN ARF SEPARATELY FROM QUESTIONNAIRE

| COMPLETE AS FAR AS FINAL OUTCOME |
|---|

1. IS THIS ADDRESS TRACEABLE, RESIDENTIAL AND OCCUPIED?

| | | |
|---|---|---|
| Yes | A | GO TO Q.3 |
| No | B | ANSWER Q.2 |

17-18

**IF NO AT Q.1**

2. WHY NOT?

| | |
|---|---|
| Insufficient address | 01 |
| Not traced (call office before returning) | 02 |
| Not yet built/not yet ready for occupation | 03 |
| Derelict/demolished | 04  *END |
| Empty | 05 |
| Business/industrial only (no private dwellings) | 06 |
| Institution only (no private dwellings) | 07 |
| Other (please give details) | 08 |

**IF YES AT Q.1**

3. ESTABLISH NUMBER OF <u>OCCUPIED</u> DWELLING UNITS COVERED BY ADDRESS:
(IF NOT KNOWN, TREAT AS OCCUPIED)

| IF NECESSARY, ASK: |
|---|

i) Can I just check, is this *house/bungalow* occupied as a single dwelling, or is it split up into flats or bedsitters?

ii) How many of those *flats/bedsitters* are <u>occupied</u> at the present time?

| | | | |
|---|---|---|---|
| NUMBER OF OCCUPIED UNITS | ☐☐ | GO TO Q.4 | 19-20 |
| No contact made with anyone at address | A | RING CODE → | 21* END |
| Information refused | B | RING CODE → | 22* END |

4. INTERVIEWER SUMMARY:

| | | |
|---|---|---|
| 1 unit only | A | GO TO Q.10 |
| 2-12 units | B | GO TO Q.5 |
| 13+ units | C | GO TO Q.7 |

**IF 2-12 UNITS**

5. LIST ALL OCCUPIED DWELLING UNITS AT ADDRESS

- in flat/room number order

or
- from bottom to top of building, left to right, front to back

| DWELLING UNIT | 'DU' CODE | DWELLING UNIT | 'DU' CODE |
|---|---|---|---|
| | 01 | | 07 |
| | 02 | | 08 |
| | 03 | | 09 |
| | 04 | | 10 |
| | 05 | | 11 |
| | 06 | | 12 |

**IF 2-12 UNITS**

6. LOOK AT SELECTION LABEL ON PAGE 1.

 i)   "PERSON/DU" ROW - Find number corresponding to total number of DUs

 ii)  "SELECT" ROW   - Number beneath total number of DUs is SELECTED DU
                       CODE NUMBER.  RING ON GRID.

 iii) **GO TO Q8.**

**IF 13+ UNITS**

7. CODE NUMBER OF SELECTED DU IS ON BACK OF PROJECT INSTRUCTIONS

**IF 2+ UNITS**

8. ENTER 'DU CODE' OF SELECTED DU                      ☐☐        21-22

9. RECORD FLAT NUMBER/DETAILS OF LOCATION OF SELECTED UNIT:

**ALL (Q.4 A-C)**

10. SEEK CONTACT WITH RESPONSIBLE ADULT AT ADDRESS AND INTRODUCE SURVEY

| | | |
|---|---|---|
| Contact made | A | **ANSWER Q.11** |
| Contact <u>not</u> made with responsible adult | B | **RING CODE** → |

23*
END

**IF CONTACT MADE**

11. ASK: Including yourself, how many people aged 18 or over live
in this *house/flat/part of the accommodation?*

| | | |
|---|---|---|
| No. of people aged 18+ | ☐☐ | **GO TO Q.12** |
| Information refused | A | **RING CODE** → |

23-24

24*
END

| INCLUDE | EXCLUDE |
|---|---|
| ● PEOPLE WHO NORMALLY LIVE AT ADDRESS WHO ARE AWAY FOR UNDER 6 MONTHS | ● PEOPLE AGED 18+ WHO LIVE ELSE-WHERE TO STUDY OR WORK |
| ● PEOPLE AWAY ON WORK FOR WHOM THIS IS THE MAIN ADDRESS | ● SPOUSES WHO ARE SEPARATED AND NO LONGER RESIDENT |
| ● BOARDERS AND LODGERS | ● PEOPLE AWAY FOR 6 MONTHS OR MORE |

**IF INFORMATION OBTAINED**

12. INTERVIEWER SUMMARY

| | | |
|---|---|---|
| 1 person only | A | **GO TO Q.16** |
| 2-12 persons | B | **GO TO Q.13** |
| 13+ persons | C | **GO TO Q.14** |

**IF 2-12 PERSONS**

13a. ASK FOR FIRST NAME OR INITIAL OF EACH PERSON. LIST IN ALPHABETICAL ORDER.

| FIRST NAME OR INITIAL | PERSON NUMBER | FIRST NAME OR INITIAL | PERSON NUMBER |
|---|---|---|---|
| | 01 | | 07 |
| | 02 | | 08 |
| | 03 | | 09 |
| | 04 | | 10 |
| | 05 | | 11 |
| | 06 | | 12 |

b. LOOK AT SELECTION LABEL ON PAGE 1

i) "PERSON/DU" ROW - Find number corresponding to total number of persons

ii) "SELECT" ROW   - Number beneath total number of persons is SELECTED PERSON NUMBER. RING ON GRID ABOVE.

iii) **GO TO Q.15**

**IF 13+ PERSONS**

14. PERSON NUMBER OF SELECTED PERSON IS ON BACK OF PROJECT INSTRUCTIONS.

**IF 2+ PERSONS**

15. ENTER 'PERSON NUMBER' OF SELECTED PERSON      [ ][ ]    25-26

ALL (Q.12 A-C)

16. RECORD FULL NAME OF SELECTED PERSON:

17. OUTCOME OF INTERVIEW ATTEMPTS

    **CODE ONE ONLY**

| | |
|---|---|
| Interview obtained: - Full | 51  * END |
| - Partial | 52 |

No interview obtained (**RING CODE BELOW AND RECORD DETAILS IN BOX**)

| | |
|---|---|
| - No contact with selected person after 4+ calls | 71 |
| - Personal refusal by selected person | 72 |
| - Proxy refusal (on behalf of selected person) | 73 |
| - Broken appointment, no recontact | 74 |
| - Ill at home during survey period | 75  * END |
| - Away/in hospital during survey period | 76 |
| - Selected person senile/incapacitated | 77 |
| - Inadequate English | 78 |
| - Other reason | 79 |

**FULL REASON FOR OUTCOME CODES 71-79**

# Appendix II
# Outline training module

The following are notes for use in a training school for new interviewers. It incorporates social skills training techniques and includes at the back a number of suggested handouts. The training session may look time-consuming at first glance but can be compressed into one and a half to two hours, if necessary. It may entail an extension of the total time normally devoted to training in doorstep techniques, but is not all additional time: some of the ground that would ordinarily be covered in interviewer training is included in this training module, such as preparation, how response rate is measured and respondent selection procedures.

**1.    Setting the scene and initial morale building**  (very brief)

Knocking on the door of a total stranger and asking them to do an interview is often the most daunting thing about interviewing at first;

BUT:    -   Most people will readily agree to take part/be pleased to see you.

           -   Most will thoroughly enjoy the interview/feel it was worthwhile.

           -   You will meet a lot of very pleasant and interesting people.

Getting a good 'response rate' *is* very important.

It is calculated like this:

e.g.    30 addresses issued, minus 4 'deadwood' (empty/businesses).  Therefore 26 addresses at which interview should be obtained.   If 21 interviews are obtained, the 'response rate' is 21 expressed as a percentage of the 26 which were the maximum that could be obtained:

$$\frac{21}{26} \quad x \quad 100 = 81\%$$

Everyone should try to get 100 per cent!  Some of you will!!  But most will get rather less; it will depend a bit on area; but also on *YOUR* skill in putting over the survey.

**2.    Preliminary preparation**

This is essential: -    a) to avoid wasting time through lack of organization and forethought;

                           b) to feel *confident* that you know what to do.

So what can you do to prepare yourself for your first trip to the field?  *Call for response from trainees then amplify the following:*

           -   Check addresses issued.

           -   Read all written instructions.

           -   Learn about the purpose of survey.

           -   Organize all materials you will need (e.g., identity card, explanatory letter).

           -   Plan route to the area and develop a strategy for tackling addresses in different parts of the area.

           -   Be thoroughly familiar with questionnaire.

**HANDOUT 1** (see end of training module notes)

**3.    Demonstration of doorstep procedure**

Points to make:

-    There is no one right way to introduce a survey; find the way that suits *you*.

-    Be flexible and adaptable to the person on the doorstep.

DEMONSTRATION OF GOOD, BAD AND INDIFFERENT INTRODUCTIONS BY TRAINER AND ASSISTANT
Demonstrate all three and then discuss. Trainees to listen and watch  critically and to be prepared to discuss and compare.

**4.    Discussion and analysis of introductions demonstrated**

-    Compare and contrast them. Which was the best? Why/in what way?

-    Lead on to establish basic principles (remember - the first goal is to be given a chance to explain what you want):

    a)    Prepare and *practise* a *short* initial introduction in advance. (Don't go into detail unless/until asked.)

    b)    Look at them and smile!  Be friendly, cheerful, interested.

    c)    Speak *clearly*, not too fast, and loudly enough to be heard.

    d)    Show identity card! Have explanatory letter, leaflet and Respondent Selection sheet to hand.

*Some rules:*

In your initial introduction, you *must:*

-    Check the address.
-    Show your identity card.
-    Mention the organization you work for.
-    Say what the survey is about (briefly).
-    Mention who the survey is for/who is funding it.

*Practice:*

-    Trainees take a few minutes to write down a basic introduction. Then work in pairs practising saying it and giving each other feedback. (Preferably stand up and face each other).

Comments and questions on this section

*Points to make:*

- Practise your introduction until it comes naturally to you and you can put yourself into it. (Get name of organization and funder tripping off your tongue.)

- There is no one right way to introduce a survey; find the one that suits you.

- Be flexible and adapt your approach according to the way the person responds.

**HANDOUT 2**     Use it to summarize and drive home main points.

**HANDOUT 3**     This is a copy of a *good* introduction. Draw attention to the points at the bottom.


## 5.     Respondent selection procedure

(The example here is for a procedure using random selection of one adult from those living at an address, addresses selected from the Postcode Address File.)

What it's for and why we need it:
- Random sampling.
- What is Post Code Address File (PAF) and why used?
- The basics of the selection process.

Ways of introducing the selection procedure. (Three examples already given in demonstration)

Being able to answer questions about the selection procedure.

Involve the contacted person in the process.

**HAND OUT SELECTION SHEET** and work through examples with trainees asking questions:
- simple one person one household example;
- two person, contacted person selected;
- three person, 'other adult' selected.

(More examples will be given at the briefing.)


## 6.     If selected person is not the one you are talking to

Continue with final example, trainee asking questions, to demonstrate and drive home:
- Avoid proxy refusals.
- Repeat basic introduction; don't assume he/she has been properly informed about the survey.
- Show identity card.

**7.    Role playing practice** (Trainer to be respondent)

Three or four trainees selected at random to role play interviewer on doorstep; to go through whole introduction including selection procedure.

Trainer to act as 'contact' on the doorstep.  The object here is to increase familiarity with *basic procedures* and thus confidence; 'contact' should be *fairly easy going*, asking for information or clarification or indicating that they can't do it just now.  (Reluctance and refusal will be dealt with later.)

When mistakes are made, ask other trainees to suggest an alternative approach.

On completion, affirm that most people will be like this, *easy to persuade to take part.*

But now we are going to move on to more difficult situations and to consider the skill involved in obtaining cooperation in more depth.


**8.    The first contact**

**a)    *What might people be doing?***

'All think back to last evening at home; at 7.00 o'clock, what were you doing?' (Trainer point at random to collect variety of different activities.)

'These are only some of the things that people might be doing when you call'.  (Ask trainees to think of others.)  How willing to stop and answer door?

**b)    *Reactions to finding a stranger on the doorstep***

'You answer the door and find a total stranger there saying something about a survey they want you to help with.  What do you think would go through your mind while listening to this?'

Also ask: How might an old lady living alone feel? A well-to-do professional business man? An 18 year old with a busy social life?

Use this to increase awareness of:

-    *Variations in willingness to stop what they're doing.* (Is the food going to burn?  Will my guests think I'm rude? etc., etc.)

-    *Possible suspicions of and reactions to a stranger on the doorstep:*
     Afraid:      Is it a thief?
     Defensive:  Is it a salesman/Jehovah's Witness?
     Angry:       Are they going to waste my time?   Are they going pressurize me into something?  Ask for a donation?  Want me to do something difficult?

### 9.    Importance of observation

'You have been thinking into the mind of the person on the doorstep; it's very important to be aware of what might be going on in their mind.  How might you be able to tell how they feel?'  (Throw the following in if not mentioned.)

- How wide do they open the door?
- Are they looking you in the eye or avoiding your eyes/glancing over their shoulder?
- Are they smiling and friendly?  Looking expressionless?  Scowling?  Looking flustered/upset/angry?
- Is their body relaxed and open or rigid and held back?
- Is their verbal greeting friendly or tense or impatient?
- Are there cooking smells?  Sounds of quarrelling?

There are many clues that you will learn to look out for.  SO BE OBSERVANT!

### 10.    How the interviewer might deal with possible adverse reactions

There are *three* main ways: REASSURE THEM, BE POSITIVE ABOUT BENEFITS, APPEAL TO THEIR ALTRUISM (ask for help).

#### Give reassurance/avoid being threatening

- Dress appropriately.
- Step back from the door.
- Relaxed friendly manner: look them in the eyes and SMILE!  (It's hard to be rude to someone who is smiling and looking at you.)
- Present your authority (identity card and, perhaps, letter).
- Don't be over-familiar (use formal politeness).
- Don't be patronizing (example of patronizing introduction).
- Verbal reassurances ('not selling'; confidentiality; police have been informed).

#### Be POSITIVE about the benefits from taking part

- Turn on the charm!  (Many agree to be interviewed because they like the interviewer.)  Sometimes it is helpful to admire the cat, the garden, the decorations etc.  (This shows an interest in them as a person.)  Perhaps make a small joke.

- Explain the purpose of the survey clearly, so that they realize it is important, serious and worthwhile.

*Appeal to altruism*

People like to help others and often respond to appeals for help

- Indicate that survey has a socially useful purpose.
- Ask for help with the survey.
- Ask for help in sorting out who to interview.

(Once a helping bond has been established, they are less likely to refuse)

### (HANDOUT 4)

### 11.    Dealing with reluctance and questions

Think of it as a continuum: most people will be very willing to be interviewed, some will be a little bit reluctant, a few will be more definitely reluctant, and one person here or there will definitely be against doing an interview.

BUT:    people will vary from time to time, according to what they are doing and how they are feeling - SO BE PREPARED TO WITHDRAW AND COME BACK ANOTHER TIME

### *Active listening technique*

Listen carefully to how the contacted person expresses reluctance and, where appropriate, use the 'active listening technique': rephrase what they have said and reflect it back to them:

Respondent:          'I'm just cooking the supper.'

Interviewer:          'I can see this isn't a good time to call.  I'll leave you this letter to read and call again another time.'

Trainer to throw out a number of different examples of reluctance and trainees to suggest 'active listening' ways of responding.

### *Role playing:*

- Trainees to introduce survey to Trainer who responds with reluctance.
- Trainees to suggest alternative ways of persuading (see below for main types of reluctance that should be illustrated).

### *Illustrate main types of reluctance:* (Aggressive as well as defensive respondents)

1   What is the survey about?/What's it for?/Who's it for?/Who did you say you were from?
2   I'm busy at the moment/I'm just cooking/I'm just going out, etc.

3   How long will it take?/I can't spare many minutes.

4   I'm much too busy/I don't have time for that sort of thing/I'm out almost every evening.

5   (Suspicions or reservations about the survey.)   Are you selling something?/I don't want to answer any personal questions.

6   Why does it have to be me?/You should talk to my husband, he's interested in that sort of thing/I don't know enough about that.

7   I'm not interested/I don't want to do it/I can't be bothered with it.

8   (Non specific.) Well, er.../I don't really think so/Well.... I don't know....

Bring out the basic principles for dealing with reluctance: (stress the three principles - GIVE REASSURANCE, BE POSITIVE, APPEAL TO ALTRUISM).

### Give reassurance and information

-   Acknowledge the reasonableness of their fear, suspicion or shortage of time ('active listening').
-   How long interview will take (don't lie).
-   Completely confidential (no names or addresses on questionnaire).
-   Can check with the police.
-   You can come back another time if now is not convenient.
-   Explain how address was selected.
-   Explain that have to select a person at random and cannot substitute anyone else.
-   Use sponsor's letter or leaflet about survey research.
-   Relaxed friendly manner; don't pressurize.  Always let them think they have the option to refuse.

### Be positive about the benefits from taking part

-   Smile and be charming and polite (however they respond).
-   'Everyone has found the interview interesting and enjoyable.'
-   Explain purpose of survey more fully - worthwhile and important.
-   An opportunity for them to give their views/to have a say in planning, etc./everyone's views equally important, not just the well informed.

### Appeal to altruism

-   Survey will help others.
-   they help to make survey successful (you are not allowed to take any substitutes/it's easy to get the views of people who are not busy, so busy people's views get less well covered).

**BE FLEXIBLE:**    Change tack - offer positive benefits as well as reassurance.

Withdraw and come back another time, especially if you feel a refusal is imminent.

**BE SENSITIVE**:    Observe and listen carefully:

Are they *afraid* to let you in because they are alone?

Are they *ashamed* to let you in because the house is untidy?

Are they upset about something/angry/worried?

**REMEMBER:**    MOST PEOPLE HATE TO SAY 'NO', ESPECIALLY TO SOMEONE WHO IS PLEASANT AND SMILING.

## 12.    Dealing with refusals

Be *extra* polite but not apologetic:

Judge whether it might be worth leaving the letter and calling again. It often is, and persistence pays off.

If you get more than one refusal, keep your morale up:

- Have a break and a cup of tea!
- Remember the pleasant and welcoming people you have met.
- Call your supervisor and tell her/him how awful it was! Discuss ways of handling the situation.
- Remember: you CAN do it!

## 13.    General morale points

- Don't go interviewing if you are upset or not well; your contacts will pick it up.
- Prepare yourself thoroughly, so that you can concentrate on putting over the introduction and OBSERVING reaction.

REMEMBER:

- Most people readily agree to be interviewed and enjoy it.
- Most people you meet will be friendly and pleasant.
- Most people hate to say no.
- Everyone gets some refusals (even supervisors).
- Withdrawing before a refusal becomes explicit and returning another day will often get the interview.

**(HANDOUTS 5, 6 AND 7)**

**HANDOUT 1**

## PREPARATION FOR FIELDWORK

1)    CHECK ........................... no. of addresses issued

2)    READ ............................ all written instructions

3)    LEARN ........................... about the purpose of the survey

4)    ORGANIZE ...................... all the material you will need.
                                        (identity card, explanatory letter, etc.)

5)    PLAN ............................. your route *to* and *within* the area

6)    GET FAMILIAR ................ with the questionnaire

**HANDOUT 2**

## DOORSTEP PROCEDURE

1)    PREPARE ........................ and *practise* your initial introduction.  Keep it short!

2)    SMILE ............................ and greet the person cheerfully

3)    SPEAK ............................ *clearly* and not too fast but loudly enough to be heard

4)    CHECK ............................ you are at the correct address

5)    SHOW ............................. your identity card

6)    INTRODUCE .................... yourself and your organization

7)    EXPLAIN ........................ what the survey is about and its purpose *(briefly)*

8)    MENTION ........................ who the survey is for

**HANDOUT 3**

## A TYPICAL INTRODUCTION

Int:          'Good afternoon.  This <u>is</u> 14A Coventry Road, isn't it?  I'm ..........
              from ........... Here's my identity card.  We are doing a survey on
              behalf of ............. to help plan future developments of the city to suit
              residents' needs.  Have you heard anything about it on the radio or
              seen it mentioned anywhere?'

Contact:      'Well, I have, but I'm not sure I can do it; I have to go out now.'

Int:          'That's quite all right.  In fact it might not be you I need to  interview.
              Could you just spare me one minute to help me find out who I need to
              ask for an interview at this address?   Then I'll come back another
              time.'

**REMEMBER:**

BE BRIEF ...............................Don't go into detail unless asked for it

BE FLEXIBLE ........................Be prepared to vary your introduction to
                                     suit the situation

FOLLOW THE RULES ............. Check address

                               Introduce self, organization (in full), show
                               identity card

                               Say who the survey is for and what it's
                               about

**HANDOUT 4**

## OPTIMIZING FIRST CONTACT

BE AWARE ............................ of all the different things that people might be doing, of how they might be feeling

BE SENSITIVE ........................ to how the person is reacting (Look! Listen!)

REASSURE BY ........................ your dress and your relaxed, friendly, smiling manner

- stepping back from the door
- presenting identity card (and perhaps letter as well)
- being polite (avoid over-familiarity)
- verbal reassurance ('not selling'; confidential; police informed etc.)

BE POSITIVE .......................... about the benefits of taking part

- Explain the purpose clearly so that the survey is presented as worthwhile, important and of benefit to them
- Be charming! Many people agree to take part because they like the interviewer

APPEAL TO ALTRUISM ............ by:

- putting over the survey as helping others
- asking for help in sorting out whom to interview
- by asking for help in making the survey a success

**HANDOUT 5**

## MAIN TYPES OF RELUCTANCE

REMEMBER:        *Most* people will be very willing to be interviewed,
                 *Some* people will be a little bit reluctant,
                 A *few* people will definitely need persuading,
                 A *tiny number* will always refuse.

BUT:             People will vary according to what they are doing and how
                 they are feeling - SO BE PREPARED TO WITHDRAW AND
                 RETURN ANOTHER DAY.


Practise dealing with these questions and expressions of reluctance


1) What's it about?          e.g.,   What is the survey about?/What's it for?/Who's
                                     it for?/Who are you from?

2) I'm busy just now         e.g.,   I'm cooking/I'm just going out/
                                     We're watching TV

3) How long will it take?    e.g.,   I can't spare many minutes

4) I'm much too busy         e.g.,   I don't have time for that sort of thing/I'm out
   (general)                         every evening/I'm going away soon and I don't
                                     have time

5) (What are you **really**  e.g.,   Are you selling something?/What's it *really*
   up to ?)                          about?/I don't want to answer any personal
                                     questions

6) Why me?                   e.g.,   Why does it have to be me?/You should talk to
                                     my husband/go next door

7) I'm not interested        e.g.,   I can't be bothered/I don't believe in surveys/I
                                     don't want to do it

8) (I want to say no but     e.g.,   Well, ... er/I don't really think so/Well, ... I
   I don't know how to)              don't know ...

**HANDOUT 6**

### SOME WAYS OF DEALING WITH RELUCTANCE

GIVE REASSURANCE AND INFORMATION
- How long the interview will take (don't lie)
- Completely confidential (no names on questionnaire)
- Can check with police
- You can come back at another, more convenient time
- Explain how address selected
- Explain about random selection of individuals (no substitutes can be taken)
- Use sponsor's letter/survey research leaflet
- Relaxed friendly manner; don't pressurize (always let them have the option to refuse)

BE POSITIVE ABOUT BENEFITS
- Smile, be charming and polite (however they respond)
- 'Everyone so far has found the interview interesting/enjoyable'
- Explain the purpose and coverage of survey more fully/worthwhile and important/will benefit people like themselves
- An opportunity for them to give views/have a say in planning/everyone's views important - not just the well informed

APPEAL TO ALTRUISM
- The survey will help others
- They can help make the survey successful (you are not allowed to take a substitute/it's easy to get the views of people who are not busy, so the views of busy people may be under represented)

BE SENSITIVE
Observe and listen carefully:
- are they afraid to let you in because they are alone?
- are they ashamed to let you in because the house is untidy?
- are they upset, angry or worried about something?

BE FLEXIBLE
- Be prepared to change your approach; mention positive benefits as well as giving reassurance
- Be prepared to withdraw and come back another time, especially if you feel a refusal is imminent

USE 'ACTIVE LISTENING'
Rephrase reluctance and then counter it: 'I can see this is a bad time to call; I'll leave you this letter to read and come back another time'; 'I appreciate that you might think it sounds uninteresting but everyone so far has enjoyed the interview. There are no right or wrong answers and no special knowledge is required.'

REMEMBER! - MOST PEOPLE HATE TO SAY 'NO', ESPECIALLY TO
                    SOMEONE WHO IS  PLEASANT AND SMILING

**HANDOUT 7**

## KEEPING YOUR MORALE UP

IF YOU HAVE A RUN OF BAD LUCK AND IT'S GETTING YOU DOWN:

*   Take a break, have a cup of tea; or go home - tomorrow is another day!

*   Remember all the pleasant, welcoming people you've met

*   Call your supervisor and have a moan! - they are there to help you


SOME GENERAL POINTS:

*   Don't go interviewing if you are upset or unwell

*   Prepare yourself thoroughly in advance so that you feel confident you can put the survey over well and answer questions about it


REMEMBER .................... Most people readily agree to be interviewed and enjoy it

Most people you meet will be friendly and pleasant

Most people hate to say 'No'

Everyone gets some refusals (even supervisors!)

Withdrawing before a refusal becomes explicit and returning another day will often get the interview


YOU **CAN** DO IT!  AND YOU WILL GET BETTER ALL THE TIME!

**Examples of introductions for demonstration (Section 3)**

*Good introduction:*  Use Handout 3 example

*Indifferent introduction:*  (gushy and speaking too fast)

Int:   'Good afternoon. I'm from .....(name of organization)..... I've got a card somewhere.....yes, here it is, that's me - (name).  This is 14A Coventry Road, isn't it?  We are doing a survey for Milton Keynes and we're asking people who live here about their jobs and their shopping - oh, and their housing and what they do in their spare time, and things like that.  You've probably heard about it - there's been lots of publicity.  Your address was selected from the post code list and I have to interview a person here so could I ask you a few questions?  It's absolutely confidential - we don't put your name on anything; and the police have been informed.'

Con   '*Who* did you say you were from - Milton Keynes Social Services?'

*Bad introduction:*   (rather familiar manner, becoming pressurizing)

Int:   'Hello!  Shocking weather, isn't it - can I just step inside to talk to you?'

Con   'Well - what do you want?'

Int:   'I'm just doing a survey, that's all.  There - that's my identity card. Is there one household living here or more than one?  Oh, by the way, this is 14A Coventry Road, isn't it? ..... Oh, that's all right then.'

Con   'What's it all about then?'

Int:   'Well, it's a survey for Milton Keynes among the people who live here; it's to help them plan what they're going to do next.  It is quite short, it only takes a few minutes, so I'd just like to ask you a few questions to find out who I have to interview.'

# Bibliography

Argyle, M. (ed) (1973), *Social Encounters: Readings in Social Interaction.* Harmondsworth: Penguin Books Ltd.

Argyle, M. (1984), 'Some New Developments in Social Skills Training', *Bulletin of the British Psychological Society,* vol.37, pp.405-410.

Argyle, M., Furnham, A. & Graham, J.A. (1981), *Social Situations.* Cambridge: Cambridge University Press.

Athey, K.R., Coleman, J.E., Reitman A.P. & Tang, J. (1960), 'Two experiments showing the effects of the interviewer's racial background on responses to questionnaires concerning racial issues', *Journal of Applied Psychology,* pp.244-246.

Babbie, E.R. (1973), *Survey Research Methods.* Belmont, Calif.: Wadsworth Publishing Co.

Barker, R.F. (1987), 'A demographic profile of marketing research interviewers', *Journal of the Market Research Society,* vol.29, no.3.

Belson, W.A. (1975), *Juvenile Theft: Causal Factors.* London: Harper & Row.

Belson, W.A. (1981), *The Design and Understanding of Survey Questions.* Aldershot: Gower.

Benson, S., Boorman, W. & Clark, K. (1951), 'A study of interview refusals', *Journal of Applied Psychology,* 35.

Bergsten, J.W., Weeks, M.F. & Bryan, F.A. (1984), 'Effects of an advance telephone call in a personal interview survey', *Public Opinion Quarterly,* vol.48, no.3.

Bingham, W.V. & Moore, B.V. (1934), *How to Interview.* New York: Harper.

Bowen, M.J. (1979), 'A survey of the general public's attitudes to market research', *Journal of the Market Research Society,* vol.21, no.2.

Bradburn, N.M., Sudman, S. & Associates (1979), *Improving Interview Method and Questionnaire Design: Response Effects to Threatening Questions in Survey Research.* San Francisco: Jossey-Bass.

Brown, C. & Ritchie, J. (1984), *Focussed enumeration: the development of sampling ethnic minority groups,* Joint report from Policy Studies Institute and SCPR, London.

Brown, P. & Levinson, S. (1978), 'Universals in language politeness phenomenon', in Goody, E.N. (ed), *Questions and Politeness: Strategies in Social Interaction. (Cambridge Papers in Anthropology, 8.)* Cambridge: Cambridge University Press.

Butcher, R. (1986), 'Influencing response rates - an example from the 1985/6 National Travel Survey', *OPCS Survey Methodology Bulletin*, no.19. London: OPCS.

Butcher, R. (1988), 'The use of the Postcode Address File as a sampling frame', *The Statistician*, vol.37, no.1.

Cannell, C.F., Groves, R.M. & Miller, P.V. (1981), 'The effects of mode of data collection on health survey data', *Proceedings of the American Statistical Association, Social Statistics Section*.

Cannell, C.F., Groves, R.M., Magilavy, L., Mathiowetz, N. & Miller, P. (1987), 'An experimental comparison of telephone and personal health surveys', *Vital and Health Statistics, series 2*, no.106. Washington: Public Health Service.

Clark, C. & Pinch, T. (1988), 'Micro-Sociology and Micro-Economics: selling by social control', in Fielding, N.G. (ed), *Actions and Structures. Research Methods and Social Theory*. London: Sage Publications.

Clarke, L., Phibbs, M., Klepacz, A. & Griffiths, D. (1987), 'General Household Survey Advanced Letter Experiment', *OPCS Survey Methodology Bulletin*, no.21, London.

Cole, D. (1956), 'Fieldwork in sample surveys of household income and expenditure', *Applied Statistics*, no.5, p.61.

Collins, M. (1982/83), 'Some response effects among older respondents', *Survey Methods Newsletter*, Winter '82/'83. London: SCPR.

Collins, M. & Sykes, W. (1987), 'The problems of non-coverage and unlisted numbers in telephone surveys in Britain', *Journal of Royal Statistical Society, Series A*, vol.150, part 3.

Collins, M., Sykes, W., Wilson, P. & Blackshaw, N. (1988), 'Nonresponse: the UK experience', in Groves et al. (eds), *Telephone Survey Methodology*. New York: John Wiley & Sons, Inc.

Colombo, R. (1983), 'Patterns of Non-Response', in Hoinville, G. (ed), *SSRC Survey Methods Seminar Series*, 1980-83. London: SCPR.

Couper, M.P. & Groves, R.M. (1991), 'The role of the interviewer in survey participation', Paper presented at a meeting of the *American Association for Public Opinion Research*.

Crespi, L. (1945), 'The cheater problem in polling', *Public Opinion Quarterly*, vol.9, pp.431-445.

Darley, J.M. & Latane, B. (1970), 'Norms and Normative Behavior', in Macaulay, J. & Berkovitz, L. (eds), *Altruism and Helping Behavior*. New York: Academic Press.

Deepchand, K. & Thomas, R. (1992), *Samples of households with telephones and entries in the public telephone directory*, Joint Centre for Survey Methods Working Paper, series no.7. London: SCPR.

DeMaio, T.J. (1980), 'Refusals, Who, Where, Why?', *Public Opinion Quarterly*, vol.44, no.2.

DeNicholas, M.E. (1987), 'Refusal to help under conditions of anger: Rejection as hedonism', unpublished doctoral dissertation, Arizona State University (quoted in Groves & Cialdinini, 1991).

Dillman, D.A., Gallegos, J.E. & Frey, J.H. (1976), 'Reducing refusal rates for telephone interviews', *Public Opinion Quarterly*, vol.4, no.1.

Dohrenwend, B.S. (1970), 'An experimental study of payments to respondents', *Public Opinion Quarterly*, vol.34, no.4.

Durbin, J. & Stuart, A. (1951), 'Differences in Response Rates of Experienced and Inexperienced Interviewer', *Journal of the Royal Statistical Society, Series A*, vol. cxiv, part II.

Eastlack, J.O., Jr. & Assael, H. (1966), 'Better telephone surveys through centralized interviewing', *Journal of Advertising Research*, vol.6, no.1.

Ferber, R. & Sudman, S. (1974), 'Effects of compensation on consumer expenditure surveys', *Annals of Economic and Social Measurement*, 3.

Fernando, E. (1977), *Survey of the Elderly in Clackmannan: Technical report*. London: SCPR.

Foreman, J. & Collins, M. (1991), 'The viability of random digit dialling in the UK', *Journal of the Market Research Society*, vol.33, no.3.

Fowler, F.J. Jr. & Mangione, T.W. (1990), 'Standardized Survey Interviewing: Minimizing Interviewer Related Error', *Applied Social Research Methods Series*, vol.18. Newbury Park, Calif.: Sage Publications, Inc.

Frankel, M.R., (1989), 'Current research practices: general population sampling including geodemographics', *Journal of the Market Research Society*, vol.31, no.4.

Gibson, D.M. & Aitkenhead, W. (1982), 'The elderly respondent: experiences from a large scale survey of the elderly', Working Paper No.30 in *Ageing and the Family Project*. Canberra: Research School of Social Sciences, Australian National University.

Goffman, E. (1967), *Interaction Ritual*. New York: Anchor/Doubleday.

Gorden, R.L. (1975) (2nd edition), *Interviewing: Strategy, Techniques and Tactics*. Homewood, Ill: Dorsey Press.

Goyder J. (1987), *The Silent Minority: Non Respondents on Sample Surveys*. Cambridge: Polity Press.

Groves, R.M., Biemer, P.P., Lyberg, L.E., Massey, J.T., Nicholls II, W.L. & Waksberg, J. (eds) (1988), *Telephone Survey Methodology*. New York: John Wiley & Sons, Inc.

Groves, R.M. & Cialdini, R.B. (1991), 'Toward a useful theory of survey participation', Paper presented at 1991 meeting of the American Statistical Association.

Groves, R.M. & Fultz, N.H. (1985), 'Gender effects among telephone interviewers in a survey of economic attitudes', *Sociological Methods and Research*, vol.14, no.1.

Groves, R.M. & Kahn, R.L. (1979), *Surveys by Telephone: A National Comparison with Personal Interviews*. New York: Academic Press.

Groves, R.M. & Lyberg, L.E. (1988), 'An overview of nonresponse issues in telephone surveys', in Groves et al. (eds), *Telephone Survey Methodology*. New York: John Wiley & Sons, Inc.

Groves R.M. & Magilavy, L.J. (1981), 'Increasing response rates to telephone surveys: A door in the face for Foot-in-the-Door', *Public Opinion Quarterly*, vol.45, no.3.

Guenzel, P.J., Berkmans, T.R. & Cannell, C.F. (1983), *General interviewing techniques: A self-instructional workbook for telephone and personal interviewer training*. Ann Arbor, MI: Institute for Social Research.

Hahlo, G. (1992), 'Examining the validity of re-interviewing respondents for quantitative surveys', *Journal of the Market Research Society*, vol.34, no.2.

Hall, Stella & Katryniak, Jackie (1990), 'The Face to Face Interviewer - An endangered species?', *Market Research Society Conference Papers*.

Hansen, R.H. (1980), 'A self perception interpretation of the effect of monetary and non-monetary incentives on mail survey respondent behaviour', *Journal of Marketing Research*, no.17.

Hansen, R.H. & Marks, E.S. (1958), 'Influence of the interviewer on the accuracy of survey results', *Journal of the American Statistical Association*, 53.

Hatchett, S. & Schuman, H. (1976), 'White respondents and race-of-interviewer effects', *Public Opinion Quarterly*, vol.39, no.4.

Henson, R., Roth, A. & Cannell, C.F. (1974), *Personal vs. telephone interviews and the effects of telephone re-interviews on reporting of psychiatric symptomatology*, Research Report, Survey Research Center, University of Michigan.

Hoinville, E. (1980), *The Relationship between Survey Non-response and Constituency Characteristics*, Methodological Working Paper no.21. London: SCPR.

Hoinville, G. (1983), 'Carrying out surveys among the elderly: some problems of sampling and interviewing', *Journal of the Market Research Society*, vol.23, no.3.

Honomichl, J. (1989), 'US research industry structure', *Journal of the Market Research Society*, vol.31, no.4.

House, J.S. & Wolf, S. (1978), 'Effects of urban residence on interpersonal trust and helping behaviour', *Journal of Personality and Social Psychology*, 36, pp.1029-1043.

Hunt, A. (1978), *The elderly at home: a survey carried out on behalf of the Department of Health and Social Security.* London: HMSO.

Hyman, H.H. (et al.) (1954), *Interviewing in Social Research.* Chicago: The University of Chicago Press.

Johnson, A.M., Wadsworth, J., Wellings, K., Bradshaw, S. & Field, J. (1992), 'Patterns of HIV risk behaviour in Britain', *Nature*, 3rd Dec.

Jones, C., Burich, M.C. & Campbell, B. (1986), 'Motivating interviewers and respondents in longitudinal research designs', Paper given at the *International Symposium on Panel Studies at American Statistical Association*, Washington DC.

Jowell, R. & Airey, C. (1975), 'Problems of empirical research on race in Britain', in Crewe, I. (ed), *The politics of race: British Political Sociology Yearbook*, vol.2. London: Croom Helm.

Kahn, R.L. & Cannell, C.F. (1957), *The Dynamics of Interviewing.* New York: John Wiley & Sons, Inc.

Kerin, R. & Peterson, R. (1983), 'Scheduling telephone interviews: lessons from 250,000 Dialings', *Journal of Advertising Research*, vol.23, pp.41-47.

Kish, L. (1949), 'A procedure for objective respondent selection within the household', *Journal of the American Statistical Association*, vol.44, pp.380-387.

Kish, L. (1965), *Survey Sampling.* New York: Wiley.

Lievesley, D. (1986), 'Unit Non Response in Interview Surveys', Joint Centre for Survey Methods unpublished paper. London: SCPR.

Lynn, P. & Lievesley, D. (1991), *Drawing General Population Samples in Great Britain.* London: SCPR.

Market Research Society (1976), 'Response rates in sample surveys: report on Working Party of the MRS's Research and Development Committee', *Journal of the Market Research Society*, vol.18, no.3.

Market Research Society (1981), 'Report on the Second Working Party on Respondent Co-operation 1977-80', *Journal of the Market Research Society*, vol.23, no.1.

Market Research Society (1989), *Code of Conduct*, Market Research Society and Industrial Marketing Research Association, London.

Marsh, C. (1986), 'Social class and occupation', in Burgess, R. (ed), *Key Variables in Social Investigation.* London: Routledge & Kegan Paul.

Marsh, C. (1991), *Hours of work of women and men in Britain*, London: HMSO (for the Equal Opportunities Commission).

Marsh, C. & Scarbrough, E. (1987), 'Quota & Random Sampling: an experimental comparison'. Cambridge: University of Cambridge, mimeo.

Marsh, C. & Scarbrough, E. (1990), 'Testing nine hypotheses about quota sampling', *Journal of the Market Research Society*, vol.32, no.4.

McCrossan, L. (1991), *A Handbook for Interviewers.* London: HMSO.

McFarlane Smith, J. (1972), *Interviewing in Market and Social Research.* London: Routledge & Kegan Paul Ltd.

McIntosh, A. (1970), 'The sampling of non-domestic populations', *Journal of the Market Research Society*, vol.12, no.4.

McIntosh, A. (1975), 'Improving the efficiency of sample surveys in industrial markets', *Journal of the Market Research Society*, vol.17, no.4.

McQueen, D. (1989), 'The stability and consistency of sensitive information obtained from face to face and computer assisted [telephone] interviewing', in *Issues in researching sexual behaviour*, London: Joint Centre for Survey Methods Newsletter, vol.10, no.1, SCPR.

Millward, N., Stevens, M., Smart, D. & Hawes, W.R. (1992), *Workplace Industrial Relations in Transition.* Aldershot: Dartmouth.

Monsees, M.L. & Massey, J.T. (1979), 'Adapting procedures for collecting demographic data in a personal interview to a telephone interview', *Proceedings of the Section on Survey Research Methods, American Statistical Association*, pp.130-135.

Moore, R.P., Lessler, J. & Caspar, R.A. (1989), *Results of Intensive Interviews to Study Nonresponse in the National Household Seroprevalence Survey*, Research Triangle Institute, Project No.257V-4190, North Carolina.

Morton-Williams, J. (1979), *Alternative patterns of care for the elderly: methodological report*. London: SCPR.

Morton-Williams, J. & Young, P. (1986), 'Interviewer strategies on the doorstep', *Proceedings of the 1986 Conference of the Market Research Society*.

Morton-Williams, J. & Young, P. (1987), 'Obtaining the survey interview - an analysis of tape recorded doorstep introductions', *Journal of the Market Research Society*, vol.29, no.1.

Moser, C.A. & Kalton, G. (1971) (2nd edition), *Survey Methods in Social Investigations*. London: Heinemann Educational Books Ltd.

Moser, C.A. & Stuart, A. (1953), 'An experimental study of quota sampling', *Journal of the Royal Statistical Society, Series A*, 116, pp.349-405.

Mowen, J.C. & Cialdini, R.B. (1980), 'On implementing the door-in-the-face compliance technique in a business context', *Journal of Marketing Research*, 17, pp.253-258.

Nelson, D. & Bowie, C. (1988), 'Non-response problems and solutions', Paper prepared for *Research Planning Conference on Human Activity Patterns, Las Vegas, Nevada*. Washington DC: U.S. Bureau of the Census.

Nicol, S. (1988), 'Analysis of recorded refusals on the General Household and Family Expenditure Survey', *OPCS Survey Methodology Bulletin*, no.22. London: OPCS.

Oksenberg, L. & Cannell, C. (1988), 'Effects of Interviewer vocal characteristics on nonresponse', in Groves et al. (eds), *Telephone Survey Methodology*. New York: John Wiley & Sons, Inc.

Parsons, T. & Bales, R.F. (1955), *Family, Socialisation and Interaction Process*. New York: The Free Press.

Pile, B. (1991), 'Setting up and managing a large-scale telephone interviewing facility', in *Telephone Surveys: the current state of the art*, Joint Centre for Survey Methods Newsletter, vol.11, no.3. London: SCPR.

Piliavin, I.M., Rodin. J. & Piliavin, J.A. (1969), 'Good Samaritanism; an underground phenomenon?', *Journal of Personality and Social Psychology*, 13, pp.289-299.

Powney, J. & Watts, M. (1987), *Interviewing in Educational Research*, Routledge Education Books. London: Routledge & Kegan Paul Ltd.

Rauta, I. (1985), 'A comparison of the census characteristics of respondents and non-respondents to the General Household Survey', *Statistical News*, 70.

Redpath, R. (1986), 'Family Expenditure Survey: a second study of differential response comparing census characteristics and FES respondents and non-respondents', *Statistical News*, 72.

Richardson, S.A., Dohrenwend, B.S. & Klein, D. (1965), *Interviewing, its forms and functions*. New York: Basic Books, Inc.

Rogers, T.F. (1976), 'Interviews by telephone and in person', *Public Opinion Quarterly*, 40, pp.51-65.

Rosenthal, R. (ed) (1979), *Skill in Non-Verbal Communication: Individual Differences*. Oelgeshlager, Cambridge, Ma.: Gunn & Hain.

Rothman, J. (1989), 'Different measures of social grade', *Journal of the Market Research Society*, vol.31, no.1.

Rothman, J. & Mitchell, D. (1989), 'General Population Sampling: UK', *Journal of the Market Research Society*, vol.31, no.4.

Schuman, H. & Converse, J.M. (1971), 'The effects of black and white interviewers on black responses in 1968', *Public Opinion Quarterly*, 35.

Scott, C. & Jackson, S. (1960), *The Use of the Telephone for Making Interview Appointments*. London: Government Social Survey (now OPCS Social Survey Division), no.M92.

SCPR (1984a), *Interviewers' Manual*. London: SCPR.

SCPR (1984b), *Field Supervisors' Manual*. London: SCPR.

Seebold, J. (1988), 'Survey period length, unanswered numbers, and nonresponse in telephone surveys', in Groves et al. (eds), *Telephone Survey Methodology*, New York, John Wiley & Sons, Inc.

Singer E., Frankel, M.R. & Glasman, M.B. (1983), 'The effects of interviewer characteristics and expectations on response', *Public Opinion Quarterly*, vol.47, no.1, pp.68-83.

Smead, R.J. & Wilcox, J. (1980), 'Ring policy in telephone surveys', *Public Opinion Quarterly*, vol.44, no.1.

Smith, D.V.L. & Bard, M. (1989), 'Everything you always wanted to know about industrial buyer behaviour, but were afraid to ask - in case it made the research too expensive', *Market Research Society 1989 Conference Papers*.

Smith, D.V.L. & Dexter, A. (1991), 'Interviewing and classifying business respondents: a guide to good practice', *Market Research Society 1991 Conference Papers*.

Smith, E. (1991), 'Telephone surveys - the business angle', in *Telephone Surveys: the current state of the art*, Joint Centre for Survey Methods Newsletter, vol.11, no.3. London: SCPR.

Social Research Association (1988), 'Ethical Guidelines', *Appendix B of SRA Directory of Members*, London.

Staveren, M. van (1990), 'Relative merits of quota and random sampling', in *Current Issues in General Population Sampling*, Joint Centre for Survey Methods Newsletter, vol.11, no.1. London: SCPR.

Steeh, C.G. (1981), 'Trends in non-response rates in 1952-1979', *Public Opinion Quarterly*, vol.45.

Stephenson, B.C. (1978), 'Probability sampling with quotas: an experiment', *Public Opinion Quarterly*, 43, pp.477-496.

Sudman, S. (1965), 'Time allocation in survey interviewing and in other field occupations', *Public Opinion Quarterly*, 29, pp.638-648.

Sudman, S. (1966), 'Probability Sampling with Quotas', *Journal of the American Statistical Association*, 61, pp.749-771.

Sudman, S. (1967), *Reducing the Cost of Surveys*, National Opinion Research Center, Monographs in Social Research, no.10. Chicago: Aldine.

Sudman, S. & Bradburn, N.M. (1974), *Response Effects in Surveys*. Chicago: Aldine.

Sutherland, K. (ed) (1991), *Researching Business Markets*, the IMRA Handbook of Business-to-Business Marketing Research. London: Kogan Page.

Swires-Hennessy, E. & Drake, M. (1992), 'The optimum time at which to conduct interviews', *Journal of the Market Research Society*, vol.34, no.1.

Sykes, W. & Collins, M. (1987), 'Comparing telephone and face-to-face interviewing in the United Kingdom', *Survey Methodology*, vol.13, no.1, pp.15-29. Statistics Canada.

Sykes, W. & Hoinville, G. (1985), *Telephone interviewing on a survey of social attitudes: a comparison with face-to-face procedures*. London: SCPR.

Tajfel, H. (1981), *Human Groups and Social Categories*. Cambridge: Cambridge University Press.

Thomas, R. (1991), 'Characteristics of households with and without telephones in 1989 and implications for the representativeness of telephone surveys', in *Telephone surveys: the current state of the art*, Joint Centre for Survey Methods Newsletter, vol.11, no.3. London: SCPR.

Trewin, D. & Lee, G. (1988), 'International comparisons of telephone coverage', in Groves et al. (eds), *Telephone Survey Methodology*. New York: John Wiley & Sons, Inc.

Turner, C.F. & Martin, E. (eds) (1981), *Surveys of Subjective Phenomena: Summary Report*. Washington DC: National Academy Press.

Turner, C.F. & Martin, E. (eds) (1984), *Surveying Subjective Phenomena*, vol.1. New York: Russel Sage Foundation.

Walsh, T.C. (1976), 'Selected Results from the 1972-73 Diary Survey', Paper presented at a seminar sponsored by the *American Marketing Association*.

Warwick, D.P. & Lininger, C.A. (1975), *The Sample Survey: Theory and Practice.* New York: McGraw-Hill.

Webber, R. (1979), *Census Enumeration Districts and Socio-economic Classifications,* OPCS Occasional Paper, no.14, London.

Weeks, M.F., Jones, B.L., Folsom, R.E. & Benrud, C.H. (1980), 'Optimal times to contact sample households', *Public Opinion Quarterly,* vol.44, no.1.

Wellings, K., Field, J., Wadsworth, J., Johnson, A.M., Anderson, R.M. & Bradshaw, S.A. (1990), 'Sexual lifestyles under scrutiny', *Nature,* vol.348, 22nd Nov.

Westerhoven, E. van (1978), 'Covering non-response: does it pay?', *Journal of the Market Research Society,* vol.20, no.4.

Williams, E. (1988), 'Reissues', *OPCS Survey Methodology Bulletin,* no.22.

Williams, J.A. Jr. (1968), 'Interviewer role performance. A further note on bias in the information interview', *Public Opinion Quarterly,* 32, pp.287-294.

Wiseman, F. & McDonald, P. (1979), 'Noncontact and refusal rates in consumer telephone surveys', *Journal of Marketing Research,* vol.16, pp.478-484.

Wish, M., Deutsch, M. & Kaplan, S.J. (1976), 'Perceived dimensions of interpersonal relations', *Journal of Personality and Social Psychology,* 33, pp.409-420.

Wood, D. (1979), *Misfortunes Compensation Study - Technical Report,* (ref. no.421). London: SCPR.

Wood, D. (1986), *Beliefs about Alcohol,* Health Education Council Research Report, no.5. London: Health Education Council.

Worcester, R. & Downham, J. (1986), *Consumer Market Research Handbook* (3rd edition). Holland: Elsevier.

# Index

Bold typeface is used to identify chapter headings; bold typeface for page numbers only indicates a subsection dealing with that topic; n after a page number indicates reference to a note